INTERCULTURAL
COMMUNICATION
THEORY

INTERNATIONAL AND INTERCULTURAL COMMUNICATION ANNUAL

Volume VII   1983

Editor
William B. Gudykunst
State University of New York at Albany

Associate Editor
Young Yun Kim
Governors State University

Book Review Editor
Dennis W. Tafoya
University of Massachusetts

Editorial Assistants
Janis Page
Lois Silverman

International and Intercultural Communication Annual
Volume VII

INTERCULTURAL COMMUNICATION THEORY

Current Perspectives

edited by

William B. Gudykunst

Published in Cooperation with
The Speech Communication Association
Commission on International and Intercultural Communication

SAGE PUBLICATIONS
Beverly Hills / London / New Delhi

For information address:

SAGE Publications, Inc.
275 South Beverly Drive
Beverly Hills, California 90212

SAGE Publications India Pvt. Ltd.
C-236 Defence Colony
New Delhi 110 024, India

SAGE Publications Ltd
28 Banner Street
London EC1Y 8QE, England

Printed in the United States of America

Library of Congress Cataloging in Publication Data

Main entry under title:

Intercultural communication theory.

(International and intercultural communication annual ; 7)
Includes index.
1. Intercultural communication—Addresses, essays, lectures. 2. Intercultural communication—Philosophy —Addresses, essays, lectures. I. Gudykunst, William B. II. Speech Communication Association. III. Series.
HM258.I524   1983   303.4'82   83-3026
ISBN 0-8039-1970-0
ISBN 0-8039-1969-7 (pbk.)

SECOND PRINTING, 1984

Table of Contents

Preface

This is the seventh volume of the *International and Intercultural Communication Annual* sponsored by the Speech Communication Association's (SCA) Commission on International and Intercultural Communication. This volume, however, is different in terms of appearance and content from former editions. In terms of appearance, this volume begins the *Annual's* association with a new publisher—Sage Publications. With respect to content, the present volume differs from its predecessors in that it has a thematic focus on theorizing in intercultural communication.

Since the inception of the *Annual* in 1974, research and teaching of international and intercultural communication has advanced by leaps and bounds. The preceding six volumes of the *Annual*, edited by Fred Casmir and Nemi Jain, contributed a great deal to this advancement. Previous editions of the *Annual* reinforced the idea that the study of international and intercultural communication is not only an interdisciplinary effort, but one that can benefit from a wide variety of orientations and approaches. The present volume continues this tradition.

Earlier editions of the *Annual* presented the top papers to emerge from a competitive selection process in any given year. This procedure worked well in the past. The result of this procedure, however, was an *Annual* that appeared to be a quarterly journal rather than a yearbook publication. The modifications that have been made with this issue are designed to make the *Annual* more closely resemble a yearbook, rather than a journal. To this end the current volume is organized around the central theme of theorizing in intercultural communication. This was accomplished in three ways: (1) by inviting participants in the 1980 SCA Seminar on Theory in Intercultural Communication to write papers specifically for publication in this issue, (2) by including manuscripts competitively selected after blind review, and (3) by inviting authors of papers on theory in intercultural communication presented at conventions to submit their work.

Since a large percentage of the papers presented in this volume are the product of an Action Caucus and Seminar on Theory in Intercultural Communication held at the 1980 Speech Communication Association (SCA) convention in New York City, a brief overview of these sessions is in order. The idea for the action caucus and seminar originated at the Commission on International and Intercultural Communication meeting at the 1979 SCA convention in San Antonio, Texas. Those present at the meeting agreed that a special program on theory development in intercultural communication should be held during the 1980 convention. Larry Sarbaugh was asked to coordinate work on developing the program(s). Sarbaugh collaborated with Nobleza Asuncion-Lande in developing the idea for the convention. From their collaboration, and discussions with members of the commission, it was decided to hold both an action caucus, to allow for the participation of relatively large numbers of people, and a seminar, to provide the atmosphere necessary for intense discussion among a smaller group of people.

The theoretical areas for the action caucus were specified and people interested in those areas identified. The areas selected formed the basis for small group discussions during the action caucus. The theoretical areas identified (and the appointed leaders and coleaders) included: (1) code and code systems (Ralph Cooley and Nobleza Asuncion-Lande), (2) constructivism (James Applegate and Howard Sypher), (3) mathematical modeling (Ed Fink and Joe Woelfel), (4) rhetorical theory (Jolene Koester and Carl Holmberg), (5) rules theory (W. Barnett Pearce and Richard Wiseman), (6) systems theory (Brent Ruben and Sharon Ruhly), (7) relationship development (Bill Gudykunst and Bob Shuter), and (8) alternative (e.g., Eastern) approaches (Molefi Asante and Erika Vora). Volunteers interested in each of the topics were asked to write position papers and circulate them to others interested in the area prior to the convention.

At the convention the action caucus began with two general presentations: William Howell discussed general issues in the area of intercultural communication, while Joe Hanna—a philosopher of social science from Michigan State—presented alternative approaches to theory in the social sciences (Hanna's paper was published in *Communication Yearbook 5*). After these two presentations, the eight groups met for approximately four hours of discussion. Discussions in the groups centered around the position papers and issues related to the use of the particular approach in developing theory in intercultural communication. The action caucus concluded with the leaders of each of the groups presenting a brief summary of their discussion.

Following the close of the action caucus, the leaders and coleaders of the eight groups met in the seminar to further discuss the issue of theory in intercultural communication. In the proposal for the seminar, Sarbaugh defined its purpose as "to provide a forum for a creative elaboration and/or resolution of the issues of general theory development." Seminar participants met for about four hours over two evenings at the convention. The seminar participants were invited to write papers for publication in this volume of the *Annual*. Leaders and coleaders were encouraged to coauthor the papers and include material from the discussions of their groups, as well as ideas articulated in the various position papers. The papers written appear throughout the volume. Further, a few of the position papers written for the action caucus, not covered in the seminar papers, have been included.

The overall quality of the manuscripts included in this volume is high. There is, however, some unevenness in the degree to which the papers *directly* address intercultural communication. For example, a few of the papers do not fully explore the implications of the particular theory under consideration for intercultural interaction; rather, they focus more upon intracultural communication. Where this occurs, I hope that you, the reader, can see the applications in intercultural situations.

As Volume 7 of the *Annual* goes to press, space in Volume 8, with a focus on methodologies for studying intercultural communication, is almost fully committed. In addition, planning for Volume 9, with a focus on intercultural communication in an organization context, is well under way.

The changes that have been made in the form and context of the *Annual* are all designed to increase the *Annual's* usefulness to you, the reader. I hope you find the modifications beneficial to you in your study of international and intercultural communication. If you have suggstions and/or comments for further improvements, please let me know.

Many people have made invaluable contributions to the publication of this volume. While it is impossible to thank all of them here, there are several who deserve to be singled out. First, I want to thank the staff of Sage Publications for their confidence in me and the *Annual*. Without their support you would not be reading this. Second, even though the

Intercultural Press is no longer associated with the *Annual*, David Hoopes and Peggy Pusch have continued to provide much needed emotional support. Next, I want to thank Young Kim, my associate editor, for her invaluable assistance and support in the preparation of this volume. The support of Bill Work, Executive Director of SCA, and the members of SCA's Commission on International and Intercultural Communication—especially Bob Shuter, the past chair, and Larry Sarbaugh, the current chair—has kept me going when I otherwise might have thrown in the towel. I also would like to express my appreciation to colleagues at Rutgers University and the State University of New York at Albany—particularly my editorial assistant Lois Silverman at Rutgers—for their encouragement and assistance in bringing this volume to completion. Finally, I must express my gratitude to the authors of the manuscripts included in this volume; their work makes the *Annual* what it is.

—*Bill Gudykunst*
Albany, New York

P.S.: Ralph Cooley, one of the contributors to this volume, passed away as this volume was going to press. Ralph will be missed by all of us in the area. I, therefore, want to dedicate this volume to his memory.

I

INTRODUCTION

1

Theorizing in Intercultural Communication
An Introduction

WILLIAM B. GUDYKUNST • *State University of New York at Albany*

A good theory is one that holds together long enough to get you a better one.

[Anonymous].

There is nothing so practical as a good theory.

[Kurt Lewin].

The focus of recent conceptual writings in intercultural communication has been on a number of sensitizing concepts that provide a framework for beginning to understand communication between people from different cultures. Sensitizing concepts, as characterized by Williams, "convey a sense of reference and orientation grasped through personal experience."[1] The major problem with the utilization of such concepts (e.g., value orientations, assumptions, sets of expectations) is that they are often discussed in isolation and never directly related to the process of communication.

It is my belief that if the study of intercultural communication is to develop further, it needs to move from a discussion of sensitizing concepts toward consistent theoretical frameworks for the analysis of communication between people from different cultures. Or, in other words, scholars in the field need to begin constructing theories in intercultural communication.

It should be noted at the outset that the position put forth here is in contrast to two recent statements. Edward Stewart has argued that "it is premature and may be irrelevant for intercultural communication to construct formal theories, test hypotheses and verify postulates following the traditional canons of the sciences. Crystallization of terms now would probably dampen development."[2] Similarly, Asante, Newmark,

AUTHOR'S NOTE: *This chapter is meant as an introduction to the issues raised in this volume of the* Annual; *it is not meant to be a complete overview of theorizing in intercultural communication.*

and Blake contend that "what is needed at this juncture is more description of the intercultural communication process; i.e., our scientists need to observe before they theorize."[3]

This "antitheory" perspective is not accepted in the field of communication in general, where interest in theory building has been on the upswing in recent years. Although this development may not have been caused by, it was at least influenced by the introduction of the rule-governed perspective by Cushman and Whiting.[4] One of the first indications of increased interest in theory building in the field of communication is McDermott's state-of-the-art essay on the classical approaches to theory construction.[5] Further theoretical introspection has taken place in two regional journals: (1) *Western Journal of Speech Communication* devoted its entire 1977 and 1978 winter issues to theoretical aspects of communication, and (2) *Communication Quarterly* devoted its 1977 winter issue to theoretical concerns in communication. In addition, *Human Communication Research* has published numerous state-of-the-art essays on different apsects of communication theory. Finally, recent overviews of theory and research in the various subareas of the field have appeared in the *Communication Yearbook* series sponsored by the International Communication Association.

Utilizing Kuhn's[6] terminology, the field of communication in general can be classified as being in a "preparadigmatic" stage of development.[7] This implies that there are several conflicting paradigms that are battling for supremacy within the discipline. These paradigms include, but are not limited to, the covering laws, systems, rules, and constructivist approaches. In contrast, the area of intercultural communication might be considered aparadigmatic. Aparadigmatic implies a somewhat immature area that has not gone through the development of its first paradigm. This is to be expected given the ambivalence of scholars in the field as to whether it is even desirable (or possible) to develop theory (or theories) in intercultural communication.

Before moving on, it is necessary to address briefly the question of why theory is necessary in intercultural communication. An alternative way of looking at this question is to ask "What is the function of theorizing in intercultural communication?" Traditionally, one or more of three possible answers are given to this question: (1) to explain, (2) to predict, or (3) to control. It should be noted that the explanation-prediction-control view of theory is directly attributable to a positivistic approach to theory development, which many people in our field (e.g., Fred Casmir)[8] have argued is not applicable to the phenomena under study.

Although there is much we can learn from the positivistic tradition, it is not necessary for intercultural theorists to buy it lock, stock, and barrel. For example, one of the most widely used texts on theory construction ignores the control aspect of theory. According to Dubin,

> Theories of social and human behavior address themselves to two distinct goals of science: (1) prediction and (2) understanding. It will be argued that these are two separate goals and that the structure of theories employed to achieve each is unique. I will not, however, conclude that they are either inconsistent or incompatible. In the usual case of building theory in the behavioral sciences, understanding and prediction are not often achieved together, and it therefore becomes important to ask why. It will be concluded that each goal may be attained without reference to the other.[9]

Dubin goes on to point out that prediction is concerned with outcomes, while understanding is concerned with interaction among variables (the units of a theory). The crux of the matter is that intercultural theorists have a choice as to which function(s) they want their theories to perform.

There is one remaining reason why theorizing is necessary in intercultural communication; namely, the area is in desperate need of conceptual frameworks that will give direction to the diverse research effort taking place within it. Saral points this out when he says:

> On the one hand, one cannot but feel overwhelmed by a huge number of studies dealing with the variables that, in one fashion or another, affect the process of intercultural communication. On the other hand, one is struck by the lack of specific focus or direction in such studies.[10]

Without some form of theorizing, research in intercultural communication will not take on specific foci or directions.

It is my contention that theorizing is necessary in intercultural communication if we are to *understand* the process of communication between people from different cultures and have guides for our future research efforts. *We must keep in mind, however, that our initial attempts at theorizing will be rough and will require much refinement.* This argument is consistent with Karl Popper: "Theories are nets cast to catch what we call 'the world': to rationalize, to explain, to master it. We endeavor to make the mesh ever finer and finer."[11] It should be noted that I am arguing that the initial goal of theory in intercultural communication is understanding, rather than prediction or control. Questions of prediction and control may be more fruitfully addressed at a later stage of development of theory in the field (i.e., when we have made the net finer).

The major question to be addressed at this point is, how do we begin to develop theory in intercultural communication? There are at least three alternative answers to this question. First, theory can be developed anew based upon research conducted specifically on intercultural communication. Robert Merton suggests this approach when he says:

> It is my central thesis that empirical research goes far beyond the passive role of verifying and testing theory: it does more than confirm or refute hypotheses. Research plays an active role: it performs at least four major functions which help shape the development of theory. It *initiates*, it *reformulates*, it *deflects*, and it *clarifies* theory.[12]

There are very few attempts at theorizing in intercultural communication that fit into this category. One excellent example, however, of theory generated from a consistent, well-thought-out line of research is Young Kim's work on the communication acculturation of immigrants.[13]

A second approach to generating theory in intercultural communication is to utilize theory generated in other disciplines involving similar social processes. One example of this approach is Gudykunst and Halsall's essay applying a theory of contraculture developed from the prison literature to research on sojourner adjustment in other cultures.[14] These writers found that there is an isomorphic relationship between prisoners' adjustment to living in prison and sojourners' adjustment to living in another culture.

The third approach to constructing theory in intercultural communication involves elaborating and/or modifying theories currently used in the field of communication in general. This approach assumes that the underlying process is similar for *intra-* and *inter*cultural communication. Larry Sarbaugh, author of one of the most recent texts in the field, suggests this position when he says:

> There appears to be a temptation among scholars and practitioners of communication to approach *intercultural* communication as though it were a different process than *intracultural* communication. As one begins to identify the variables that operate in the communication being studied, however, it becomes apparent that they are the same for both intercultural and intracultural settings.[15]

Sarbaugh goes on to suggest that since all communication is intercultural to a certain extent, we can use homogeneity and heterogeneity of the participants to discern the degree of interculturalness.

Specific attempts to apply different perspectives from the general study of communication to the intercultural area were sparse prior to the action caucus on theory in intercultural communication at the 1980 Speech Association convention. Examples of early attempts include Gudykunst's[16] application of Miller and Steinberg's[17] developmental approach to interpersonal communication; Davey's discussion of cultural patterns and interaction sets;[18] Wiseman's application of a rules perspective;[19] and Wright's examination of social network analysis and its utility in intercultural communication.[20]

More recently, several writers have begun to extend theorizing on the coordinated management of meaning to other cultures.[21] These extensions include, but are not limited to, Alexander and her associates' research on topic sequencing and information gain in relationship development;[22] Stanback and Pearce's work on dissembling, passing, shucking, and toming;[23] and Wolfson and Pearce's study of the implications of self-disclosure for subsequent conversation.[24] Similarly, Cushman and his associates' work on rules in the mate-formation process[25] has been extended to consider cross-cultural comparisons.[26]

In addition to work on rules theory, several authors have recently examined theories of initial interaction from either a cross-cultural or intercultural perspective. For example, Shuter compared interracial and intraracial dyads involved in initial interactions,[27] while Gudykunst and Singh[28] examined uncertainty reduction theory[29] in initial intracultural and intercultural interactions, and in low- and high-context cultures.[30]

This volume of the *Annual* is devoted to building upon the foundation provided by earlier work by further exploring issues of theorizing in intercultural communication. The two remaining chapters in Part I examine general issues covered throughout this volume. For example, Okabe examines the cultural assumptions underlying communication theory from Eastern (Japan) and Western (United States) perspectives. The final essay in Part I by Sarbaugh and Asuncion-Lande synthesizes the papers emerging from the Action Caucus on Theory in Intercultural Communication held at the 1980 Speech Communication Association convention.

The chapters in Parts II, III, and IV can be seen as falling into the three approaches to theorizing outlined above (extending intracultural communication theory to intercultural settings, developing theory anew, and borrowing from other disciplines). Part II presents five chapters that extend theory developed to explain intercultural communication within the United States, including (1) Applegate and Sypher's extension of the constructivist approach, (2) Pearce and Wiseman's examination of the implications of rules theory for intercultural communication, (3) Cronen and Shuter's discussion of the development of interpersonal relationships between people from different cultures, (4) Koester and Holmberg's plea for a return to rhetoric for studying intercultural communication, and (5) Ruben's system-theoretic view of communication between people from different cultures.

Part III presents four new theoretical developments in intercultural communication. The first chapter, by Mowlana, presents an integrated theory of mass media and culture, while Barnett and Kincaid outline a mathematical theory of cultural convergence. The third chapter by Ellingsworth develops an adaptive theory of intercultural communication, and Tafoya presents a theory of the perceptions of the roots of conflict in intracultural and intercultural settings.

The final section, Part IV, includes six chapters that draw upon other disciplines to examine intercultural communication. The first two chapters, by Cooley and Asuncion-Lande, argue for the use of language and linguistic theory to explain communication between people from different cultures. The third chapter, by Ehrenhaus,[31] builds upon his earlier work and discusses culture's influence on the attribution process. The application of phenomenology is examined by Pilotta, while Blackman suggests the use of grounded theory to develop theories in intercultural communication. The final chapter, by Asante and Vora, argues for the use of multiple philosophical approaches in the study of intercultural communication.

Each chapter included in this volume taken alone is a laudible step in improving the state of theorizing in intercultural communication. Taken together, they lay the foundation for significant improvement in the near future. This volume must, however, be considered an initial attempt to outline the issues and various perspectives available for theorizing in intercultural communication. If it stimulates future development of theory in intercultural communication, the volume can be considered successful.

NOTES

1. K. R. Williams, "Reflections on a Science of Communication," *Journal of Communication*, 23 (1973): 243.

2. E. Stewart, "Outline of Intercultural Communication," in *Intercultural and International Communication*, ed. F. Casmir (Washington, DC: University Press of America, 1978), p. 265.

3. M. K. Asante, E. Nemark, and C. Blake, *Handbook of Intercultural Communication* (Beverly Hills, CA: Sage, 1979), p. 12.

4. D. P. Cushman and G. Whiting, "An Approach to Communication Theory: Toward a Consensus on Rules," *Journal of Communication* 22 (1972): 217-38.

5. V. McDermott, "The Literature on Classical Theory Construction," *Human Communication Research 2* (1975): 83-103.

6. T. S. Kuhn, *The Structure of Scientific Revolution*, 2nd ed. (Chicago, University of Chicago Press, 1979).

7. Some people would disagree with this statement. For example, B. Ruben contends that there is a paradigm that has been accepted in communication by default. He argues that this paradigm is "message sent equals message received." Ruben further argues that much of the early writing in the field was meant to clarify this paradigm, but we are now at a stage of transition from this old paradigm to an as yet unknown new paradigm. See B. Ruben, *Communication and Human Behavior* (New York: Macmillan, forthcoming). Obviously, I would tend to disagree with Ruben. It is my opinion that "message sent equals message received" does *not* constitute a paradigm in the sense of the term in which Kuhn uses it.

8. F. Casmir, ed., *Intercultural and International Communication* (Washington, DC: University Press of America, 1978).

9. R. Dubin, *Theory Building* (New York: Free Press, 1969), pp. 9-10.

10. T. Saral, "Intercultural Communication Theory and Research: An Overview," in *Communication Yearbook 1*, ed. B. Ruben (New Brunswick, NJ: Transaction, 1977), p. 393.

11. K. Popper, *The Logic of Scientific Discovery* (New York: Science Editions, 1968).

12. R. Merton, *On Theoretical Sociology* (New York: Free Press, 1967), p. 157.

13. Y. Kim, "Toward an Interactive Theory of Communication-Acculturation," in *Communication Yearbook 3* ed. D. Nimmo (New Brunswick, NJ: Transaction, 1979).

14. W. Gudykunst and S. Halsall, "The Application of a Theory of Contraculture to Intercultural Communication: Searching for Isomorphic Processes," in *Communication Yearbook 3*, ed. D. Nimmo (New Brunswick, NJ: Transaction, 1979).

15. L. Sarbaugh, *Intercultural Communication* (Rochelle Park, NJ: Hayden, 1979), p. 5.

16. W. B. Gudykunst, "Toward a Theoretical Framework for the Study of Intercultural Communication" (Paper delivered at the Speech Communication Association Convention, Washington, DC, November 1978).

17. G. R. Miller and M. Steinberg, *Between People* (Chicago: Science Research Associates, 1975).

18. W. G. Davey, "Cultural Patterns and Communication: Analyzing Interaction Sets and Interaction Outcomes" (Paper delivered at the Speech Communication Association Convention, Minneapolis, MN, November 1978).

19. R. Wiseman, "Intercultural Communication: A Rules Perspective" (Paper delivered at the Speech Communication Association Convention, Minneapolis, MN, November 1978).

20. J. Wright, "The Application of Social Network Analysis to the Study of Intercultural Communication" (Paper delivered at the Speech Communication Association Convention, Minneapolis, MN, November 1978).

21. W. B. Pearce, "The Coordinated Management of Meaning," in *Explorations in Interpersonal Communication*, ed. G. Miller (Beverly Hills, CA: Sage, 1976).

22. A. Alexander, V. Cronen, K. Kang, B. Tsou, and J. Banks, "Patterns of Topic Sequencing and Information Gain: A Comparative Study of Relationship Development in Chinese and American Cultures" (Paper delivered at the Speech Communication Association Convention, New York, November 1980).

23. M. H. Stanback and W. B. Pearce, "Talking to 'The Man': Some Communication Strategies Used by Members of 'Subordinate' Social Groups," *Quarterly Journal of Speech* 67 (1981): 21-30.

24. K. Wolfson and W. B. Pearce, "A Cross-Cultural Comparison: Implications of Self-Disclosure for Subsequent Conversation" (Paper delivered at the International Communication Association Convention, Minneapolis, MN, May 1981).

25. See, for example, D. P. Cushman, B. Valentinsen, and D. Dietrich, "A Rules Theory of Interpersonal Relationships," in *Comparative Theories of Human Communication*, ed. F. Dance (New York: Harper & Row, 1981).

26. D. P. Cushman and E. Kunimoto, "A Rules Theory of the Mate Relationship in Two Subcultures of the United States," in *Communication from an Eastern and Western Perspective,* ed. L. Kincaid and D. Cushman (forthcoming).

27. R. Shuter, "Initial Interactions of American Blacks and Whites in Interracial and Intraracial Dyads," *Journal of Social Psychology* 117 (1982): 45-52.

28. W. Gudykunst and I. Singh, "An Exploratory Study of Uncertainty Reduction in Initial Intracultural and Intercultural Encounters" (Paper delivered at the Speech Communication Association Annual Convention, New York, November 1981).

29. C. Berger and R. Calabrese, "Some Explorations in Initial Interaction and Beyond," *Human Communication Research* 1 (1975): 99-112.

30. W. Gudykunst, "Uncertainty Reduction and Predictability of Behavior in Low- and High-Context Studies: An Exploratory Study," *Communication Quarterly* (in press).

31. P. Ehrenhaus, "The Application of Attribution Theory to Intercultural Communication," in *Communication Yearbook 6*, ed. M. Burgoon (Beverly Hills, CA: Sage 1982).

2

Cultural Assumptions of East and West
Japan and the United States

ROICHI OKABE • *Nanzan University*

There has been a growing interest over the past decade in intercultural theory of communication and rhetoric among scholars of the social sciences, philosophy, and the humanities. Many students of communication have become conscious of the critical roles that intercultural perspectives of communication theory assume both theoretically and practically.

Despite this spreading awareness of the importance of the study of communication theory from diverse approaches across national boundaries, the dominant perspective toward communication, and consequently nearly all of the studies in this field, come out of the United States. Very few researchers, for example, have examined the nature, function, and scope of both the theory and the practice of Japanese communication and rhetoric from intercultural perspectives.

The purpose of this chapter is to present one alternative way, namely an Eastern way, of looking at human communication by analyzing and categorizing cultural assumptions, values, and characteristics of communication and rhetoric as they are found in Japanese culture in comparison and contrast with those in the American counterpart.

More specifically, the first part of my chapter will concern itself with a preliminary exploration and analysis of cultural values as found in both societies along the line of Robert L. Scott's nuclear concepts in communication and rhetoric. He lists such concepts as "substance," "form," "strategy," "style," and "tone" as key constituents of communication.[1] This will be followed, in the second section of this study, by an analysis of how cultural assumptions and values of these two societies characterize the function, scope, and patterns of communication in each.

On the basis of the assumption of divergences between the two cultures under discussion, I will set out in this study to describe in dichotomous terms cultural values and assumptions as found in Japan and the United States. All these contrasting assumptions, however, should be viewed as differing in degree or in emphasis rather than as strictly dichotomous in substance. In other words, all these pattern variables should be taken, not as binary distinctions, but as means of pointing out a relative degree of the preponderance of one characteristic over the other. I will, therefore, employ the modifier "predominantly" frequently to indicate relatively high degrees of specific characteristics, as in "predominantly dependent," "predominantly interdependent," and so on.

CULTURAL VALUES IN JAPAN AND THE UNITED STATES

Substance

Rober L. Scott lists rhetorical "substance" as the first nuclear concept in communication, and defines it as "that which enables the speaker to link the stuff of his commitments to those of his listeners."[2] He has in mind value assumptions that speakers and their listeners tend to share.

Values play an important role in rhetorical communication. Speakers or writers will try to link arguments whenever possible to positions generally held by the audience or reader. "An argumentation," the Belgian rhetorician Chaim Perelman asserts, "depends for its premises—as indeed for its entire development—on that which is accepted; that which is acknowledged as true, as normal and probable, as valid."[3] It is fair to assume that in an *intra*cultural setting a communicator and a receiver invariably share some views, desires, and values that can serve as the bases upon which a receiver-conscious communicator builds a receiver-centered case. This assumption, however, does not apply to *inter*cultural communication, where persons of diverse cultural backgrounds interact. This is why an analysis should be made of the cultural values of the Japanese and the Americans that will inevitably characterize the function, scope, and patterns of intercommunication between the two cultures under discussion.

I will here compare and contrast predominant value assumptions held by the Japanese and the Americans concerning their respective society and culture, their attitudes toward nature itself, their human relationships, and their thinking (or thought) patterns.

Values concerning the nature of society and culture. There are two key concepts for understanding the nature of Japanese society and culture: homogeneity and verticality. Whereas heterogeneity in race, language, habit, and mores is predominant in America, Japan's unusual homogeneity as a people should be emphasized as a key to explaining its culture. One cultural anthropologist, Masao Kunihira, calls Japan an "endogamous society," by which he means that "the members share a great many aspects of their daily life and consciousness."[4] Closely related to this dual concept of homogeneity and heterogeneity is that of verticality and horizontality. "In abstract terms," Chie Nakane observes, "the essential types of human relations can be divided . . . into two categories: *vertical* and *horizontal.*"[5] Nakane then attempts to explain through the vertical principle the unique structure of Japanese society, which contrasts with the more horizontal nature of American society.[6]

A horizontal society, typically, is one based on the principle of assumed equality or egalitarianism. "Running through the American's social relationships with others," writes Edward C. Stewart, "is the theme of equality. . . . Interpersonal relations are typically horizontal, conducted between presumed equals."[7] One obvious contrast between Japanese and American societies is the much greater Japanese emphasis on hierarchy.[8] The concept of hierarchy remains fundamental and all-pervasive in Japanese culture, thus coloring its character and determining its shape. Japanese society is divided into numerous groupings, each structured along multiple status layers. This vertical, hierarchical arrangement is quite evident in many organizations, notably government bureaucracies and business firms. Such a speciality of the culture of Japan as the principle of homogeneity and veriticality may be attributed to its unique natural conditions, its geographical isolation, and its mild climate. The Japanese have escaped invasions from the outside as well as large-scale famines.

A couple of cultural typologies may serve to explain the above-mentioned characteristics of Japanese versus American cultures. In her remarkable pioneer effort right after World War II to paint a coherent picture of Japanese culture, Ruth Benedict uses a combination of the concepts of "shame" and "guilt." She characterizes Japan as having a shame, rather than a guilt culture such as that of the United States. This means, she explains, that shame before the judgment of the society or the world is a stronger conditioning force than guilt before God. Benedict makes the distinction clear: "True shame cultures rely on external sanctions for good behavior, not, as true guilt cultures do, on an internalized convictions of sin."[9]

Another unique typology should be insightful for a contrastive analysis of Japanese and American cultures. The noted philosopher, Masao Maruyama, describes American culture as being like the *sasara,* a bamboo whisk used in the Japanese tea ceremony and characterized by the outward spreading of many fine wood strands made by carefully slitting one end of a piece of bamboo. He characterizes Japanese culture, on the other hand, as being like the *takotsubo,* or octopus pot, an urn-shaped trap that catches octopi simply by drawing them inside it. American culture, in other words, reaches outward; Japanese culture draws inward. Maruyama cites as one manifestation of the *takotsubo* character the tendency of Japanese scholars to work in a vacuum—that of taking in only what they feel is needed for their own academic pursuits and of never venturing out of their self-sufficient cubicles. While meaningful dialogues in the West are conducted among scholars in diverse branches, the only true communication and information exchange in homogeneous, vertical Japan may be observed within a single cubicle.[10]

To account for the difference between Japanese and American cultures, Maruyama and others offer yet another typology of the "doing" and the "being" orientations.[11] Such American expressions as "getting things done," "How are you doing?" "I'm doing fine—how are you coming along?" all indicate that "doing," as Stewart asserts, "is the dominant activity for Americans."[12] In a feudalistic, vertical society such as that of Japan, an individual's birth, family background, age, and rank tend to be more important than his or her later achievement and development.[13] "What he *is,*" in other words, carries a greater significance than "what he *does.*" For those who have been reared in American culture, peace, for instance, is something that must be built. They face outward to build peace and at the same time work for internal changes that will make peace more effective in the totality of things. In contrast to this American doing/building consciousness, the Japanese see peace as the status quo and something for them to preserve. They think of things happening or being of themselves. Even things that have been decided upon are thought of as having happened. Asked what they have been doing, Japanese are likely to answer not "I did such and such," but "Things happen to be so and so."[14]

Still another typology that serves to explain the distinction between the two cultures under consideration is that of "pushing" and "pulling" cultures. The pushing culture, according to Shinya Takatsu, a journalist, has a practical and scientific orientation represented by the development of computers and electronics. The United States represents this sort of culture. Japanese culture, by contrast, is traditionally pulling in nature in that its orientation is humanistic and aesthetic, as seen in the development of its unique, traditional music, art, and literature. Takatsu hastens to add, however, that these two seemingly contrastive modes of cultures should be seen as complementary rather than as symmetrical or diametrically opposed.[15]

Kyoto University Professor Yuji Aida sets forth one last typology to differentiate the American from the Japanese culture: that of the *omote* ("exterior" or "outside") and the *ura* ("interior" or "inside") cultures. In the heterogeneous, egalitarian, *sasara*-type, doing, pushing culture of the United States, there is no distinction between the *omote* and the *ura* aspects of culture. The predominating *omote* aspect is always taken at face value and always carries its own meaning. In the hierarchical, *takotsubo*-type, being, pulling culture of Japan, on the other hand, a clear-cut distinction should always be made between the *omote* and the *ura* dimensions of culture, the former being public, formal, and conventional, and the latter private, informal, and unconventional. The Japanese tend to conceive of the *ura* world as being more real, more meaningful.[16] This tendency of the Japanese to distinguish between the *omote* and *ura* aspects of culture is closely related to their inclination to make the sharp discrimination between belongers to (or "ins" of) a given *takotsubo* group and outsiders (or "outs").[17] At national and international levels, all foreigners are lumped together as *gaijin* (literally "outsiders") and treated as such. This exclusive attitude tends to create, as one journalist puts it, "the Japan-is-different syndrome."[18] This at best frustrates mutual exchange of information and ideas between the insiders and the outsiders in Japan.

Attitudes toward nature. The American mode of living is characterized by confrontation with and exploitation of the external world and by humanity's being armed against it. The conquest of natural conditions is the dominant assumption in the United States. Condon calls the American's relationship with nature a "master-slave relationship . . . with man the master of nature."[19] "The American's formidable and sometimes reckless drive to control the physical world,"[20] however, is diametrically opposed to the adaptative attitude of the Japanese toward nature. They tend to look at humanity and nature in total harmony and in eternal inseparability. They have the subtle wisdom to devise comfortable conditions for human living by adapting themselves to their natural surroundings.

Values concerning interpersonal relationships. The value of independence is predominant in the horizontal, doing culture of the United States. The independent "I" and "you" clash in argument and try to persuade each other. They go so far as to enjoy argument and heated discussion as a sort of intellectual game.[21] The principle underlying this high value set on independence is the notion that each individual is solely responsible for his or her fate. What others think and say is of little significance. In contrast, it is the value assumption of interdependence that dominates the stratified, vertical, and being culture of Japan. Here pronouns such as "I" and "you" are truly "relative" in that their correct forms can only be determined in relation to the others in the interaction. Generally, "we" predominates over "I" in Japanese interpersonal relations. What others think and say is of greater importance than what the individual does. This value of interdependence, if taken to the extreme, turns to that of *amae*, namely "dependence, the desire to be passively loved, the unwillingness to be separated from the mother-child circle and cast into a world of objective 'reality.' "[22] The propensity to continue to seek dependent gratification is directly related to Japanese primary association. Commenting on this concept of *amae* as it relates to the social structure, Takeo Doi, originator of the idea, states that "*amae* is a key concept for the understanding not only of the psychological makeup of the individual Japanese but of the structure of Japanese society as a whole. The emphasis on vertical relationships . . . could . . . be seen as an emphasis on *amae*."[23]

The concept of *amae* also underlies the Japanese emphasis on the group over the individual, the acceptance of constituted authority, and the stress on particularistic rather than universalistic relationships. There would appear to be two distinct and diametrically opposed cultural concepts affecting both the individual and national cultures of peoples, which James Moloney, borrowing from Hamlet's famous quandry, calls "the 'to be free' concept and the 'not to be free' concept."[24] American political theory, he says, emphasizes individualism, the "to be free" idea. The American value of individualism encourages self-assertion and frank expression of opinions and shows up in the American propensity to argue back when challenged.[25] In the homogenous, vertical society of Japan, on the other hand, the dominant value is conformity to or identity with the group: The Japanese insist upon the insignificance of the individual. The group emphasis has affected the whole gamut of interpersonal relationships in Japan. A group player is more liked than a solo player, for instance. As the old Japanese saying goes, the nail that sticks out gets banged down. The Japanese, therefore, display great cautiousness in expressing personal opinions and in modifiying their opinions to be consistent with those of others around them. [26]

In the American model, each individual asserts himself or herself to other individuals who are presumed to be his or her equals. This creates symmetrical relationships, based as they are "on an assumption of likeness, or similarity." The interaction between equals is predominantly the American value assumption. Japanese culture, however, values the contrastive pattern of complementary relationships based "on assumptions of differences, which complement each other to make a whole."[27] John Condon summarizes the key difference between the two cultures under discussion along the dual concept of symmetry and complementality:

> As a culture, Americans place great value on symmetrical relationships, minimizing differences that might suggest inequality. Americans tend not to like titles or honorifics that suggest some superior/subordinate relationship. . . .
>
> Symmetrical relationships maximize similarities of age, sex, role, or status and serve to encourage the apparent differences of each individual as an individual. . . . Complementary relationships [in a culture like that of Japan] maximize differences in age, sex, role, or status and serve to encourage the mutuality of the relationship, the interdependence.[28]

Because they are presumed to be equal and symmetrical in their relationships, the Americans tend to maximize their "public self," that is, to expose more of themselves than the Japanese, who are apt to keep their "private self" to a maximum in their interaction with others. As a result, Americans are likely to express their inner feelings and emotions openly, while Japanese tend to conceal them in an effort to maintain harmonious relations with the people around them.[29]

Another aspect of the difference between American and Japanese cultures is found in the diametrical values of informality and formality. Americans tend to treat other people with informality and directness. They shun the use of formal codes of conduct, titles, honorifics, and ritualistic manners in their interaction with others. They instead prefer a first-name basis and direct address. They also strive to equalize the language style between the sexes.[30] In sharp contrast, the Japanese are likely to assume that formality is essential in their human relations. They are apt to feel uncomfortable in some informal situations. The value of formality in the language style and in the protocol allows for a smooth and predictable interaction for the Japanese, "who cannot communicate until they know the status of the other person since the language requires different forms to correspond to the status of the listener."[31]

Values concerning thinking (or thought) patterns. Cultural differences in patterns of thinking are important issues for both American and Japanese communicators. Analytical thinking, first of all, characterizes the thought pattern of Americans. They tend to analyze and dissect things into elements in order to understand them properly. Their emphasis is upon the parts rather than upon the whole of things. They tend to be quite strong in classification and categorization and to pursue absolute dichotomies such as good and bad, God and the devil, the individual and the whole.

Contrary to this American way of thinking, the Japanese are likely to employ synthetic thinking patterns—synthetic in that they try to "grasp reality in its suchness or isness, or in its totality, seeing things as they are in themselves. . . ."[32] They do not analyze or divide things into categories, so much as they synthesize elements into a unified whole. In this sense, their emphasis is upon the "whole."[33]

Another cultural difference in thinking patterns may be found in the American inclination toward absolutism and in the Japanese tendency toward relativism. In a society that sees itself as made up of independent and equal individuals, as indeed the United States does, any thinking pattern must predominantly be universalistic and absolutistic, applying to all individuals equally. The concepts of right and wrong, for instance, must be clear and invariable, regardless of one's personal status. In a society in which people view themselves primarily as members of groups, however, specific relationships may take precedence over universal principles. Criteria, in other words, may be more situational than absolutistic.[34]

The distinction between another set of thinking patterns, realism and idealism, should also be mentioned here. Realism is factual. It puts its focus on objective facts. This is predominantly the thinking pattern of Americans, who value objectivity, specificity, and precision.[35] In sharp contrast, Japanese thinking is predominantly that of idealism. It puts greater stress on subjective ideas than on objective facts. The Japanese tend to think introspectively and do not show too much interest in the precise details of factual events. The Japanese people, in this sense, are subjective in thinking and orientation.

This discussion of the differences in thinking patterns between the United States and Japan will be concluded with a reference to one last typology—that of "line" versus "point/dot/space." In American culture communication is not established unless the words follow a certain route. The logicality of the English language may be thought of as a line. The listener proceeds toward understanding what the speaker says as he or she follows the coherent, linear route of the speaker. In a hetero-geneous and egalitarian society very little is take for granted in com-munication. As a result, the logical route should be solidly paved and the listener, too, must take care not to stray from its bounds. The Japanese language, on the other hand, tends to make for a pointlike, dotlike, spacelike thinking. The speaker organizes his or her ideas and thoughts in a stepping-stone mode: The listener is supposed to supply what is left unsaid. In the homogeneous society of Japan much commonality is taken for granted, so that the Japanese tend to value those loose modes of communication that leave much room for various interpretations.[36]

I have thus far discussed the divergences in rhetorical substance, namely the value assumptions held by American and Japanese communicators. I will now turn to an analysis of how these value assumptions influence the theory and practice of communication and rhetoric as found in American and Japanese cultures.

Form

Robert L. Scott lists rhetorical forms as the second nuclear concept in communication. Form is concerned with the problem of ordering and organizing a discourse.[37] The first difference in discourse organization between the two cultures under discussion is that of the speaker's perspective. If, as in America, the goal of the speaker in relation to his or her audience is confrontation and persuasion, then his or her form should stress those points where he or she differs with his or her opponent. The debater's case is a prime example of a point—a polarized, dichotomous, confrontational mode of organization. If the speaker's goal is harmony and consensus in a homogeneous cultural context, as in Japan, however, the communicative form is likely to be "cautious, tentative, complementary toward the others, incomplete and seeking others to make the position complete."[38] In such an aggregative form, the speaker takes great care in structuring his or her discourse before arriving at his or her point.

Allied closely to this dichotomy between polarization and aggregation in rhetorical form is that of linear and circular forms of argumentation. American logic and rhetoric value step-by-step, chainlike organization, as frequently observed in the problem-solution pattern or in the cause-to-effect or effect-to-cause pattern of organization. In this kind of communicative form, logic is tossed continuously and aggressively between the speaker and the listener, and throughout there is a sense of reinforcing each other's independence. By contrast, Japanese logic and rhetoric emphasize the importance of a dotted, pointlike method of structuring a discourse. No sense of rigidity or logicality is required in the Japanese-speaking society, where there is instead a sense of leisurely throwing a ball back and forth and carefully observing the other's response.

One of the main features of composition in the English language is the construction of a coherent and unified paragraph, a series of sentences that develop one central topic in a clear and forceful manner. Americans are encouraged to start a paragraph with a topic sentence, to develop it with specific details, and to conclude with a return to a general statement in the summary sentence. Rhetorical composition in America values a harmonious proportion between the theme and the details. "As a general rule in English composition and speaking," John Condon aptly points out, "the clearest and most appreciated presentations or explanations are those which contain a balance between the abstract and the specific."[39]

Due to the lack of the paragraph sense on the part of the Japanese, however, I find it difficult, or almost impossible, as an instructor of English and communication, to teach Japanese students of English to write a coherent English paragraph. A paragraph or even a whole composition is usually marked either by a *hosomi* form or by a *zundo* form. *Hosomi*, which literally means "slender," is a way of organizing a discourse with only specific details. *Zundo*, literally "stumpy," is a form of structuring a composition with only general statements. Excessive reliance either on the general or on the specific is a hallmark of form in Japanese rhetoric.

Americans' emphasis on a balance between the general and the specific leads them to place their strongest, most interesting points at the beginning of the series in each major part of a discourse. To put its another way, they tend to follow primacy and anticlimactic principles of organization. By contrast, Japanese communication predominantly favors recency and climactic principles of rhetorical form, saving the most interesting points for the end of the series.[40]

One last distinction in form may be observed in the American emphasis on process versus the Japanese reliance on product. Japanese is often defined as a language of product, a "terminal" language that skips process and goes immediately to a conclusion. The way the Japanese use their language involves what may appear to be leaps in logic. The English language, on the other hand, is described as the embodiment of logic, which is the process itself. Americans value the logical process by which a conclusion is to be drawn. The main difference in rhetorical mode of organziation is that Japanese communication is directed toward the object "what" from the beginning, while the English language stresses the steps leading up to the "what," namely the "how" or "why."

Strategy

Value assumptions influence how each culture views not only form but also strategy in rhetorical communication, which Robert Scott defines as the instruments of rhetoric that the speaker uses for eliciting the intended response from the listeners.[41] Here will be compared and contrasted the way the respective culture looks at three modes of proof in rhetoric, namely ethos, logos, and pathos, and the way each culture under consideration proceeds toward making decisions.

Rhetorical proof. Since the days of Corax and Tisias, Western rhetorical theorists have been concerned with the role of ethos in communication. During this 2400-year period, Aristotle's view that such dimensions of ethos as intelligence, character, and good will are the most potent means of persuasion has seldom been challenged.[42] Plato, Isocrates, Cicero, and Quintilian all express similar views.[43] It is a surprising fact that almost without exception, modern empirical and experimental studies have demonstrated the theoretical importance of ethos in rhetorical communication.[44]

As a general principle, ethos may be viewed as the dominant factor in rhetorical communication across cultures. However, what constitutes ethos may differ from culture to culture. Here again, the value assumptions of each culture under discussion will give a clue to discovering the ideal constituents of ethos. Americans, for example, still tend to accept such constituents of ethos as intelligence, competence, and character as potent in communication. These qualities are achieved rather than ascribed: the speaker, in other words, has acquired them through his or her own efforts and initiative. The Japanese, on the other hand, have a tendencey to subscribe to such ascribed characteristics as seniority, sex, and family background. If the speaker is old, male, and from a reputable family, he may be able to depend on these ascribed qualities in rhetorical communication. Takeshi Naruse observes that in evaluating a person's competence and qualifications, what matters in Japan is not what he or she has learned, but where he or she has learned it—more specifically, what school he or she attended.[45] Thus, as the constituents of the concept of ethos may differ from culture to culture, their influences should be taken seriously in attempting to understand intercultural communication.

The concept of logos provides another example of the difference in rhetorical theory between the two cultures. The American values of specificity, objectivity, and precision tend to lend support to the importance of using as logical proof facts, figures, and quotations from authority. These values also require exactness in citing what others have said.[46] Exact quotation is possible in a society where the unification of spoken and written forms is the rule, and not the exception. This is not the case with Japan, however. Since Japanese culture values the assumptions of subjectivity and ambiguity, the Japanese communicator is inclined to shun relying on specific facts, figures, and quotations from authority. If he or she must resort to quotations, he or she will usually paraphrase rather than quote verbatim what others have said. The main reason for the necessity of paraphrasing is that the separation of spoken and written forms is often the case with the Japanese language.

As has been discussed and analyzed in the section on thinking patterns, Americans value logical consistency, or line logic, in contrast to the extra- and paralogic, or point logic, practiced by the Japanese. Americans, in other words, are more inclined toward hard, mindlike logic than the Japanese, who tend to adopt soft, heartlike logic. As a result, Americans have a tendency to show greater preference for logos, reason, and cognition, whereas the Japanese have a tradition of highly developed words for expressing sympathy, appreciation, and encouragement. The Japanese speaker, therefore, is extremely skillful in expressing complicated emotional nuances, though he or she is weak in employing logic for the precise expression of intents and purposes.[47]

The components of rhetorical proof are thus more complicated than they might first appear to those reared in the tradition of Western rhetoric. They are strongly colored by cultural and national differences. Their nature and function should be analyzed carefully before they can be successfully introduced into intercommunication among cultures and nations.

Decision-making strategy. Decisions in American democracy are ideally made by the majority for the greatest good of the greatest number without infringing on the basic rights of the minority or the individual. Open conflict of views and the resolution of differencs of opinions through rational discussion and by simple majority voting are both at the heart of the democratic system of the United States. Americans prefer a rational, specific, issue-oriented strategy of decision-making—issue-oriented in that they analyze the problem at hand with little regard to the human relations involved and then select the best possible solution.[48]

The Japanese, on the other hand, assume that differences of opinions can best be resolved and the most suitable decisions made not by argument and voting, but by more subtly seeking a consensus of feeling in a slow, cumbersome, and roundabout manner. Ideally, the Japanese prefer to avoid decisions, if they can, "letting nature take its course as long as the course is acceptable" for the sake of maintaining harmonious relations among members of the group.[49] Making a decision is analogous to resolving a conflict, and the ideas of conflict and confrontation are serious breaches of the Japanese values of harmony and interdependence. This is a diffuse, human-relations-oriented strategy to decision-making.[50] But when they must make a decision to resolve a conflict, the Japanese resort to the unique modes of *nemawashi*, the *ringi* system, and go-betweens.

The Japanese try to involve all relevant parties in the decision-making process. This process is called *nemawashi* or "root binding," which literally means binding the roots of a plant before pulling it out, and refers to the Japanese practice of broad consultation before taking actions for a decision. The functions of *nemawashi* include "to give each group ample time to adjust to the emerging decisions, to explain the goals of the decision and to let them understand the information that leads to this conclusion."[51] Through this method the group is in a position to elicit from its members widespread support for its final solution.

Another popular strategy employed for decision-making is the *ringi* system, which literally means "a system of reverential inquiry about the superior's intentions."[52] This system is the wide circulation of a document to which large numbers of persons affix their seals as a sign that they have seen it and approved what it says or proposes. The *ringi* system enables a group to arrive at unanimity and consensus. Referring to the considerable difference between American and Japanese methods of decision-making, Kazuo Nishiyama observes as follows: "The notion of 'decision by a majority' does not exist in the traditional Japanese process of decision-making or *ringi-seido*, because every member concerned must approve the proposal; it must be a unanimous decision. There is no decision, in the American sense, which is obtained through reasoning."[53]

To avoid confrontation and maintain group solidarity, the Japanese also tend to resort to go-betweens. In delicate interactions a neutral person seeks out the views of the two sides concerned and finds ways of resolving differences or else terminates the negotiations without the danger of loss of face on either side.[54]

Style

Rhetorical style is the fourth nuclear concept in communication. Robert Scott defines it as "the way in which language works to embody the communicative intentions of its users."[55] Here, too, the rhetorical canon of style is subject to the influence of cultural values and assumptions.

Reflecting the cultural value of precision, Americans' tendency to use explicit words is the most noteworthy characteristic of their communicative style. They prefer to employ such categorical words as "absolutely," "certainly," and "positively," even to the point of playing the devil's advocate. The English syntax dictates that the absolute "I" be placed at the beginning of a sentence in most cases, and that the subject-predicate relation be constructed in an ordinary sentence.[56] Americans are also inclined to value overstatement, exaggeration, and even oversimplification. They like to use superlative ranking phrases such as "the greatest," "the biggest," "the longest." In their eagerness to oversimplify the reality, they tend to describe it in a dichotomous, either-or pattern. In addition, they lean toward relying on "square words" with "square logic."

By contrast, the cultural assumptions of interdependence and harmony require that Japanese speakers limit themselves to implicit and even ambiguous use of words. In order to avoid leaving an assertive impression, they like to depend more frequently on qualifiers such as "maybe," "perhaps," "probably," and "somewhat."[57] Since Japanese syntax does not require the use of the subject in a sentence, the qualifier-predicate is a predominant form of sentence construction. This omission of the subject often leaves much room for ambiguity. The "I" is not dominant, as in English; its nature is rather determined by its relationship with others. In this sense, it is truly a relative pronoun. Another source of ambiguity in style is found in the preference of Japanese for understatement and hesitation rather than for superlative expressions. Lastly, they are likely to resort to "round words" with associative, "round logic."

Due to the influence of the doing/making orientation in American culture, English sentences are predominantly studded with action verbs. The cultural value of being orientation, on the other hand, requires speakers of Japanese to depend on state verbs that indicate their adherence to the status quo.

A doing-oriented culture is remarkable for its informality, spontaneity, and freedom from adherence to strict stylistic patterns. Americans try very hard to equalize their language and their interpersonal relations, despite differences of age, status, and sex, through an extensive use of informal, colorful, and at times humorous expressions in communication. Humor, in particular, is taken as an effective leveler of differences in interpersonal relations.

It is equally natural for the Japanese to shape their hierarchical relationships through the use of prescribed expressions. Japanese ceremoniousness in style is usually expressed in the varying degrees of honorific language, which differ not only in vocabulary but also in grammar. Failure to choose the correct word may mean offending someone. Consequently, they tend to think it safer to resort to platitudes, cliches, and set phrases than to devise fresh expressions for each interaction. The Japanese, in this sense, are more conscious about the form than about the content of communication.[58]

Another way of looking at the differences in American and Japanese rhetorical styles is to examine the degree of reliance upon what Basil Bernstein calls "elaborated" and "restricted" speech patterns.[59] In a "low-context" culture, namely a "highly individualized, somewhat alienated, fragmented" culture like that of the United States, the lack of shared assumptions requires the American speaker to verbalize his or her message to make his or her discrete intent clear and explicit.[60] Americans are thus more inclined to resort to "the verbal elaboration of meaning."[61] By contrast, Japanese is a typical "high-context" culture, in which "people are deeply involved with each other . . . information is widely shared . . . [and] simple messages with deep meaning flow freely."[62] In such a culture the people have traditionally established and preserved a great number of specific rules of conduct and forms of expression. They do not have to elaborate their speech codes. They can indeed safely depend on restricted codes of speech, which may be taken as "status-oriented speech system . . . [which] reinforces the form of the social difference."[63] With this speech system the Japanese speaker tends to minimize extra- and paraverbal aspects of communication. Bernstein sums up the characteristics of restricted codes as follows:

> The "how" of the communication would be important rather than the "what." The discrete intent of the speakers, the "I" of the speakers, would be transmitted not through varying the verbal selections, but through varying the expressive features of the communication, through changes in gestures, physical set, intonation, facial modifications.[64]

My assumption is that differences in style such as these between the two cultures under consideration here must be taken into account for understanding intercultural communication. These are acquired habits indicating widely shared assumptions held by the communicators within a particular culture. Cultural influences on rhetoric and communication are thus more complicated and far-reaching than they might first appear to be.

Tone

I have thus far discussed cultural assumptions of rhetoric as they concern the nuclear concepts of substance, form, strategy, and style. My discussion will now turn to the last nuclear concept, what Robert Scott calls "tone." By tone Scott has in mind "the speaker's attitude toward his listeners."[65]

In American rhetoric the speaker tends to view himself or herself as an agent of change, manipulating and persuading his or her listeners in a confrontational setting. There is a clear differentiation of roles between the speaker and the audience. The speaker is a transmitter of information, ideas, and opinions, while the audience is a receiver of these speech messages. The theory of Western rhetoric has long emphasized the importance of audience adaptation, but this concept, too, carries the implication that audience adaptation is a mere rhetorical technique always to be viewed from the side of the speaker. The speaker still remains the central, potent agent of attitude change and persuasion. To communicate well means, for the American speaker, to express himself or herself logically and persuasively. Focus on the expressive is a hallmark of American rhetoric.

By contrast, the rhetoric of Japan is remarkable for its emphasis on the importance of the perceiver. The Japanese people, in a sense, are excellent perceivers, capable of accurately tuning in to the faintest of signals. There is not a clear differentiation, but rather an integration of roles between the speaker and the audience. The speaker, therefore, always attempts to adjust himself or herself to his or her listeners. In a culture of *sasshi* or *omoiyari* (both words meaning "considerateness"), to communicate well means, for the Japanese speaker, to understand and perceive the inexplicit, even to the point of deciphering the faintest nuances of nonverbal messages. *Sasshi ga ii,* or "being a good mind reader," and *omoiyari ga aru,* or "being considerate about other's feelings," are both considered virtues in Japanese culture.[66] *Im*pressive or perceptive emphasis remains a potent orientation in the rhetoric of Japan.

The *erabi* ("selective") and *awase*("adjustive") typology proposed by Kinhide Mushakoji will here serve to illustrate the crucial difference in the concept of tone between speaker-centered and perceiver-centered cultures.[67] The *erabi* or selective view holds that human beings can manipulate their environment for their own purposes, as the speaker consciously constructs his or her message for the purpose of persuading and producing attitude change. *Erabi* means choosing the best from a range of alternatives to effect such change.

The *awase* or adjustive view, on the other hand, assumes that human beings will adapt and aggregate themselves to the environment rather than change and exploit it, as the speaker attempts to adjust himself or herself to the feelings of his or her listeners. *Awase is the logic not of choosing between but of aggregating several alternatives. Mushakoji succinctly describes communication patterns in awase* culture as follows:

> *Awase* logic does not depend upon standardized word meanings. Expressions have multifarious nuances and are considered to be only signals which hint at reality rather than describing it precisely. Words are not taken at face value; it is necessary to infer the meaning behind them. In contrast to *erabi* culture in which the face value of words is trusted most and one is expected to act on it, in *awase* society it is possible to "hear one and understand ten." It is interesting to note that in Japan it is considered virtuous to "catch on quickly" . . . to adjust to someone's position before it is logically and clearly enunciated.[68]

The first part of this chapter has thus discussed how cultural values, assumptions, and presuppositions of American and Japanese cultures both reveal and shape the kind of rhetorical theory practiced in each society under the influence of substance composed of value assumptions on the rhetorical concepts of form, strategy, style, and tone.

THE INFLUENCE OF VALUES ON COMMUNICATION

Overall Nature of Rhetoric and Communications

The second part of this chapter will briefly summarize, again in contrastive terms, the overall natue of the theory and practice of rhetoric and communication as understood in the United States and in Japan. It should be stressed once again that these summary views should be taken to indicate differences in degree rather than strict dichotomies in substance.

Functions of rhetoric and communications. Rhetoric, in the Western sense of the word, is concerned with persuasion pursued at public forums. The prototype of the American speaker consciously uses symbols to create an understanding and to form, strengthen, or change an attitude on the part of his or her listeners. American rhetoric, in this sense, is basically argumentative and logical in nature.[69] It is also confrontational in that the speaker as an independent agent always stands face to face with the listener as another independent agent. Confrontation carries a positive connotation in American rhetoric: It is seen as a dynamic force for the advancement of Western civilization.[70]

The Japanese, on the other hand, value harmony and view harmony-establishing and/or harmony-maintaining as a dominant function of communication. They seek to achieve harmony by a subtle process of mutual understanding, almost by intuition, avoiding any sharp analysis of conflicting views. The result is that Japanese rhetoric functions as a means of disseminating information or of seeking consensus. It is by nature intuitive, emotional, and adaptive.

Dominant modes of rhetoric and communication. There are at least two completely different systems of communication: dialogue and monologue. Dialogue, in the Western sense of the word, aims to clarify the points of disagreement. The dialogical or dialectical mode of communication is a dominant characteristic of American rhetoric and an especially effective means of resolving differences between two parties with diverse interests or backgrounds. Dialogue in this sense of the word, however, will not often appear between Japanese. Even when the mode of communication appears to be dialogical on the surface, its content is no more than alternating monologue; in their eagerness that their views conform, the two sides do not truly engage each other in discussion. Japanese communication tends to be monologic, since Japanese is basically a "chamber" language, not suitable for public discussion or speech at a big hall. In this sense Japanese is quite different from English, which fulfills the requirements of a "public hall" language.[71]

The digital and analogical dimensions of expression proposed by Watzlawick and his colleagues also serve to explain dominant modes of communication.[72] In a digital mode of communication there is no necessary connection between what is expressed and how it is expressed. Since the relationship is arbitrarily assigned, it must be learned. The digital is more characteristic of the American mode of communication. In an analogical mode of expression, however, the relationship between the content and the form is so close that with little training one can guess at the meaning of many analogical forms. The Japanese language is more inclined toward the analogical: its use of ideographic characters, its reliance on onomatopoeia, and its emphasis on the nonverbal aspect.

The excessive dependence of the Japanese on the nonverbal aspect of communication means that Japanese culture tends to view the verbal as only *a* means of communication, and that the nonverbal and the extra-verbal at times assume greater importance than the verbal dimension of communication. This is in sharp contrast to the view of Western rhetoric and communication that the verbal, especially speech, is *the* dominant means of expression.

In a low-context culture, like that of the United States, where very little is taken for granted, greater cultural diversity and heterogeneity are likely to make verbal skills more necessary and, therefore, more highly prized. One of the chief qualifications of a group leader, indeed, is his or her ability of verbal expression. Group leaders should be able to analyze and outline varying positions, clarify their differences, and invite open discussion and confrontation.

In a high-context culture, such as Japan's, however, cultural homogeneity encourages suspicion of verbal skills, confidence in the unspoken, and eagerness to avoid confrontation. The Japanese have even developed *haragei*, or the "art of the belly" for the meeting of minds or at least the viscera, without clear verbal interaction. Verbal ability is not necessarily required of Japanese leaders. They are, indeed, expected to perform this *haragei* art.

Other Characteristics of Rhetoric and Communication

The goal of Western societies, including the United States, is a civilization of the dialogue and public speaking. The spirit of Western civilization is the spirit of inquiry. Its dominant theme is the logos. Nothing is to remain undiscussed. Everybody speaks their minds eloquently and persuasively. The exchange of ideas is held to be the path to the realization of the potentialities of each society. America, in this sense, is a communication-active society.

In the tradition of rhetoric and communication, however, Japan stands out in marked contrast to much of the world. The feudalistic, hierarchical society of Japan is most notable for its emphasis on writing and for its total lack of a tradition of public speaking. Modesty, humility, and supression of self are moral ideals in this communication-passive society. These moral qualities lead to a shyness in communication behaviors rare in the age of aggressive self-assertion.

As a corollary to all of this, the Japanese have developed "aesthetics of silence" in place of rhetoric and logic. They tend to view silence as essential to self-realization and sublimation. This is diametrically opposed to the American way of looking at silence as symptomatic of a problem. It is a fairly recent development, and a good sign for students of intercultural communication, though, that in communication-active American society some attention is being paid to the importance of silence as an emerging area of rhetorical research.[73]

CONCLUSION

The first and second parts of this chapter have stressed the divergence and difference in cultural values, assumptions, and presuppositons as investigated and taught in American and Japanese theories of rhetoric and communication. It has been repeatedly called to mind throughout this chapter that the contrasting views outlined and analyzed here should be taken not as strictly dichotomous in substance but as differing more in degree. Although the main concern of this chapter has been with a comparison and contrast of "A" (for "American")-type theory and "J" (for "Japanese")-type theory of rhetoric and communication, this study implies some possibility of A-type theory coming closer to J-type theory and vice versa. This also suggests the possibility of constructing a Z-type theory of communication, an amalgam or an aggregation of both A-type theory and J-type theory, which could bridge the schism in communication among cultures and nations.[74]

My future interest will be in investigating to what extent these seemingly dichotomous assumptions of rhetoric and communication might converge on the continuum and under what conditions this convergence will be made possible. I take it as a good sign for students of intercultural communication that some scholars of an A-type theory have gradually directed their attention to the rhetorical significance of silence, a unique concept in J-type theory. It should be pointed out at the same time that some Japanese reared in J-type theory have found it necessary, or almost inevitable, to approach intercultural communication with something of A-type orientation to communication. They will have to "consciously construct and organize verbal messages" for the purpose of "persuading" their listeners of divergent cultural backgrounds, if they are to be successful in communicating across national and cultural boundaries. They will have to avoid "yes-no" ambiguity and to learn "how to agree to disagree" at international conferences and negotiations.[75]

It is to be hoped that this chapter will respond to the schism that might exist in Western and Eastern communicologists' understanding of intercultural communication and offer one impetus for encouraging joint explorations by communication scholars on both sides of the Pacific as to the possibility of constructing a Z-type theory of cultural rhetoric and communication.

NOTES

1. Robert L. Scott, "The Generative Power of Rhetorical Problems," in *The Speaker's Reader: Concepts in Communication* (Glenview, IL: Scott, Foresman, 1969), pp. 2-22.

2. Scott, *The Speaker's Reader*, p. 9.

3. Chaim Perelman, *The Idea of Justice and the Problem of Argument*, trans. John Petrie (New York: Humanities Press, 1969), p. 159. For a discussion of the importance of

values in communication, see Wayne C. Minnick, *The Art of Persuasion* (Boston: Houghton Mifflin, 1957), pp. 207-22.

4. Masao Kunihiro, "The Japanese Language and Intercultural Communication," in *The Silent Power: Japan's Identity and World Role*, ed. Japan Center for International Exchange (Tokyo: Simul Press, 1976), pp. 57-58.

5. Chie Nakane, *Japanese Society* (Berkeley: University of California Press, 1970), p. 23.

6. The theme of Nakane's other books is also centered around the vertical principle in Japanese society. See her *Tateshakai no ningenkankei* [Interpersonal Relationships in a Vertical Society] (Tokyo: Kodansha, 1967) and *Tateshakai no rikigaku* [Dynamism in a Vertical Society] (Tokyo: Kodansha, 1978).

7. Edward C. Stewart, *American Cultural Patterns: A Cross-Cultural Perspective* (Pittsburgh, PA: University of Pittsburgh, 1971), p. 46, and Edwin O. Reischauer, *The Japanese* (Tokyo: Charles E. Tuttle, 1977), p. 157.

8. Reischauer, *The Japanese*, pp. 151-157.

9. Benedict, *The Chrysanthemum and the Sword: Patterns of Japanese Culture* (Cleveland, OH: World Publishing Co., 1946), p. 223. See also Bin Kimura, " 'Ma' to kojin" ["Space" and the Individual], ed. Takehiko Kenmouchi (Tokyo: Kodansha, 1981), pp. 232-33, and Yujiro Shinoda, *Hokori to nihonjin* [Pride and the Japanese People] (Kyoto: PHP Institute, 1980), pp. 123-52.

10. Masao Maruyama, *Nihon no shiso* [The Intellectual Tradition in Japan] (Tokyo: Iwanami Shoten, 1961), pp. 123-52.

11. Maruyama, *Nihon no shiso*, pp. 153-80: Stewart, American Cultural Patterns, pp. 31-33; John C. Condon and Fathi S. Yousef, *An Introduction to Intercultural Communication* (Indianapolis, IN: Bobbs-Merrill Co., 1975), pp. 71-73, 137; Yuji Aida, *Nihonjin no ishiki kozo* [The Structure of the Japanese Consciousness] (Tokyo: Kodansha, 1972), pp. 36-37; Shichihei Yamamoto, *Nihonjin teki hasso to seiji bunka* [The Japanese Way of Thinking and Political Culture] (Tokyo: Nihon Shoseki, 1979), p. 208. The most recent book on this topic published in Japanese is Yoshihiko Ikegami, *"Suru" to "naru" no gengogaku* [The "Doing" and the "Becoming" Linguistics] (Tokyo: Taishu-kan Shoten, 1981).

12. Stewart, *American Cultural Patterns*, pp. 31-32.

13. Maruyama, *Nihon no shiso*, pp. 158-59.

14. Aida, *Nihon no shiso, pp. 36-37.*

15. *Shinya Takatsu, Hiku bunka osu bunka* [Pulling" Culture and "Pushing" Culture] (Tokyo: Kodansha, 1977), p. iv.

16. Aida, *Nihonjin no ishiki kozo*, pp. 57-59.

17. Maruyama, *Nihon no shiso*, p. 139.

18. Fumi Saisho, *Nihongo to eigo* [Japanese and English] (Tokyo: Kenkyusha, 1975) p. 11.

19. Condon, *Intercultural Communication*, p. 103.

20. Stewart, *American Cultural Patterns*, p. 59.

21. Reiko Naotsuka, *Obeijin ga chinmoku suru toki: Ibunka kan komyunikeishon* [When Europeans and Americans Keep Silent: Intercultural Communication] (Tokyo: Taishukan Shoten, 1980), pp. 116-17.

22. Takeo Doi, *Anatomy of Dependence,* trans. John Bester (Tokyo: Kodansha International, 1973, p. 7.

23. Doi, *Dependence,* p. 28.

24. James Clark Moloney, *Understanding the Japanese Mind* (Tokyo: Charles E. Tuttle Co., 1954), p. 2.

25. Takao Suzuki, *Kotoba to bunka* [Language and Culture] (Tokyo: Iwanami Shoten, 1973), pp. 202-203 and Stewart, *American Cultural Patterns*, pp. 68-71.

26. Shinoda, *Hokori to nihonjin,* pp. 204-5 and Reischauer, *The Japanese,* pp. 127-35.

27. John C. Condon, *Interpersonal Communication* (New York: Macmillan Publishing Co., 1977), p. 52.

28. Condon, *Interpersonal Communication,* pp. 53-54.

29. Dean C. Barnlund, *Nihonjin no hyogen kozo* [The Structure of Japanese Way of Expression], trans. Sen Nishiyama (Tokyo: Simul Press, 1973), pp. 35, 59. See also Barnlund, "The Public Self and the Private Self in Japan and the United States," in *Intercultural Encounters with Japan: Communication—Contact and Conflict,* eds. John C. Condon and Mitsuko Saito (Tokyo: Simul Press, 1974), pp. 27-96.

30. Stewart, *American Cultural Patterns,* pp. 49-50 and Condon, *Intercultural Communication,* pp. 86-87.

31. Stewart, *American Cultural Patterns,* p. 50.

32. Charles A. Moore, *The Japanese Mind: Essentials of Japanese Philosophy and Culture* (Tokyo: Charles E. Tuttle, 1967), p. 290.

33. For a discussion of the relation between the parts and the whole, see Hideo Yamashita, *Nihon no kotoba to kokoro* [The Japanese Language and Mind] (Tokyo: Kodansha, 1979), pp. 33-34.

34. Nobutane Kiuchi, "Fushigi na kuni' nihon o tsukuriageta nihonjin" [Japanese Who have Made up a "Wonderland Japan"], in *Nihonjin ni tsuite no jisho* [Ten Chapters on Japanese], ed. Yasutaka Teruoka (Tokyo: Chobunsha, 1981), p. 53.

35. John C. Condon, "The Values Approach to Cultural Patterns of Communication," in *Intercultural Encounters with Japan,* p. 150.

36. Shinoda, *Hokori to nihonjin,* pp. 208-15. For a discussion of line like and point like thinking patterns, see Shigehiko Toyama, *Nihongo no ronri* [The Logic of Japanese] Chuo Koronsha, 1975), and *Shoryaku no bungaku* [Omission in Literature] (Tokyo: Chuo Koronsha, 1976).

37. Scott, *The Speaker's Reader,* pp. 6-9.

38. Condon, *Intercultural Communication,* p. 243.

39. John C. Condon, *Words, Words, Words: What We Do with Them and What They Do to Us* (Tokyo: Seibido, 1977), p. 33. For a discussion of the general-specific balance, see also Condon, *Semantics and Communication* (New York: Macmillan, 1966), pp. 39-45.

40. Naotsuka, *Obeijin ga chinmoku suru toki,* pp. 245-45, and Shigehiko Toyama, *Kotowaza no ronri* [The Logic of Proverbs] (Tokyo Shoseki, 1979), pp. 204-11.

41. Scott, *The Speaker's Reader,* pp. 11-12.

42. Lane Cooper, trans., *The Rhetoric of Aristotle* (New York: Appleton-Century-Crofts, 1932), p. 92

43. W. M. Sattler, "Conceptions of Ethos in Ancient Rhetoric," *Speech Monographs,* 14 (March 1947): 55-65.

44. For a modern interpretation of the concept of ethos see James C. McCroskey, *An Introduction to Rhetorical Communication,* 3rd ed. (Englewood Cliffs, NJ: Prentice-Hall, 1978, pp. 67-85.

45. Takeshi Naruse, *Kotoba no jikai* [The Magnetic Field of Language] (Hiroshima: Bunka Hyoron Shuppan, 1979), p. 60.

46. Shichihei Yamamoto, *Nihonteki hasso to seiji bunka,* pp. 208-11.

47. For a discussion of the relation between reason and emotion see Yuichi Aira, "Shiron 'nihonjin' " [Personal Views on the Japanese], in Teruoka, *Nihonjin ni tsuite no jissho,* p. 177, and Tadanobu Tsunoda, *Nihonjin no no: No No hataraki to tozai no bunka* [The Japanese Brains: Their Functions in Eastern and Western Culture] (Tokyo: Taishukan Shoten, 1978), p. 85.

48. Kinhide Mushakoji, *Kodo kagaku to kokusai seiji* [Behavioral Sciences and International Politics] (Tokyo: Tokyo University Press, 1972), p. 232.

49. Richard Halloran, *Japan: Images and Realities* (Tokyo: Charles E. Tuttle, 1969), p. 90.

50. Mushakoji, *Kodo kagaku to kokusai seiji*, p. 233.

51. Ezra F. Vogel, *Japan as Number One: Lessons for America* (Cambridge, MA: Harvard University Press, 1979), 94.

52. Kiyoaki Tsuji, "Decision-Making in the Japanese Government: A Study of *Ringi-sei*," in *Political Development in Modern Japan*, ed. Robert E. Ward (Princeton, NJ: Princeton University Press, 1968), p. 457.

53. Kazuo Nishiyama, "Interpersonal Persuasion in a Vertical Society—The Case of Japan," *Speech Monographs*, 38 (June 1971): 149.

54. Condon discusses the role of go-betweens in communication in his *Interpersonal Communication*, pp. 55-58.

55. Scott, *The Speaker's Reader*, p. 13.

56. Hideo Kishimoto, "Some Cultural Traits and Religions," in Moore, ed., *The Japanese Mind*, pp. 110-11.

57. Condon, *Intercultural Communication*, pp. 217-18.

58. Yasushi Haga, *Nihonjin wa ko hanashita* [This Is How the Japanese Spoke] (Tokyo: Jitsugyo no Nihonsha, 1976), pp. 233-34 and Akiko Jugaku, *Nihongo no urakata* [The Background of the Japanese Language] (Tokyo: Kodansha, 1978), 29.

59. Basil Bernstein, "Elaborated and Restricted Codes: Their Social Origins and Some Consequences," *American Anthropologist*, 66 (December 1964) (Special Publication): 55-69.

60. Edward T. Hall, *Beyond Culture* (Garden City, NY: Anchor Books, 1976), p. 39.

61. Bernstein, "Elaborated and Restricted Codes," p. 63.

62. Hall, *Beyond Culture*, p. 39.

63. Bernstein, "Elaborated and Restricted Codes," p. 63.

64. Bernstein, "Elaborated and Restricted Codes," p. 61.

65. Scott, *The Speaker's Reader*, p. 14.

66. Takeo Suzuki, *Kotoba to shakai* [Language and Society] (Tokyo: Chuo Koronsha, 1975), pp. 65, 84-85; Takao Suzuki, *Kotoba to bunka*, pp. 201-2; and Aida, *Nihonjin no ishiki kozo*, p. 98.

67. Kinhide Mushakoji, "The Cultural Premises of Japanese Diplomacy," in *The Silent Power*, pp. 35-49.

68. Mushakoji, "The Cultural Premises," p. 43.

69. Condon, *Intercultural Communication*, pp. 190, 213, 232.

70. Hideaki Kase, *Nihonjin no hasso seiyojin no hasso* [The Japanese Way of Thinking and the Western Way of Thinking] (Tokyo: Kodansha, 1977), p. 31.

71. Takehide Kenmochi, "Nihongo to 'ma' no kozo" [The Japanese Language and the Structure of "Space"], in *Nihonjin to "ma,"* p. 26, and Shigehiko Toyama, *Hajime ni kotoba ariki* [In the Beginning Was the Word] (Tokyo: Kodansha, 1981), pp. 128-30.

72. Paul Watzlawick, Janet Beavin, and Don Jackson, *Pragmatics of Human Communication* (New York: W. W. Norton, 1967).

73. For a discussion of the importance of silence in communication, see Thomas J. Bruneau, "Communicative Silences: Forms and Functions of Silence," ETC, 30 (1973); and Richard L. Johannesen, "The Functions of Silence: A Plea for Communication Research," *Western Speech*, 38 (Winter 1974): 25-35.

74. The terms A-type theory, J-type theory, and Z-type theory are directly taken from a best-selling book by William G. Ouchi, professor of business administration at UCLA,

who has most recently proposed the importance of Z-type theory of business management, an amalgam of A-type and J-type theories of organizing and managing businesses. See his *Theory Z: How American Business Can Meet the Japanese Challenge* (Reading, MA: Addison-Wesley, 1981).

75. The *Asahi Shimbun*, an influential daily in Japan, recently commented on the marked change in the communication patterns of the Japanese participants at the Fifth Japan-U.S. Shimoda Conference held in September 1981. The participants from the Japanese side actively expressed their opinions and voiced their disagreements aggressively at times. See *Asahi Shimbun*, Evening ed., September 4, 1981: 3.

3

Theory Building in Intercultural Communication
Synthesizing the Action Caucus

L. E. SARBAUGH ● *Michigan State University*
NOBLEZA ASUNCION-LANDE ● *University of Kansas*

This chapter, a synthesis of papers on theoretic perspectives coming out of the Action Caucus and Seminar on Theory in Intercultural Communication, will focus on three tasks: a context for the action caucus, a summary of the reports from the eight work groups, and an effort to draw out the uniqueness and complementarities among the eight groups.

A CONTEXT FOR THE ACTION CAUCUS

Intercultural and cross-cultural communication studies have proliferated in the social and behavioral sciences during the past ten years. The proliferation is shown by the dramatic increase of published books and articles. Since 1973 ten text/reference books on intercultural communication have been published. Two journals—the *International and Intercultural Communication Annual,* and the *International Journal of Intercultural Relations*—have begun publishing exclusively on the topic. Further evidence of the growing interest is the increasing number of papers presented at national and international conferences of professional and scholarly organizations, and by the increase in courses in this area at universities and colleges in other countries as well as in the United States.

While this productivity attests to a growing popularity of the subject as an area of study, the quality of research that has been produced has varied widely. The field has become very popular and attracted many amateurs. While this is a favorable sign for the development of the field, in the sense that it demonstrates that the subject can be approached from a variety of perspectives, nevertheless, most amateurs do not recognize certain problems that this type of research poses and sometimes do not adhere to established standards for scientific research. The intent of the Action Caucus and Seminar on Theoretic Perspectives in Intercultural Communication was to provide a firmer base for continuing study in this field.

Early studies in the field of intercultural communication consisted mainly of subjective impressions based on travel or short-term contacts with other cultures. Some provided personal insights obtained by practitioners in a different cultural or in a multicultural setting. Some were the result of questionnaire surveys of small samples of informants from which general conclusions about patterns of communication behavior or culture were made. More recent studies, however, reflect fairly sophisticated research designs that could lead to the formulation of common basic concepts upon which the nature of communication across culture can be explained.

Several readers[1] and state-of-the art reviews[2] on the status of intercultural communication study reflect the fact that there are serious issues that need to be resolved if the area of intercultural communication is to continue to develop a basic set of propositions for research and practice.

Those planning the Action Caucus and Seminar on Theoretical Perspectives in Intercultural Communication for the 1980 SCA Convention were guided by the following three assumptions:

(1) Intercultural communication is an extension of the study of communication phenomena generally. The communication variables being studied are the same in both intercultural and intracultural settings. The values of the variables between the settings differ, but the same basic variables are employed in analyzing communication in both. Support for this view is expressed by Ellingsworth and Sarbaugh.[3]

(2) The uniqueness of intercultural communication as a field of study lies in its focus on the cultural factors that impede communication among or between persons or groups of differing cultures. Support for this assumption can be found in recent books on intercultural communication.[4]

(3) Major theoretic perspectives that underlie the study of human communication can provide fruitful directions to guide the study and the practice of intercultural communication.

Among the theoretic perspectives examined at the Action Caucus and Seminar were (1) codes and code systems, (2) constructivism, (3) different philosophical perspectives (non-Western), (4) mathematical modeling, (5) relationship development, (6) rhetorical theory, (7) rules perspective, and (8) systems theory. Participants at the Action Caucus were preassigned to work groups concentrating on each of the eight different perspectives.

At least two members of each group were asked to prepare "stimulator" papers dealing with that perspective. These papers were then sent to individuals who had indicated an interest in participating in the discussion. The Action Caucus was followed by a seminar that involved only the leaders of each group, and included the chairperson and the coordinator/participant observer of the joint sessions.

The seminar served as a mechanism to pull together the key ideas discussed at the work group sessions. The point of convergence of the different communication perspectives, their distinct properties, and the implications for theory building in intercultural communication were examined.

Although the caucus and seminar continued for a day and a half, the time and energy of the participants were not adequate for a thorough analysis and synthesis of the eight perspectives. The leader and coleader for each work group had several days of work following the convention to bring together the points of view expressed in their groups. The chapters in this issue of the *Annual* reflect the work both at the convention and following the convention.

AN ASSESSMENT OF THE EIGHT PERSPECTIVES

As one reviews each of the eight group reports, it becomes apparent that those in each group found themselves engrossed in discussions of both theory and methodology. It will become apparent also that there are some unique aspects presented by each perspective and that there are some commonalities among the various perspectives. It also will be noted that together and individually they have raised some provocative questions for those studying and practicing intercultural communication.

Codes and Code Systems

Cooley and Asuncion-Lande stressed the centrality of codes to any study of communication and especially to the study of intercultural communication. Cooley noted, however, that a review of four major communication journals from 1969 to 1979 by H. W. Cummings revealed only sixty articles on language, even when one uses a very relaxed definition of language (codes). Their point was that although codes are central to the study of communication, relatively little of the effort has been directed to this aspect of the communication process.

They define code as a culturally defined, rule-governed system of shared arbitrary symbols used to transmit (and elicit)[5] meaning. Included within the concept of code are language, paralinguistic phenomena, nonverbal phenomena, silence, language choice, multilingual behavior, interruptions, turn-taking, and organization of talk. Cooley and Asuncion-Lande said that the term code system is a redundancy since the term code entails systematicity.

Descriptions of complex code behaviors may be studied through linguistic theory, sociolinguistic theory, psycholinguistic theory, ethnomethodology, and ethnography of speaking. In their report, Cooley and Asuncion-Lande focused on sociolinguistics, ethnomethodology, and ethnography of speaking as the most fruitful for intercultural study. Their choice of these perspectives was based on a belief that it is more fruitful to study language in use so that the impact of context is included in the findings.

The strengths noted for sociolinguistics are the use of rigorous linguistic analytic methods to examine language in use; along with that, they sought to demonstrate the relationship between the language behaviors of interest and the social norms of the community. This also allows for the study of changes in codes or creation of new codes between two communities that do not share a common language.

The ethnomethodologists study how people construct their everyday activities and use those constructions to make their behaviors accountable and reportable. Cooley pointed out that although the ethnomethodologists do not have the rigorous set of analytic methods, they do systematically handle large amounts of data to determine patterns, interpret them, and generalize from those interpretations. This he found of great value.

A strength of both sociolinguistic and ethnomethodological approaches is their reliance on context. The code group saw this as a highly important consideration for the study of codes in intercultural communication. They said that only by placing context in the middle of the investigation can we arrive at some understanding of the meanings that attach to the behaviors we are interested in.

The report of the codes work group argues for some set of principles for organizing contexts according to the place they have in a given society's organization of its everyday world. It is proposed that ethnographic analysis of the communicative conduct of a community is the way to achieve this set of principles. The claim for ethnographic analysis is that it will inevitably result in a body of data that can be organized according to the communicative contexts within and across cultures. That will lead to a start at understanding the range of events serving to express and perpetuate values within a culture. Then one can begin to engage in cross-cultural comparisons.

Throughout the report of the work group on codes there is the suggestion of the interdependence between codes and culture and their centrality to the communication process. The importance of language (codes) has been generally accepted as a vital factor in intercultural communication. A counter-concern has been that the focus on language might obscure the importance of other aspects of the process. Nevertheless, the questions posed by the codes group and their emphasis on studying codes in natural settings offer a direction for continuing fruitful theorizing and research.

Constructivism

Applegate and Sypher, reporting as coleaders of this group, emphasized the importance of learning about intercultural communication throughout the study of everyday actions, as did the code group and others. Again, we see a recognition of the importance of contextual domain in our theorizing and research, and we would add, especially in the area of intercultural communication.

The set of assumptions with which they opened the report and the presentation of their statement of constructivism in relation to the study of intercultural communication does a number of useful things for us in our efforts to strengthen the theoretic base for our study and practice.

First, they stressed that what is needed is a coherent theory of communication. This suggests that if we could firmly establish such a coherent thoery, then the application to special areas of communication, such as intercultural communication, would carry us further than trying to establish special categories of theories for special types of communication. This position is consistent with the position that emerged in the seminar following the Action Caucus. It highlights the destination between intercultural communication theory and theoretic perspectives for intercultural communication.

Another useful contribution of the constructivism group was their focus on studying the relationship between communication and culture. They recognized the ways in which the culture and the social world into which one is born contribute to developing the cognitive schemes by means of which one interprets the world. While they would not rule out comparative studies across cultures, they would opt for studying the interrelationship between communication and culture at least as a first stage.

In keeping with their assumption that theories should be interpretive in nature, they showed how constructivism takes interpretation as one of its key concepts. The affinity developed between constructivist notions and the concept of culture should make obvious the potential value of approaching the study of intercultural communication from a constructivist perspective.

Their brief presentation of the basic concepts of constructivism—interpretation, action, interaction, communication, cognitive schemes, and the like—should be very useful to the intercultural communication scholar as a starting point. And their listing of some of Halliday's taxonomy of the functions of language should also be a useful guide for the intercultural communicator.

They noted that constructivism has utilized many of the existing methodologies—experimental, interaction analysis, psychometric tests, and naturalistic observation. However, there has been a central concern with an overt preference for naturalistic observation and free response data-collection techniques. This preference is to achieve responses more closely representing natural real-world responses to which one seeks to generalize.

Another aspect of this perspective, which should commend its serious consideration, is that covered in their discussion of the variety of forms that cognitive schemes may take for construing reality—linear, causal, spatial, temporal, balance, or bipolar templates. This would seem to provide the latitude for dealing with differing philosophical systems among the populations we study. One of the arguments for different approaches to study of communication (generally signifying non-western) is that persons of different cultures operate from different world views, different philosophies. What seems to be implied in the plea for considering differing approaches is a recognition of different schemes for construing reality.

Different Philosophical Perspectives

A major concern of this group is that the study of intercultural communication from a predominantly Western philosophical perspective will present a limited, if not distorted, view of the process. One of their contentions was that studies of interactions should start with a systematic observation of intercultural dyads, rather than with ready-made hypotheses.

It is unclear as to how this approach would be more Asian or African or Eurocentric than what they have labeled a Western perspective. Scholarship in the Western mode also encompasses inductive generalization from observation of numerous cases. That generally is the starting point of learning. From those generalizations, the observers then go on to make predictions and base future behaviors on these predictions and the outcomes of behaviors based on those predictions. Anthropologists have reported numerous examples of those patterns of observation, generalization, prediction, explanation, observation, generalization, and so on through recurring cycles.

Hanson,[6] writing about the role of theory in discovery and explanation, used the example of Kepler and Tycho Brahe watching the sun at the rim of the horizon. One saw the sun moving above a stationary horizon; the other saw a moving horizon move down from a stationary sun. Hanson refers to this as the distinction between "seeing" and "seeing that." The seeing is what is recorded on the retina of the eye. The seeing that is what is interpreted from that image; it is the combination of what appears, and the theoretic base from which one views that determines what gets interpreted from the sense data received.

If this is the point uppermost in the concern of the group exploring different philosophies for studying intercultural communication, it is a very important one; and it may be getting close to the metatheory they desire. It brings into focus the operation of the construct system of the constructivists in interpreting and responding to stimuli, with the context being part of the stimulus system. If this is the point, the challenge then becomes to make explicit the philosophic (theoretic) base from which the "seeing that" derives. We believe it is contingent upon every observer, to the extent possible, to share the base from which the observing has been done. Otherwise, reports of observations will add further confusion rather than clarification that would permit improved explanation, prediction, and appreciation of the process we call intercultural communication.

This group said that what is needed is a methatheory capable of generating hypotheses and research projects that can accommodate intercultural interactions, and presumably, a metatheory powerful enough to accommodate the range of philosophical bases from which researchers would be observing, thus allowing an understanding of the differences in "seeing that" which may occur. This has been one of the goals of the Action Caucus and Seminar on Theory in Intercultural Communication. It would seem that this exercise has provided a start and that the development of the metatheory will be a continuing process in itself.

The different approaches group cited three categories of studies they believe are necessary:

(1) *Studies of interactions, starting without ready-made hypotheses, will provide data from which generalizations can be made.* By this the group may mean starting without explicit hypotheses, since there are some implied theoretic positions and hypotheses involved in deciding what one will record all the things in communication environment. The label "systematic observations" in itself suggests that some decisions have already been conciously made as to how one will observe, and the "how" impacts on "what."

(2) *Studies of rituals and myths—examining the imbedded structure of myths and rituals can provide researchers with a view of culture expansive enough to generate theories.* Again, it may be more accurate to say one will expand, refine, and modify theories through the study of rituals and myths, since the contention of the authors of this synthesis is that there is an underlying theory in all action. The distinction is how explicitly and rigorously it has been stated and how logically coherent it is.

(3) *Studies of interpersonal attraction—which is a social context factor— also would aid our theory building.* The group states that this provides an element of personal choice to that of cultural choice, and that there is an interaction of the two. This set of investigations would concentrate on identifying the elements of personal choice and cultural choice and the points of intersection, and the theory would be developed from this.

The overall thrust of the statement from the different approaches group seems to focus on inductive processes. The authors of this synthesis have no difficulty with that approach, but would urge that as scholars we do more than add to the existing mass of observations. The systematic synthesizing of those observations is very much needed, followed by rigorous testing of the generalizations under varied conditions in order to see the range of their applicability.

Again, it is interesting to note that yet another of the groups has emphasized the importance of taking into account the social context in which the communication is occurring and has also emphasized the importance of collecting data in natural settings.

Mathematical Modeling

Mathematical modeling is a method for theory development and specification. The product from modeling then becomes the theoretic statement. One such model, developed by Barnett and others, allows the description and prediction of the pattern of convergence when two or more cultures come into contact. This product would then become the theoretic statement of the process and the relationship involved.

Math modeling can give to intercultural communication precise description and projections of the outcomes of communicative acts. Another advantage of the math model is that the mathematical relationships can be worked out independent of a specific communication event. This can save time, permit test applications to a range of situations, and often may suggest or call attention to elements and relationships previously overlooked. It aids the "seeing that" phase of the investigation process. By coupling math modeling with other perspectives, we may increase understanding of the process of communication and improve the ability to achieve communicator goals.

Relationship Development

Joe Hanna,[7] philosopher of science and outside resource person for the Action Caucus and Seminar, observed that the Intercultural Communication Action Caucus and Seminar was in itself highly intercultural. While the accuracy of that observation was apparent in all of the groups, it was quite apparent in the relationship development group, where several different perspectives were considered.

In the paper developed by Cronen and Shuter to reflect the deliberations of the groups, they reviewed and critiqued three approaches to the study of interpersonal relationships; they then presented two alternatives they believed are superior to the other approaches. The two they offered are the Coordinated Management of Meaning (CMM) and the Values/Communication approach. At the same time, they appear to find some use in the other approaches— exchange, uncertainty reduction, coorientation, rules, and adaptive approaches. They note weaknesses of each, then go on to develop the alternatives that undoubtedly will also possess some vulnerable spots.

It would be interesting to have a short statement of the historical base from which the authors generate their positions. There appear to be strands of the George Herbert Mead symbolic interactionist school; the structural-functionalism of Merton, Parsons, and others; the existentialism of Kierkegard and others; the values orientation of Strodtbeck and Kluckhohn; and some hints of gestalt psychology and transactional analysis. Given Cronen and Shuter's own models of relationship development, it is interesting to speculate on how closely their models predict their outcomes as reflected in their paper, given the cultural base from which the task was approached.

This group worked on some ways of doing what the different approaches group was asking for, namely, to study interpersonal interactions. They spoke of the actor in a communication transaction (interaction) as being a unique synthesis of relationship and selfhood, along with conceptions of culture and communicative episodes and acts. Perhaps that statement catches the kernel of the point of convergence between CMM and the Values/Communication approach. It recognizes the impact of values coming out of the historical cultural base of the actor and at the same time recognizes the individual uniqueness of the actor.

While CMM focuses on rules as organizations of meanings for and by the individual rather than as a social pattern, it does recognize the contribution of the social milieu to the individually unique sets of meanings. This is reflected in the suggestion that when persons of two relatively distinct cultures meet to interact, they may form a third culture with the generation of a new system of managing meaning in the context (level). Several different levels are suggested at which transactions may occur, and it is suggested that as the contextual level changes, the ways in which the relationship gets initiated, structured, and progresses will vary. The suggestion also is present that there are identifiable patterns in the development process for the differing contextual levels.

Without much strain, one can see affinity between this approach and that of a sociolinguistic approach. Consider the similarity of concerns as one moves from the verbal and nonverbal behavior (stimuli) available to one's senses, to the cultural pattern level in which are imbedded the essential ways of knowing and acting defined for the social collectivity of which the actors are a part. The focus is on communicative acts within a social context.

The Values/Communication approach appears to emphasize the cultural pattern level. This is evident in the focus on the basic value orientations developed in the Strodtbeck and Kluckhohn work: good-evil, time orientation, humanity-nature relation, modality of human activity, and modality of relation to other persons. The suggeston that communication patterns will differ as basic value orientations differ is intriguing, makes intuitive sense, and has some support in empirical work.

The challenge now is to derive from descriptions of the process of relationship development the recurring patterns and individual and group characteristics in which these patterns are anchored. What social context, what set of meaning rules, or what set of values make the most difference in how a relationship develops and as to the kind of relationship it becomes.

Rhetorical Theory

The group considering rhetorical theory and its usefulness in studying intercultural communication also discovered a high degree of diversity within their group. There was consensus on the point that rhetorical
perspectives, in addition to the Aristotelean view, should be incorporated in any rhetorical analyses.

There also was agreement that rhetorical analyses offer a useful tool
in the study of intercultural communication. It seems that the differences among those in the group offer some alternative methods for gaining
increased understanding of the process of intercultural communication
through rhetorical analyses.

Rhetorical scholars in the past have studied the rhetoric of various
ethnic groups under several types of situations. They have compared
speaking styles of Native Americans, Blacks, religious movements, and
so on. These types of studies were considered useful by the rhetorical
perspectives groups in the Action Caucus. They would suggest a wider
range of possibilities for learning to anticipate the outcomes of various
types of rhetorical efforts in the international domain.

They also pointed to the potential for learning about the values of
various cultural groups via rhetorical analysis of a range of message
samples—books, broadcasts, speeches, and artistic productions. Such
analyses could reveal communication styles, communication rules, linguistic structures, norms, values, and belief systems, including beliefs
about developing relationships. From this perspective, it would seem
that the rhetorical theorists and critics could well work in partnership
with scholars who claim one of the other seven perspectives as their
primary focus for intercultural studies.

Three central concepts that appear to be points of convergence in
rhetorical study include "rhetorical theory," the "critical method," and
the "rhetorical object." All have specific applications to intercultural
communication study:

(1) A specific conception of rhetorical theory is appropriate for
intercultural communication because it is related to a specific cultural
context. The study of community-specific rhetorics that function
within a given cultural milieu may yield knowledge about cultural
rhetoric, which in turn may illuminate the nature of intercultural encounter between individuals from different suasory traditions. The
analysis of suasory encounters between individuals within a given
cultural milieu also may be compared to suasory encounters between
these individuals and individuals from a differing milieu.

(2) The critical method is grounded in the study of the rhetorical act. The
critic goes directly to the object itself and builds interpretation from

that direct confrontation. This aspect of the critical method suggests that intercultural communication be studied by going directly to the interaction for the express purpose of description, understanding, and interpretation. Such interactions would encompass the primary communicative act in speeches, story, film, newspapers, advertisement, sculpture, music, and painting.

(3) This rhetorical approach to studying intercultural communication might well be combined with a linguistic analysis, with a study of communication rules, a search for patterns of relationship development, or a search for how patterns of constructing reality may be revealed in rhetorical objects. The combined approaches might well increase the richness of the findings.

Rules Perspective(s)

Once again, an Action Caucus group identified several orientations within the perspective within which they were working. Wiseman and Pearce have provided a useful and concise comparison of three views of the nature of rules. And they have evaluated each in terms of its usefulness in communication study generally and intercultural communication specifically.

They found the *rule-following* orientation lacking in three important ways:

(1) It is faced with the dilemma of either ignoring the hierarchical nature of communication or of equating behavior from different levels of meaning.
(2) It is incapable of specifying the necessity for human behavior.
(3) The generality of explanation is limited.

For the *rule-governing* view, as presented by Wiseman and Pearce, the rule is the actor's belief about what should be done or what probably will occur as a consequence of his or her action. The problems that they find with this orientation are:

(1) The generality is limited to those situations in which the social group is predictable.
(2) It is difficult to assess whether actors know a rule without teaching it to them, and there is evidence that actors know rules they cannot state and may not recognize when stated.
(3) This perspective also depends on the assumption that persons act purposefully, and this assumption does seem to always pertain.

For Pearce and Wiseman, the *rule-using* approach is preferred by default. It envisions a matrix of social rules as the grounds on which persons act.

In the study of intercultural communication, this perspective has in common with other approaches the consideration of culture as "subjective culture." It looks at the linkages that the actor perceives among meanings. It would seem to offer the potential for studying the variation in rules used by actors as they move from one context to another; and it would permit an assessment of the variations in rules among persons of differing amounts of cultural differences as they interact in differing contexts. As Pearce and Wiseman suggest, an excitement has developed around the heuristic potential of the rules perspective.

One of the areas in which the rules perspective is being applied is in the area of negotiation. Here the concern is with what rules are used in negotiation situations, and what happens when there is a deviation from the expected pattern of rules in the negotiation setting. In applying this to the intercultural communication area, a further question could be asked as to the differences in rules pertaining in the negotiation setting as the level of homogeneity-heterogeneity of the participants varies. Are there predictable patterns of rules for given social-psychological variations among the participants?

To strengthen the understanding of the rules perspective, a reading of Piaget[8] on the development of rules and principles by individuals and groups would likely be helpful to anyone who uses this approach to intercultural study.

Systems Perspective

If we ask what permeates all of the approaches considered in the Action Caucus and Seminar, it would have to be the concern with structure, pattern, system, and rules. The system perspective provides a general theoretic framework for considering system in whatever context it occurs. And Brent Ruben, in the paper reporting the work of the systems group, began by reviewing the basic concepts and propositions of general systems theory.

He also called attention to the wide-ranging generality of a systems approach. Here he noted that systems theory has been the outgrowth of various fields of study, noting several general conceptions appearing across the fields. These are the problems of organization, wholeness, dynamic interaction, boundary, part-whole relationships, adaptation, and interdependence.

Perhaps more than any other perspective, the systems perspective forcefully calls attention to the interdependence of multiple elements in every communication transaction of whatever kind, at whatever time, among whatever persons, in whatever place. In the intercultural area, it brings this into focus in several ways; the first is the notion that culture derives and persists through communication, and is in turn affected by the cultural milieu in which it occurs and the cultural heritage of the participants.

The interconnection of the systems perspective with the others discussed in this series becomes evident when culture is defined in the systems paper as "those symbols, meanings, images, rule-structure, habits, values, and information-processing and transformation patterns and conventions that are shared in common by members of a particular social system." Here we can see the overlapping concerns with those of the code and code system group, with the constructivism group, with the rule perspective group, and so on.

In looking to ways of using a systems perspective in intercultural investigation, a number of possibilities are opened to the scholar; among these are the concept of adaptation and related propositions. How do various elements in a system, or introductions into a system, respond in achieving adaptation and balance (equilibrium) within the system? This provides a framework for considering cross-cultural adjustments when persons move from one system (or subsystem) to another and seek to communicate with persons from the other system. Systems theory suggests general sets of adaptive mechanisms that may be very suggestive for the cross-cultural interloper.

Cultural shock, a phenomenon frequently discussed as occurring when persons cross cultural boundaries, may be viewed from the perspective of how systems and elements within a system respond under stress. A basic proposition here from systems theory is that when two or more differing systems come into contact with one another, stress will result in the process of achieving accommodation through adaptation.

A systems definition of communication stresses the processing and transfer of information to adapt to one's environment, and to adapt to one's environment to one's needs and condition. The adaptation view of the communication process would suggest the potential for creation of new forms arising from transactions between and among differing cultural groups of individuals. One could look at different types of adaptation from general systems theory and predict the types of adaptation that might be most probable in transactions involving persons of varying levels of heterogeneity.

The systems perspective in its conceptualization of open and closed systems, and the propositions about the flow of information and the consequences of that flow and other relationships pertaining to openness and closedness, provides a framework for generating propositions about communication within and between social systems with varying levels of open-closedness. Some of this base may be especially useful in looking at some of the issues pertaining to free flow of information, types of cultural change that may occur with increasing potential for information exchange, and so on.

A part of the boundary setting that might be suggested by systems perspective is the agreement that when we speak of a national culture or subculture, for example, the Japanese, we are referring to some modal set of persons within that society and those shared elements we consider when we seek to define culture. It seems that some of the literature in intercultural communication tends to overlook that aspect of our labeling. We speak of the possibility that the within-variance may be as great as the variance between some of the groups we label as culture. Yet we seem to forget that in our labeling and in our discussions of behaviors of persons included in those labels.

CONCLUSION

The hope for the Action Caucus and Seminar was that they would stimulate some new ways of thinking about the study and practice of intercultural communication. We believe that this is occurring and that as the Commission for International and Intercultural Communication, we should continue to explore the potential contributions of many theoretic perspectives to the understanding of that communication we label intercultural.

All the perspectives considered in the Action Caucus seemed to place a high value on studying intercultural communication in natural settings to the greatest extent possible. All seemed to recognize the centrality of language in the broad sense of code systems in any study of communication. And the physical, social, and psychological contexts were implicit, if not explicit, concerns in all of the perspectives. The relative emphasis given to the psychological and to the sociological aspects of a communication varied, but the interdependence of both was recognized.

The interculturalness of the members of the Commission on International and Intercultural Communication will undoubtedly continue to persist. There undoubtedly will be those who wish to move toward the extensional end of Jo Hanna's theory continuum and those who prefer to operate more intensionally. Just as the transactions among persons of differing cultures may create new forms for all participants, the continued transactions among members of the commission should create new perspectives that will expand our understanding of intercultural communication.

NOTES

1. Among the readers are Larry A. Samovar and Richard E. Porter, *Intercultural Communication: A Reader* (Belmont, CA: Wadsworth Publishing Co., Inc., 1972; 2nd edition, 1976); Alfred G. Smith, *Communication and Culture* (New York: Holt, Rinehart & Winston, 1966); Michael Prosser, *Intercommunication Among Nations and Peoples* (Boston: Houghton Mifflin, 1973).

2. Two early state-of-the-art reviews are Michael Prosser, *The Cultural Dialogue: An Introduction to Intercultural Communication* (Boston: Houghton Mifflin, 1978); Tulsi Saral, "Intercultural Communication Theory and Research: An Overview of Challenges and Opportunities," *Communication Yearbook 3* (New Brunswick, NJ: Transaction Books, 1979).

3. Huber, W. Ellingsworth, "Conceptualizing Intercultural Communication," *Communication Yearbook 1* (New Brunswick, NJ: Transaction Books, 1977); L. E. Sarbaugh, *Intercultural Communication* (Rochelle Park, NJ: Hayden Book Co., Inc., 1979).

4. L. S. Harms, *Intercultural Communication* (New York: Harper & Row, 1973); Andrea Rich, *Interracial Communication* (Harper & Row, 1974); John Condon and Fathi Yousef, *An Introduction to Intercultural Communication* (Indianapolis, IN: Bobbs-Merrill Co., Inc., 1975); John A. Blubaugh, John A. Pennington, and Dorthy L. Pennington, *Crossing Difference . . . Interracial Communication* (Columbus, OH: Charles E. Merrill, 1976); R. Brislin and P. Pedersen, *Crosscultural Orientation Programs* (New York: Gardner Press, Inc., 1976); Sharon Ruhly, *Orientations to Intercultural Communication* (Chicago: Science Research Associates, 1976); K. S. Sitaram and Roy T. Cogdell, *Foundations of Intercultural Communication* (Columbus, OH: Charles E. Merrill Publishing Co., 1976); Edward Hall, *Beyond Culture* (Garden City, NY: Anchor Books/ Doubleday, 1976); Carley H. Dodd, *Perspective on Cross-Cultural Communication* (Dubuque, IA: Kendall/Hunt, 1977); Fred Casmir, ed., *International and Intercultural Communication* (Washington, DC: University Press, 1978); Michael Prosser, *The Cultural Dialogue: An Introduction to Intercultural Communication* (Boston: Houghton Mifflin, 1978); M. Asante, E. Newmark, and C. Blake, eds., *A Handbook of Intercultural Communication* (Beverly Hills, CA: Sage, 1978); L. E. Sarbaugh, *Intercultural Communication* (Rochelle Park, NJ: Hayden Book Co., Inc., 1979); Richard Brislin, *Cross-Cultural Encounters: Face-to-Face Interactions* (New York: Pergamon Press, 1981); Larry A. Samovar, R. Porter, and Nemi Jain, *Understanding Intercultural Communication* (Belmont, CA: Wadsworth Publishing Co., 1981).

5. Our position is that we do not transmit meanings; we transmit symbols that serve as stimuli to elicit meanings in the person receiving the stimuli.

6. Russell N. Hanson, *Patterns of Discovery* (Cambridge: Cambridge University Press, 1958), pp.1-30.

7. Professor Joseph Hanna, Professor of Philosophy, Michigan State University.

8. Jean Piaget, *Moral Judgment of the Child* (New York: Free Press, 1965).

II

THEORIES BASED ON TRADITIONAL COMMUNICATION PERSPECTIVES

4

A Constructivist Outline

JAMES L. APPLEGATE • HOWARD E. SYPHER • *University of Kentucky*

Essays forwarding a theoretical framework for studying culture and communication must (if implicitly) embody assumptions about the nature of theory, the relation of theory and research, and the very nature of culture and communication. In a theory-building forum such as this, where different theoretical orientations to the study of culture and communication are being presented and compared, it is important that such assumptions be elaborated. Conflicts between theories over these types of assumptions cannot (or at least are unlikely to be) resolved through direct empirical testing. The relative merit of such sets of assumptions as a basis for the construction of theory must be established in explication and rational argument among members of the scientific community. In the following section we present the general assumptions we believe should guide us in constructing theory-based cultural research programs. An outline follows of a constructivist approach to cultural communication studies embodying these assumptions.

ASSUMPTIONS OF AN INTERPRETIVE APPROACH TO THE STUDY OF COMMUNICATION AND CULTURE

First, we argue that what is needed is not a theory of *inter*cultural, *cross*-cultural, or *inter*racial communication, but at base, a coherent theory of communication whose focus of convenience encompasses accounts of the probable impact of historically emergent forms of group life on the various forms and functions communication assumes in everyday life. If our theories give us no clear, independent conceptualization of the core features of communication, attempts to compare communication across cultural communities are doomed to produce amorphous research results. Researchers are left with little guidance in deciding *what* to call communication, in generating expectations for *which* of the myriad facets of cultural life might be expected to influence communication, or for *how* they would do so.[1]

Second, we argue that our theories should be interpretive in nature. They should embody a philosophical anthropology that treats people as active interpreters of their social environment: one that rejects determinism and recognizes the falsity of the nature/nurture dichotomy.[2] Interpretive theories should focus upon the interpenetration of the developing symbolic capacities of human organisms and the historical structures of culture within which the former emerge.[3]

Third, following from this interpretive focus we argue that research methods arising from such theories should provide as dense and detailed accounts as possible of the everyday interactions of cultural participants. Intimate involvement in the detailed and specific features of communication offers the best hope to elaborate and validate theoretical abstractions that speak to what is generic within them. As Geertz has argued,

> Our double task is to uncover the conceptual structures that inform our subjects' acts, the "said" of social discourse, and to construct a system of analysis in whose terms what is generic to those structures . . . will stand out against the other determinants of human behavior. . . . The office of theory is to provide a vocabulary in which what symbolic action has to say about itself—that is about the role of culture in human life—can be expressed.[4]

In short, if we are to assume people are active interpreters then we must focus upon their interpretations. It is there that the culture we seek to explain is created and maintained. However, we hasten to add that while the logic of constructivism demands use of methods that more naturally capture cultural participants' first-order constructions of reality, it does not preclude the use of a variety of more structured methods of data collection and analysis. This methodological point and the general commitment of constructivism to a reflective empiricism is addressed in more detail later in this essay.

Fourth, we argue that the focus of our study in this area should not be exclusively, nor even primarily, upon comparative studies of cultures, but rather upon the nature of the relationship between culture and communication. Hence, we forward constructivism as an approach to cultural communication studies rather than to inter- or cross-cultural communication. Comparative studies can throw light on this relationship. They have practical value in explaining and reducing specific problems in encounters between individuals from different cultures. However, to wed our studies primarily to comparisons of specific similarities and differences between cultures is to omit the central issue: the relationship between culture and communication.[5]

Having unpacked at least this much of the assumptive baggage with which we approach the study of the relationship between culture and communication, we now turn to an outline of a constructivist approach to cultural communication studies that builds on these foundations.

THE CONSTRUCTIVIST CONCEPTION OF COMMUNICATION

As an approach to communication study, constructivism gives primary attention to analysis of stable interrelations among, and individual and group differences in, the cognitive and behavioral processes underlying the emergent quality of communication in different contexts. The logic of the approach is developmental in nature.[6] Specifically, the theory embraces the comparative developmental logic forwarded within Heinz Werner's comparative organismic theory, capsulized in Werner's Orthogenetic Principle: "Whenever development occurs it proceeds from a state of relative globality and lack of differentiation to a state of increasing differentiation, articulation, and hierarchic integration."[7] Specific dimensions of cognitive and behavioral development are derived from this principle (e.g., globality-differentiation, concreteness-abstractness, diffuseness-integration), which are used in comparative analysis of the quality of child, adolescent, and adult communication.[8]

Constructivist theory emphasizes the intrinsically social nature of these developmental processes. The development of interpretive systems is accomplished through interaction with and accommodation to cultural forms of life. Hence, in studying situated communication we are confronted simultaneously with some part of the shared backcloth of cultural knowledge that has been integrated within individual world views and, in relief, individual differences in interpretive systems produced by a lifetime of creative attempts to adapt to particular social situations.

Analysis of the development of the various processes employed by individuals to give meaning to and direct behavior is organized around distinctions made between interpretation, action, interaction, and communication. We briefly define these concepts before describing their relevance for analyses of cultural influences on communication. *Interpretation* is the most pervasive and general of these features of social life. It is accomplished through the development and application of *cognitive schemes* that segment the ongoing stream of social life into domains of experience (e.g., physical, interpersonal, moral/religious) creating relatively differentiated and hierarchically integrated schematic structures within and across domains. Such schemes emerge from interactions with the environment. They may assume a variety of forms: linear causal, spatial, temporal, balance, or bipolar templates for construing reality. The organization and degree of utilization of particular types of schemes may vary across cultures and/or particular domains of experience within cultures. Given the constructivist conception of *communication* (see below) cognitive schemes employed in the interpersonal domain (those used to interpret people) have received primary attention. Conceptualization of the organization and operation of interpersonal schemes has been derived from George A. Kelly's theory of personal constructs.[9]

The cognitive schemes employed by individuals define intentions and imply alternative lines of action within situations. Individuals choose a line of action on the basis of their situated intention(s). What results is *action* organized into *strategies* designed to actualize the intention to behavior. Actions, and the strategies produced utilizing them, are defined by the goals they are designed to accomplish. Various goals and strategies may be incorporated within a particular line of action. The actor is often only *tacitly* aware of the goals and strategies guiding his or her communication.

Interaction involves the coordination of individual lines of action (and the strategies they embody) through the application of shared schemes for the organization of action itself. Such interactional schemes are of two types: interpretive principles and organizing schemes. We deal only with the latter type here given its greater relevance for the study of cultural influences on communication.[10] Organizing schemes are tied to the content of interaction. They may link particular acts (e.g., adjacency paris), define a script for routine interactions between individuals within ascribed roles in institutional settings (e.g., teacher-student interaction), or offer a general plan for an entire speech event (e.g., the meeting of a college class). Such schemes are seen as hierarchically organized within particular social settings (e.g., certain adjacency pairs embedded within schemes for routine teacher-student interactions, embedded within even more general schemes for the organization of classroom meetings). Most importantly for our purposes such schemes are inherently social and often culturally shared.[11]

Finally, there is *communication*, defined as a special form of interaction characterized by participants' desire to express (make publicly available) some private state, their recognition of a similar desire in another, and the organization of interaction around those communicative intentions. Communication "is not defined by its products or goals but by its peculiar structure of reciprocal intentions."[12] Hence, in constructivism, communication is by its very nature linked to the interpretation of people and their intentions (i.e., utilization of constructs embodied in the interpersonal cognitive system). However, communication is more than interpretation. It is made up of strategically organized actions, but it is more than goal seeking. It involves coordination of action through utilization of interactional schemes, but it is a special case of interaction in which the mutual desire to express intentions is the focus for coordinating action.

Armed with this set of concepts, we can begin to outline foci for research aimed at abstracting from situated communication those shared qualities of cognitive schemes, strategic action, interactional organizing schemes, and communication that reflect the influence of culture on communication.

ANALYZING IMPLICIT CULTURAL COMMUNICATION THEORIES

Sociolinguists have argued that human groups develop linguistic rules at the semantic and pragmatic levels that encourage particular ways of forming and organizing social relationships (i.e., communicating). These rules are seen as organized within "sociolinguistic codes" characterizing particular "speech communities."[13] Much of the theoretical and empirical analysis in this area is compatible with the logic of constructivism. However, for reasons elaborated elsewhere (e.g., the concept neglects the role of individual psychological processes in communication), constructivist theory eschews use of the "code" concept as traditionally employed.[14] Rather, cultural influences are seen as organized within implicit cultural communication theories. Through socialization, the theory is actively incorporated as an implicit feature of individual world views, visible in much the same way as one may see the influence of a dominant theory of art embedded in the individual creative works of its period.

The order of the presentation of foci for research investigating the effect of implicit cultural communication theories on situated communication presented below is dictated by the logical relationship of cognitive schemes, strategic action, interactional schemes, and communication within constructivist theory. While research efforts initially should focus on situations in which communication, as defined here, is present, the agenda for cultural analyses from that point may vary. We subscribe to a modified version of Geertz's argument that

> one can start anywhere in a culture's repertoire of [communication-relevant] forms and end up anywhere else. One can stay . . . within a single, more or less bounded form, and circle steadily within it. One can move between forms in search of broader unities or informing contrasts. One can even compare forms from different cultures to define their character in reciprocal relief. But whatever the level at which one operates, and however intricately, the guiding principle is the same: societies, like lives, contain their own interpretations. One has only to learn how to gain access to them.[15]

The goal of the constructivist program is to make available the nature of and relationship between communication-relevant forms (e.g., strategic action schemes and interactional organizing schemes) defined in implicit cultural communication theories implicitly shared by cultural participants. Ultimately, comparisons can be offered of implicit cultural communication theories along dimensions derived from the logic of comparative developmental analysis.

Cultural Influences on Cognitive Schemes

In attempting to fully elaborate how an implicit cultural communication theory influences individuals' communication, we must include investigations of shared qualities of the systems of cognitive schemes employed by cultural participants to place and organize events within larger contexts of meaning and expectation. As noted above these schemes are the grounding from which particular communications emerge.

Constructivist research to date articulates a complex picture of the nature of cognitive schemes within the interpersonal domain, the course of their structural development, and their impact on strategic action and communication. This work and, more generally, analyses of cognitive schemes provided by schema theorists in psychology[16] provide a rich conceptual base from which to generate what Charles Frake calls "ethnographies of cognitive systems": particularly of the interpersonal cognitive subsystem.[17]

Frake's own work and that of others in the area of cognitive anthropology and ethnosemantics offer a starting point for research investigating the shared (cultural) content and structural features of cognitive systems. Frake suggests that such ethnographies should include a focus on the differentiation and hierarchic integration of such schemes and argues that such schemes may be fruitfully seen as "contrast sets": A notion very similar to the constructivist conception of a "construct."[18]

Analyses of culture's influence on cognition may include ethnographies outlining the typical structure and quality (i.e., degree of differentiation, integration, abstractness) of cognitive systems. In addition, content analysis of schemes employed in particular social domains (e.g., interpersonal, moral, political) may be useful in assessing the impact of culturally shared features of cognition on communication.

Cultural Influences on the Goals and Strategic Organization of Action

Cultural communication theories also may influence individual communication by defining the important functions of communication and the most appropriate strategic means of accomplishing those functions. In his insightful analysis of the functions of language, M.A.K. Halliday argues that language is best conceptualized as a resource capable of use in accomplishing a variety of potential objectives. Halliday and others have begun the task of constructing taxonomies of the major functions of language around which action is organized.[19] Those typologies reflect an emerging consensus on the major language functions guiding human action. A selective list is presented below:

personal	elaborating subjective feelings, motives, needs; negotiating conflicts in perspectives
regulative/control	effecting change in others thinking and behavior
referential	describing objects and objectives relationships in the external world
imaginative	experimenting with language for the sheer enjoyment of creating new ways of seeing the world
identity management	creating a desired self-image

Investigations of language used across cultures will enlarge our understanding of the potential objectives of action and the types of strategies that may be employed to accomplish them. However, a taxonomy of major functions should not be open to infinite growth (especially when focused on functions emerging across cultures) if we closely tie analyses to situated action. Such a contention is based on the assumption that there is something out there called a social order that is not random and is amenable to abstraction and typification.

Creation of such taxonomies within and across cultures enables us to translate the notion that communication is multifunctional into a powerful analytic tool for strategy analysis "since assumed or already negotiated aspects of social reality culture can be seen as taken for granted . . . constraints upon strategy selection."[20] In analyzing these constraints, we are about the business of unpacking another part of a culture's implicit communication theory. We begin to answer such questions as: What goals of action are most valued by the culture? Are goals differentially valued across social/institutional contexts within the culture? What types of strategies are deemed most appropriate for the accomplishment of particular goals? How do our answers to these questions differ across cultures? What are the implications of such differences for communication across cultures? Having answered these questions, we can better explain the impact of culture on the development of the repertoire of strategies individuals employ in communication (e.g., the differentiation, degree of integration, level of egocentrism, and so on of the strategies possessed).

Cultural Influences on Organizing Schemes in Interaction

Evidence of cultural influence can be found in organizing schemes embodied in many types of interaction. Many such interactions do not represent instances of communication, since that process has been defined here (e.g., the coordination of driving behavior at a busy intersection). Such interactions are certainly worth study and may even be useful in explaining related communicative interactions (e.g., the interaction between two drivers after colliding at the intersection). Nevertheless, the focus of constructivist analyses is upon interactions of the latter type. Uncovering consistencies in the nature and hierarchic structuring of organizing schemes that emerge in various contexts for communication within a cultural community defines yet another important avenue of cultural influence on communication.[21]

As an example of how such an analysis might proceed, let us elaborate on our earlier reference to classroom communication, asking the following types of questions. What are the culturally common features of the organizing schemes for classroom interaction? Are there embedded within this general scheme different subsets of schemes for organizing persuasive actions (e.g., disciplining procedures) and personal action (e.g., dealing with disappointment)? Are there types of adjacency pairs more typical of one or the other type of interaction (e.g., question-answer pairs more prevalent in persuasive contexts; question-question pairs in personal contexts)? Finally (and this is the question to be asked of findings of cultural influence on cognition and strategic action as well), how do the schemes employed affect the typical outcome and quality of communication in this type of setting in this culture (e.g., its adaptive quality, the degree and type of coordination of intentions and understanding achieved)? For those with macrosociological concerns, such an analysis could provide useful insights into the function of education in the culture or the nature of authority relationships: this in addition to further elaborating the nature of the culture's implicit communication theory.

Cultural Influences on the Process of Communication

Analyses of culturally shared qualities of cognitive schemes, strategies, and organizing schemes employed in communicative relationships, all document cultural influences on communication. They help us understand how and why communication assumes the form and function it does within the culture. However, to fully understand the impact of culture on communication, we must examine the nature of cultural attitudes toward the general usefulness and appropriate form for this special relationship in which interaction is reciprocally focused on the coordination of individuals' intentions.

Specifically, we must address questions such as: To what extent is communication valued (if at all) as a means of accomplishing goals? Is communication more valued as a means of accomplishing goals in some functional contexts than in others (e.g., personal as opposed to regulative/control)? Finally, even where communication is encouraged, does the culture constrain what may be appropriately expressed and negotiated and/or the appropriate means of expression (e.g., verbally or nonverbally)?[22]

METHODOLOGICAL PRIORITIES

To this point we have focused upon constructivism's philosophical and theoretical underpinnings. We have suggested several substantive questions about the impact of culture on communication to be addressed with this perspective and sought to identify other positions compatible with this approach. As all such theoretical discussions must, this one has implied certain methodological priorities. We now make these explicit.

Wedding Theory and Methodology

Some scholars have viewed constructivism and its tenents as a radical departure from traditional research practices.[23] However, as Delia made clear, "constructivists endorse many of the canons of traditional research practice."[24] For example, it seems less than radical to contend, as this position does, that one's theory be based upon a firm and consistent philosophical foundation, or that one's research practices and preferences be guided by one's theoretical orientation. For reasons best argued elsewhere we believe that such theoretical-methodological consistency is the best way to proceed.[25]

Constructivism has been criticized for an over-reliance upon free response data-collection techniques and a tendency to lean on softer methods in its analyses of communicative behavior. However, it should be clear, given the conceptual framework outlined, that such methods are consistent extensions of the theory in that they provide researchers with a rich understanding of respondents' categories for interpreting the world (rather than the researcher's) and call upon the investigator to beware of his or her conceptual baggage. However, the position does not require that one reject more structured techniques of analysis.

Delia has called constructivist methodology "reflective empiricism," and posited that

> such an orientation to research calls on the researcher to become as self aware as possible of the ordering principles embedded in his questions and research tools while recognizing the necessity for commitment to particular points of view and methods in learning anything about the empirical world.[26]

The constructivist position does not reject traditional social science methods (although constructivists have been highly critical of methodological abuses). Constructivists have for some time called upon researchers to recognize and beware of the ideological and theoretical assumptions embedded within research procedures and questions. A similar concern has been voiced by scholars who point out the Western bias pervading most intercultural communication research and methodology. However, recognition of this shortcoming does not require that we abandon the techniques and procedures we have been trained to use. Indeed, the realization that our methodological biases need probing and continual reexamination should comfort us, for it is through careful self-reflection that fruitful endeavors emerge.

Methodological Appropriateness

The major methodological question confronting us is not whether or not to utilize a method, but *which method is the most appropriate for the task at hand.* It appears obvious to most that standardized questionnaires developed in one culture may be appropriate in another. Further, one would expect different cultures to exhibit unique forms of valued communication. Communication researchers, like our colleagues in other disciplines, are often guilty of utilizing rigid, inappropriate categories or variables and of simply attacking too many problems with the same methodological implement.

What sort of methods are appropriate? Again, this requires that we first ask, "What is the question?" Some concerns call for psychometric considerations, some for the creation of specific rating scales, others for subject-guided and provided elicitations, while naturalistic observation might be best suited for others. Constructivist research to date has utilized a variety of methodological strategies, including experimental manipulations, interaction analysis techniques, naturalistic observation, and standard psychometric test construction methods.[27]

There has been a central concern and overt preference for naturalistic and free response data-collection techniques. This methodological preference lies at the core of constructivists' beliefs about the way that research should be conducted. What is important about these approaches is that a more spontaneous response is elicited, a response that is more closely representative of natural real-world responses to which we seek to generalize. However, constructivists do not advocate "data without structure." Instead, as Delia points out, "the issue is not whether to introduce structure or not, but how much to introduce, when to introduce it in the research process, and the ends to which it is introduced."[28] To date, constructivist researchers have shown a clear preference for utilizing theoretically grounded coding schemes adapted to the emergent quality of respondents' conceptualizations and accounts.

Another major advantage of free response data-collection is its flexibility. That is, free response data can be coded in a number of different ways. For example, in one instance, the same data base served in studying strategic elaboration of messages and in establishing the independence of cognitive complexity and loquacity.[29] So this form of data lends itself easily to multiple analyses and questions.

What we suggest is that systematic programs of research are hindered if one severs theoretical from methodological issues. We believe that such concerns are especially valid in the intercultural context, where methodology has often preceded theory development. Method, theory, and research are interdependent considerations forming an eternal braid.

Research requires that one become intimately familiar with the object of study. Lacking such familiarity, researchers are prone to utilize their own implicit theories of culture. Unfortunately, one often finds these implicit theories bear only superficial resemblance to what is being studied. As we have previously argued, many central questions about the form and function of communication in differing cultures are not immediately amenable to investigation with standardized data analysis techniques.

CONCLUSION

We have presented only a general outline of what a constructivist approach to cultural communication studies might look like. Obviously, anyone interested in applying such an approach should survey the more in-depth treatment of the concepts and methods introduced and found in the sources referenced. Some current research has successfully applied the theory to the study of specific cultural antecedents to communication development.[30] The logic of the position allows for, and in fact demands, analyses that abstract from situated communication those shared qualities linked to forms of cultural organization constituting the central interpretive challenge to the developing individual. Specific research efforts have produced encouraging results.[31] Moreover, the general success of applications of constructivist theory to a wide variety of other communication issues argues for its status as a sound general communication theory in which to ground cultural communication studies.[32] Our hope is that this outline will aid in the formulation of such theory-based research.

At present we can only argue for the promise of constructivist theory as a basis for cultural communication studies. We have only begun to mine the vein. That endeavor has already made clear the relevance of a variety of other theoretical approaches to our work. In this essay, and others referenced here, we have pointed to what we hope is a theoretically self-conscious integration of aspects of speech-act, ethnomethodological, symbolic interactionist, and certain sociolinguistic theories. Similarly, we have begun to assess the relevance of a variety of methodological techniques for our research. In doing so, we have tried to avoid the vitiating effects of philosophically naive eclecticism.

Constructivism grants a central role to culture in the process of individuals' social cognitive and communicative development. This essay elaborates how that role may be studied and how differences in the substance of implicit cultural communication theories may be assessed in terms of their influence on the quality of communication within and across cultural boundaries.

This volume reflects the increasing theoretical self-consciousness of researchers interested in the relationship of culture and communication. We recognize the need to step back and survey the various theoretical positions available to us: to assess the assumptions they make, the conception of communication they forward, and the foci for cultural research they suggest. This process will aid in the production of programs of theory-based research from a variety of perspectives, providing us with a more sound basis for future judgments of the relative usefulness, scope, parsimony, and precision of explanations provided by various theories. Such an approach is essential if we hope to provide any sort of coherent understanding of the "terrible complexity" characterizing the relationship of culture and communicatoin: If we are to "descend into detail, past misleading tags, past the metaphysical types, past the empty similarities to grasp firmly the essential character of not only the various cultures but the various sorts of individuals within each culture."[33]

NOTES

1. Without such a general theory, research takes the form of variable analysis research. For critiques of the many problems embodied in this tradition see Herbert Blumer, "Sociological Analysis and the Variable," *American Sociological Review*, 21 (1956): 683-90; Jesse G. Delia, "Constructivism and the Study of Human Communication," *Quarterly Journal of Speech*, 63 (1977): 66-83.

2. For arguments regarding the false nature of this dichotomy and the damage done to the quality of research by its acceptance see: H. G. Furth, "Piaget, IQ and the Nature-Nurture Controversy," *Human Development*, 16 (1973): 61-73; W. F. Overton, "On the Assumptive Base of the Nature-Nurture Controversy: Additive versus Interactive Conceptions," *Human Development*, 16 (1973): 74-89; especially see Melford E. Spiro, "Culture and Personality," *Psychiatry*, 14 (1951): 19-41.

3. For elaboration of a conceptual framework within which to conceptualize such a process of interpenetration see Peter Manicas, "The Concept of Social Structure," *Journal for the Theory of Social Behavior*, 10 (1980): 65-82; James L. Applegate and Jesse Delia,

"Person-Centered Speech, Psychological Development, and the Contexts of Language Usage," in *The Social and Psychological Contexts of Language*, ed. Robert St. Clair and Howard Giles (Hillsdale, NJ: Lawrence Erlbaum, 1980), pp. 245-82.

4. Clifford Geertz, *The Interpretation of Cultures* (New York: Basic Books, 1973), 27.

5. Basically the same argument has been forwarded for cultural psychology in Douglas Price-Williams, "Toward the Idea of a Cultural Psychology," *Journal of Cross-Cultural Psychology*, 11 (1980): 75-88.

6. See Jesse G. Delia, Barbara J. O'Keefe, and Daniel J. O'Keefe, "The Constructivist Approach to Communication," in *Comparative Human Communication Theory*, ed. Frank E. Dance (New York: Harper & Row, forthcoming).

7. Heinz Werner, "The Concept of Development from a Comparative and Organismic Point of View," in *The Concept of Development*, ed. D. B. Harris (Minneapolis: University of Minnesota Press, 1957), p. 126. See also Heinz Werner and Bernard Kaplan, *Symbolic Formation* (New York: John Wiley, 1963).

8. For a summary addressing the relevance of this work to cultural analyses see Applegate and Delia, "Person-Centered Speech."

9. George A. Kelly, *The Psychology of Personal Constructs*, vols. 1 and 2 (New York: W. W. Norton, 1955).

10. Interpretive principles are universal schemes necessary for the accomplishment of any interaction and hence, by definition, subject to little cultural variation. Of course, identification and validation of the existence of such universals (e.g., Cicourel's reciprocity of perspectives principle) will require studies of interaction across cultures. For a detailed account of the distinction between interpretive principles and organizing schemes (what Cicourel labels "surface rules") see Aaron V. Cicourel, *Cognitive Sociology: Language and Meaning in Social Interaction* (New York: Macmillan, 1974), especially pp. 42-73; Delia, O'Keefe, and O'Keefe, "Constructivist Approach to Communication." For an example of how such principles may be employed in accounting for the organization of interaction, see Sally Jackson, "Rule Knowledge and Role Knowledge: Conversational Implicature in Children's Discourse" (Paper delivered at the Speech Communication Association Annual Convention, New York, 1980).

11. For examples of constructivist work addressing the nature of organizing schemes see Barbara J. O'Keefe, Jesse G. Delia, and Daniel J. O'Keefe, "Interaction Analysis and the Analysis of Interactional Organization," in *Studies in Symbolic Interaction*, vol. 3, ed. Norman K. Denzin (Greenwich, CT: JAI Press, 1980); Sally A. Jackson and C. S. Jacobs, "Adjacency Pairs and the Sequential Description of Arguments" (Paper delivered at the Speech Communication Association Annual Convention, Minneapolis, 1978); Stephen A. Taylor, "The Acquisition of the Roles of Conversation: A Structural-Developmental Perspective and Methodological Comparison" (Ph.D. doctoral diss. University of Illinois at Urbana-Champaign, 1977).

12. Delia, O'Keefe, and O'Keefe, "Constructivist Approach to Communication."

13. For examples of this work see Dell Hymes, *Foundations in Socioloinguistics*, (Philadelphia: University of Pennsylvania Press, 1974); M.A.K. Halliday, *Language as Social Semiotic* (Baltimore: University Park Press, 1978); Basil Bernstein, ed., *Primary Socialization, Language and Education*, 9 vols. (Boston: Routledge & Kegan Paul, 1971).

14. Applegate and Delia, "Person-Centered Speech," offer a reconceptualization of the code concept and a general analysis of sociolinguistic research in terms of its relevance to constructivism.

15. Geertz, *Interpretation of Cultures*, p. 453.

16. For an introduction to relevant work in this area see R. Schank and R. Abelson, *Scripts, Plans, Goals, and Understanding* (Hillsdale, NJ: Lawrence Erlbaum, 1977); Reid Hastie et al., *Person Memory: The Cognitive Basis of Social Perception* (Hillsdale, NJ: Lawrence Erlbaum, 1980).

17. Charles Frake, "The Ethnographic Study of Cognitive Systems," in *Readings in the Sociology of Language*, ed. Joshua A. Fishman (The Hague, Netherlands: Mouton, 1968), pp. 434-446.

18. For a brief introduction to the work in cognitive anthropology and ethnosemantics discussed here see Phillip K. Bock, *Continuities in Psychological Anthropology* (San Francisco: W. H. Freeman, 1980), especially pp. 227-246.

19. For example see M.A.K. Halliday, *Explorations in the Functions of Language* (London: Edward Arnold, 1973); Ruth Anne Clark and Jesse G. Delia, "Topoi and Rhetorical Competence," *Quarterly Journal of Speech*, 65 (1979): 187-206; Applegate and Delia, "Person-Centered Speech."

20. Clark and Delia, "Topoi and Rhetorical Competence," 199.

21. Our argument for drawing linkages between the internal organization of interaction and more general consistencies in cultural world views is not new. Attewell, Cicourel, and others suggest that discourse (or interaction) analysis research (e.g., that done with ethnomethodological and speech-act frameworks) is in need for just such an enlargement in focus. See Paul Attewell, "Ethnomethodology Since Garfinkle," *Theory and Society*, 1 (1974): 179-210; Aaron V. Cicourel, "Three Models of Discourse Analysis: The Role of Social Structure," *Discourse Processes*, 3 (1980): 101-131.

22. The work of Bernstein and his colleagues begins to address these questions in examining communication in the British lower and middle classes. See also Martha C. Ward, *Them Children: A Study in Language Learning* (New York: Holt, Rinehart & Winston, 1971); and James L. Applegate, "Person- and Position-Centered Communication in a Day Care Center," in *Studies in Symbolic Interaction*, vol. 3, ed. Norman K. Denzin (Greenwich, CT: JAI Press, forthcoming).

23. See, for example, Gerald R. Miller and Charles R. Berger, "On Keeping The Faith in Matters Scientific," *Western Journal of Speech Communication*, 42 (1978): 44-57.

24. Jesse G. Delia, "The Research and Methodological Commitments of a Constructivist" (Paper delivered at the Speech Communication Association Annual Convention, Minneapolis, 1978), p. 1.

25. For a discussion of this and related issues see Jesse G. Delia, "Constructivism and the Study of Human Communication," *Quarterly Journal of Speech*, 63 (1977): 66-83.

26. Delia, "Commitments of a Constructivist," (1978), p. 3.

27. See Applegate, "Communication in a Day-Care Center"; Jesse G. Delia and Walter H. Crockett, "Social Schemas, Cognitive Complexity, and the Learning of Social Structures," *Journal of Personality*, 41 (1973): 413-429; Jesse G. Delia, Ruth Ann Clark, and David E. Switzer, "Cognitive Complexity and Impression Formation in Informal Social Interaction," *Speech Monographs*, 41 (1974): 299-308; Daniel J. O'Keefe and Jesse G. Delia, "Cognitive Complexity and the Relationship of Attitudes and Behavioral Intentions," *Communication Monographs* (in press).

28. Delia, "Commitments of a Constructivist," (1978), p. 6.

29. Applegate and Delia, "Person-Centered Speech"; Brant R. Burleson, James L. Applegate, and Cindy M. Neuwirth, "Is Cognitive Complexity Loquacity? A Reply to Powers, Jordan, and Street," *Human Communication Research* (forthcoming).

30. For example see Jesse G. Delia, James L. Applegate, and Judy L. Jones, "Person-Centeredness of Mother's Communication Strategies and Individual Differences in

Children's Social Cognitive and Communication Development" (Paper delivered at the Speech Communication Association Annual Convention, New York, 1980); Judy L. Jones, Jesse G. Delia, and Ruth Anne Clark, "Person-Centered Parental Communication and the Development of Communication in Children" (Unpublished, University of Illinois at Urbana-Champaign, 1979.

31. For example see Applegate, "Communication in a Day-Care Center"; Applegate and Delia, "Person-Centered Speech"; J. L. Nicholson, "The Development of Role-Taking Abilities and Sociolinguistic Competence in Three Interpersonal Communication Domains Among Caucasian, Black, and Spanish-American Fourth-, Fifth-, and Sixth-Grade Children" (Ph.D. diss. University of Illinois at Urbana-Champaign, 1976); Judy L. Jones, Jesse G. Delia, and Ruth Anne Clark, "Socio-Economic Status and the Developmental Level of Second- and Seventh-Grade Children's Persuasive Strategies" (Unpublished, University of Illinois at Urbana-Champaign, 1979).

32. For the most current summary of the various issues addressed within the theory see Delia, O'Keefe, and O'Keefe, "Constructivist Approach to Communication."

33. Geertz, *Interpretation of Cultures*, p. 53.

5

Rules Theories
Varieties, Limitations, and Potentials

W. BARNETT PEARCE ● *University of Massachusetts*
RICHARD L. WISEMAN ● *California State University, Fullerton*

Only a few years ago, Cushman and Whiting introduced the concept "rule" to the speech/communication discipline as a principle for explaining human action.[1] In a surprisingly brief time, a substantial literature has developed exploring the heuristic value of the concept for the traditional concerns of the discipline and—more tentatively—for new concerns. For example, Nofsinger, Sanders, and Hooper have done conversational analysis from a rules perspective;[2] Donohue has studied negotiation;[3] Reardon has reanalyzed the processes of persuasion;[4] Cushman et al. and Harris have studied relational/family communication;[5] Philipsen has studied social roles and social settings;[6] Cronen and his colleagues have studied pathological or at least aberrant forms of conversation;[7] and Wiseman, and Kang and Pearce have argued that the rules perspective provides a uniquely advantageous perspective for studying intercultural and cross-cultural communication.[8]

The rules perspective caught on so quickly for three reasons. First, a number of other approaches to the study of communication had not fulfilled their early promise and were failing the ultimate test of a paradigm: the next generation of graduate students were not joining up. The efforts of researchers for three-quarters of a century were unable to identify *any* laws of behavior. The intellectual excitement of systems theorists paled in the application to the real world. The time was right for a new intellectual approach—either a fad or new paradigm.

Second, the rules perspective was consistent with many of the assumptions about humankind and social action that had bedeviled the behaviorists. Koch's acerbic history of the successive revisions of the behavioristic dogma describes at comfortable distance generations of frustrated and soul-searching researchers who found their intellectual underpinnings untenable.[9] The alternative to the behavioristic assumptions had always been action theory, and "rulesers" could blithely adopt these as foundational rather than look on them as problems.

Third, the rules perspective really is not new, so when it was recently introduced to this field, it had an instant intellectual heritage. Rules theorists could trace their lineage back to Kant, Wittgenstein, and other academic heroes, and could look laterally to ethnoscience, ethnomethodology, phenomenology, hermaneutics, sociolinguistics, generative linguistics, cognitive psychology, and the like for cognate studies and even research exemplars.

Based on an analysis of the history of rules perspectives in other disciplines, we have come to these conclusions:

(1) The rules perspective is particularly relevant for a theory of communication that can transcend cultural conventions. Kang and Pearce developed an argument that communication theory per se requires transcultural concepts.[10]

(2) The rules perspective as it currently exists in the communication discipline is dysfunctionally diverse, with substantive disagreements about the most basic concepts.

(3) All existing rules perspectives have inherent limitations on their explanatory power that precludes them from being a *sufficient* structure for a theory applicable to intercultural and cross-cultural communication.

(4) A theory adequate for intercultural and cross-cultural communication must include multiple explanatory principles, one of which is a rules perspective.

THE VARIETIES OF THEORETICAL EXPERIENCE

There are three issues about which various rules theorists have chosen differently, the combination of which determines the form of theory they construct. These issues are:

(1) What is the nature of sociation? Is it based on a homogeneous social order or a heterogeneous aggregate of inividual interpretive processes?

(2) What is a rule?

(3) What is the relation between an actor and a rule? In what sense does the rule explain or cause behavior?

The Nature of Sociation

The nature of the social order has been perceived differently by rules theorists. Donohue, Cushman, and Nofsinger have described these differences as positions along a continuum of social-order-as-homogeneous to social-order-as-heterogeneous.[11] The former position assumes that communicators act within a homogeneous social order and rely on standard ways to make sense of utterance sequences. These standard interpretive procedures are the rules enabling actors to know how to perform conversation. Generally, researchers attempt "to describe microscopically *how* bits of conversation are created."[12]

A second position assumes that even though the social order is heterogeneous, individuals manage to coordinate their actions through communication rules. Those communication rules that are relatively conventionalized and useful for obtaining desired goals are known as *standardized usages*.[13] Researchers working from this perspective attempt to determine how actors use talk to accomplish goals rather than how they make talk. Cushman et al.'s analysis of relationships exemplifies this approach and Wiseman has depicted how this perspective could be applied to intercultural communication.[14]

A third position, articulated in Pearce, Cronen, and Conklin's research on the coordinated management of meaning (CMM),[15] assumes an even more heterogeneous social order. Rules are defined *intrapersonally* as descriptions of the way particular persons intepret their world and decide how to act. Persons strive to coordinate their acts with others, but do so in principle from within a system of rules that is idiosyncratic and, to an extent not fully knowable by the actor, unlike that of the other persons with whom they interact. Harris's analysis of communication competence in the interpersonal domain and Pearce and Branham's analysis of the ineffable in intercultural communication are exemplary of research from this perspective.[16]

The differences between these conceptualizations have important implications. Depending on the theorist's concept of sociation, the phenomena selected for study and the form of explanation used in the theory differ.

The Nature of "Rules" and Their Relation to Action

The different concepts of rules are grounded in the perspectives of the theorist, requiring the reader of this section to engage in multiple perspective-taking. The form of the sentences various researchers use to state rules indicates some dimensions of these perspectives. Some use probability statements, having the form "if X, then people usually do Y"; some use prescriptive statements, "if X, then you should do Y"; and some use descriptive statement of deontic relations, "if X, then this person thinks she should do Y."

By explicating the assumptions that make these various types of statements seem appropriate, it is possible to identify three perspectives represented in the literature.[17]

Rule-following behavior. This perspective, which departs least from the old paradigm (to use Rom Harre's term), envisions persons as acting with some degree of regularity. The rule is the observer's description of this regularity: The particular truth-claim is that a particular form of behavior happens "as a rule."

From this perspective, a rule is simply an empirical generalization and functions like a weak law. That is, the rule purports to describe a regularity, and the rule becomes the major premise in a categorical or dysjunctive syllogism. The form of explanation looks like this:

If X, then people usually do Y;
X;
Therefore, this person will probably do Y.

This perspective on rules has been used, among others, by interaction analysts as they compute the probability that particular types of utterances are followed by other types, and predict that the sequence will recur.[18] It is an appropriate form of explanation if one assumes that sociation is homogeneous.

There has been considerable cross-cultural and intercultural research on nonverbal communication illustrating the rule-following approach. First, the research on the display rules for the facial expression of emotion exemplifies research on the following of regulative rules, that is, those rules that inform us of the channels, circumstance, or manner of communication.[19] Display rules are socially learned instructions that specify which management technique is to be applied to which facial behavior in which context.[20] Ekman and Friesen have found that these display rules vary culturally.[21] Second, Morris et al.'s cross-cultural research on the meaning of various gestures illustrates research on the following of constitutive rules, i.e., those rules that delineate the meaning of symbols.[22] Morris, Collet, Marsh, and O'Shaughnessy attempted to ascertain the meanings of twenty different gestures across forty nations. The results of their investigation suggest that there are often significant differences in the constitutive rules operative in various cultures. In both of the cross-cultural approaches to nonverbal communication, researchers attempted to find regularities (and differences) in individuals' rule-following behavior.

There are three major limitations on the rules theory that emerge from the rule-following perspective. First, it either excludes a major aspect of communication behavior or confuses levels of abstraction. Typically, rule-following theorists attempt to develop a comprehensive set of discrete categories; however, the work of Bateson and his associates clearly shows that communication occurs on multiple levels simultaneously and that the meanings of these levels importantly affect each other. Coding categories are faced with the dilemma of either ignoring the hierarchical nature of communication or equating behaviors from different levels of meaning. The first adds to the error term while restricting the range of communication that can be studied; the latter commits a classic form of the fallacy of logical typing.

Second, this perspective is incapable of specifying the nature of the necessity for human behavior. Achinstein convincingly argues that any scientific theory must explain as well as describe, and explanation consists of identifying the necessity, or that which makes observed regularities *have* to be the way that they are.[23] The explanatory power of the rule-following behavior perspective consists of predicting that whatever happened before will happen again.

Finally, the generality of explanation is limited. Achinstein and McClelland both argue that a scientific statement must be preceded by some term that describes the category, such as "some," "most," or "all."[24] Further, a well-formed scientific statement will indicate the boundary conditions within which the relationship among the variables obtains. The rule-following theorist tends to neglect these two forms of generality.

Rule-governed behavior. This perspective is consistent with the action theorists' argument that human behavior is conscious, meaningful, and purposive. The rule is the actor's belief about what should be done or what probably will occur as a consequence of his or her action. The truth-claim includes a statement (1) that a regularity or prescription exists; (2) that the actor knows the rule; and (3) that the actor sees to it that his or her behavior conforms to the rule.[25] These statements are framed in the third-person practical syllogism as an explanatory model:

Person A wants Y;
Person A knows that s/he must do X if Y is to occur;
Therefore, Person A sets him/herself to do X.[26]

This perspective has been articulated by Cushman and Pearce, has been used by Cushman et al. in their recent work on relational communication, and, with the practical syllogism translated into Toulmin's argument structure, by Shimanoff.[27]

Although there has been very little empirical research on intercultural communication from the rule-governed approach,[28] several theoretical papers have articulated how this approach can be applied. Wiseman has examined the dynamics of communication rules in intercultural encounters.[29] In his analysis the communication rules of individuals in intercultural settings could vary in a number of ways; for example, definition of the rule or the generative mechanism producing the rule. Since individuals from different cultures often bring different rule systems to their intercultural encounters, Sigman suggests that individuals may use "socially patterned negotiation strategies for the establishment of a new set of rules; this would indicate that the new rules—while unique at one level of analysis—are not totally an individual creation."[30] The nature of these negotiation rules has signficiant implications for both the intercultural researcher and practitioner.

This perspective does specify a necessity—the desires and volitional acts of the person—and the approach is viable if three conditions are met. First, the social group in which the action takes place must be perceived by the actor as homogeneous enough to permit the calculation of plans of action. This may occur, as Cushman argues, only in those domains where there are standardized usages, or as Nofsinger argues, when rules for meaning in conversation may be well-distributed through a population.[31] Jackson's return potential model provides a conceptualization and measurement protocol for the empirical assessment of the *degree* of homogeneity in any given group.[32] The generality of this perspective is limited to those situations in which the social group is predictable.

Second, this perspective assumes a great burden of empirical proof. Before the explanation can be given, the researcher must demonstrate that the actor knows the rule. It is difficult to assess whether actors know a rule without teaching it to them, and there is good evidence that actors know rules they cannot state and perhaps do not recognize if stated. These empirical problems do not militate against this perspective *in principle*, but do restrict its region of utility.

Finally, the perspective depends on the assumption that persons act purposefully. However, some research has indicated that persons do not always act purposively, or—better—do not often act totally purposively.[33] To the extent that these critiques of action theory are valid, the rule-governed perspective becomes a poor basis for explanation.

Rule-using behavior. This perspective envisions a matrix of social rules as the ground on which persons act. It assumes that persons know the rules and decide whether to see to it that their actions conform to them. From this perspective, the competence of actors to find and/or create alternatives and the competence of rules systems to permit actors to decide whether to follow rules can both be assessed.

The explanatory device consistent with this approach is a description of the rules as known by the actor, the actor's intention, and an account of how the act accomplishes the intention. When the rule system is homogeneous and the content of the rules provides a standard means of accomplishing one's purposes, the practical syllogism or Toulmin's model of argument may be used as an explanation: The rule-governed behavior perspective is taken as a special case of the rule-using behavior perspective. The virtue of the rule-using perspective is that it applies to those conditions to which the rule-governed perspective does not; however, it does not offer—at least yet—a formal structure for explanation comparable to those in the other perspectives. Harris has developed a taxonomy for systems and individuals that describes the characteristics of persons who can create new behavioral options and of systems that facilitate the creation of new options.[34] Thus far, her research suffices to establish the existence of exemplars of the types identified in these taxonomies, and to verify some aspects of her characterizations of them, but not to explain why persons or systems develop these characteristics. Hewitt and Stokes's concept of aligning actions is consistent with the rule-using perspective, but is limited to identifying types of communication that indicate that persons are acting upon the rules by creating options or narrowing options.[35] Bowers, Elliott, and Desmond's study of devious messages also shows that rule-using behavior occurs, but does not develop a formal explanatory mechanism.[36]

DISCUSSION

Despite its relatively immature status, we believe that a rules theory in our discipline that will survive the problems on which those in other disciplines have floundered exists, namely the rule-using behavior perspective. The rule-following perspective is flawed *in principle*: Even if it does as well as possible, it has no necessity and limited generality. The rule-governed approach is adequate if one limits the theory to the relatively narrow range of phenomena in which the requisite conceptual and methodological conditions obtain. However, these exclude the most interesting forms of human sociation, including most intercultural communication. By default, the rule-using perspective is preferred, and the absence of an adequate explanatory framework consists of an agenda for further development rather than a reason for avoiding the perspective.

The line of research Pearce et al. are pursuing has produced some empirical findings that indicate the need for a theory that includes several explantory principles.[37] The lowest level is the statement of a rule, which simply describes the linkages that the actor perceives among meanings, and which has little explanatory power in itself. The second level is the calculation of logical force and a description of the type and amount of order in the system of rules. Finally, the research can assess the extent to which a person is enmeshed within or able to move among various systems of rules.

This concatenated explanatory model appears to have considerable utility in explaining intercultural communication, acculturation, and the differences betwen cultures. Further, it contains what appears to be the basis for a satisfactory response to the criticisms successfully brought against rules approaches in other disciplines.

NOTES

1. Donald P. Cushman and Gordon C. Whiting, "An Approach to Communication Theory: Toward Consensus on Rules," *Journal of Communication,* 22 (1972): 217-38.

2. Robert E. Nofsinger, Jr., "On Answering Questions Indirectly: Some Rules in the Grammar of Doing Conversation," *Human Communication Research,* 2 (1976): 172-81; Robert E. Sanders, "The Question of a Paradigm for the Study of Speech-Using Behavior," *Quarterly Journal of Speech,* 59 (1973): 1-10; Robert Hooper, "How to Make a Point" (Paper delivered at the Speech Communication Association Convention, San Antonio, Texas, November 1979).

3. William A. Donohue, "Development of a Model of Rule Use in Negotiation Interaction" (Paper delivered at the Speech Communication Association Convention, New York City, November 1980).

4. Kathleen K. Reardon, *Persuasion: Theory and Context* (Beverly Hills, CA: Sage, 1981).

5. Donald P. Cushman, Barry Valentinsen, and Gordon Whiting, "The Self-Concept as Generative Mechanism for Interpersonal Choice" (Paper delivered at the Speech Communication Association Convention, New York, November 1980); Linda M. Harris, "Interaction Management and Communication Competence" (Paper delivered at the International Communication Association Convention, Chicago, May 1978).

6. Gerald Philipsen, "Speaking 'Like a Man' in Teamsterville: Cultural Patterns of Role Enactment in an Urban Neighborhood," *Quarterly Journal of Speech* 61 (1975): 13-22; Gerald Philipsen, "Places for Speaking in Teamsterville," *Quarterly Journal of Speech* 62 (1976): 15-25.

7. Vernon E. Cronen, W. Barnett Pearce, and Lonna Snavely, "A Theory of Rule Structure and Types of Episode, and a Study of Perceived Enmeshment in Unwanted Repetitive Patterns," in *Communication Yearbook 3,* ed. Dan Nimmo (New Brunswick, NJ: Transaction, 1979).

8. Richard L. Wiseman, "Towards a Rules Perspective of Intercultural Communication" (Paper delivered at the International Communication Association, Acapulco, Mexico, May 1980): Kyungwha Kang and W. Barnett Pearce, "Reticence: A

Transcultural Analysis" (Paper delivered at the Speech Communication Association, New York, November 1980).

9. Sigmund Koch, "Psychology and Emerging Conceptions of Knowledge as Unitary," in *Behaviorism and Phenomenology*, ed. T. W. Wann (Chicago: University of Chicago, 1964), pp. 1-41.

10. Kang and Pearce, "Reticence."

11. William A. Donohue, Donald P. Cushman, and Robert E. Nofsinger, Jr., "Creating and Confronting Social Order: A Comparison of Rules Perspectives," *Western Journal of Speech Communication,* 44 (1980): 5-19.

12. Ibid., p. 6.

13. Cushman and Whiting, "Approach to Communication Theory."

14. Cushman, Valentinsen, and Whiting, "Self-Concept as a Generative Mechanism"; Wiseman, "Towards a Rules Perspective"; Richard L. Wiseman, "Functional Systems and Culturally-Determined Cognitive Differences" (Paper delivered at the Western Speech Communication Association Convention, Portland, OR, February 1980).

15. W. Barnett Pearce, Vernon E. Cronen, and Forrest Conklin, "On What to Look at When Analyzing Communication: A Hierarchical Model of Actors' Meanings," *Communication* 4 (1979): 195-221; W. Barnett Pearce and Vernon E. Cronen, *Communication, Action, and Meaning: The Construction of Social Realities* (New York: Praeger, 1980).

16. Harris, "Interaction Management"; W. Barnett Pearce and Robert J. Branham, "The Ineffable: An Examination of the Limits of Expressibility and the Means of Communication," in *Communication Yearbook 2*, ed. Brent Ruben (New Brunswick, NJ: Transaction, 1978), pp. 351-62.

17. This analysis is indebted to but differs in some ways from Joan Ganz, *Rules: A Systematic Study* (The Hague: Mouton, 1971).

18. For example, see B. Aubrey Fisher and Leonard C. Hawes, "An Interact System Model: Generating a Grounded Theory of Small Groups," *Quarterly Journal of Speech,* 57 (1971): 16-32

19. For a distinction between constitutive and regulative rules, see John Searle, *Speech Acts: An Essay in the Philosophy of Language* (Cambridge: Cambridge University Press, 1969).

20. Jerry D. Boucher, "Display Rules and Facial Affective Behavior: A Theoretical Discussion and Suggestions for Research," in *Culture Learning: Concepts, Applications, and Research*, ed. Richard W. Brislin (Honolulu: East-West Center, 1977), pp. 131-46.

21. Paul Ekman and Wallace V. Friesen, "The Repertoire of Nonverbal Behavior: Categories, Origins, Usage, and Coding," *Semiotica,* 1 (1969), 49-98.

22. Desmond Morris, Peter Collett, Peter Marsh, and Marie O'Shaughnessy, *Gestures* (New York: Stein & Day, 1979).

23. Peter Achinstein, *Laws and Explanation* (Oxford: Oxford University Press, 1971).

24. Achinstein, *Laws and Explanation*; Peter McClelland, *Causal Explanation and Model Building in History, Economics, and the New Economic History* (Ithaca, NY: Cornell University Press, 1975).

25. Ganz, *Rules*.

26. Georg von Wright, *Explanation and Understanding* (Ithaca, NY: Cornell University Press, 1971).

27. Donald P. Cushman and W. Barnett Pearce, "Generality and Necessity in Three Types of Theories, with Special Attention to Rules Theory," *Human Communication Research*, 3 (1977): 344-53; Cushman, Valentinsen, "Self Concept as a Generative Mechanism"; Susan Shimanoff, *Communication Rules* (Beverly Hills, CA: Sage, 1980).

28. Two exceptions to this statement are Jack Bilmes, "Rules and Rhetoric: Negotiating the Social Order in a Thai Village," *Journal of Anthropological Research*, 32 (1976): 44-57; Gerry Philipsen, "Speaking 'Like a Man' in Teamsterville."

29. Wiseman, "Towards a Rules Theory of Intercultural Communication."

30. Stuart J. Sigman, "On Communication Rules from a Social Perspective," *Human Communication Research*, 7 (1980): 45.

31. Cushman and Whiting, "Approach to Communication Theory"; Nofsinger, "On Answering Questions Indirectly."

32. Jay Jackson, "A Conceptual and Measurement Model for Norms and Roles," *Pacific Sociological Review*, 9 (1966): 35-47.

33. W. Barnett Pearce, Linda M. Harris, and Vernon E. Cronen, "The Coordinated Management of Meaning: Human Communication Theory in an New Key," in *Rigor and Imagination: Essays on Communication from an Interactional View*, ed. Paul Weakland and Carol Wilder-Mott (New York: Praeger, 1980).

34. Harris, "Interaction Management."

35. John P. Hewitt and Randall Stokes, "Disclaimers," *American Sociological Review*, 40 (1975): 1-11.

36. John W. Bowers, N. D. Elliott, and Roger J. Desmond, "Exploiting Pragmatic Rules: Devious Messages," *Human Communication Research*, 3 (1977): 235-42.

37. Pearce, Harris, and Cronen, "The Coordinated Management of Meaning."

6

Forming Intercultural Bonds

VERNON E. CRONEN • *University of Massachusetts*
ROBERT SHUTER • *Marquette University*

Forming interpersonal relationships has never been easy. Consider this story about the skills of an Eastern European matchmaker: A certain matchmaker regaled a young man with the boundless virtues of a particular young woman. "To look at her," he said, "Well—she's like a picture." After meeting this beauty the young man came back to the matchmaker and told him: "Like a picture! Her eyes are crossed, her nose points to one side, and when she smiles one half of her mouth goes down. . . ." "Just a minute," the matchmaker interrupted, "Is it my fault you don't like Picasso?"

Even in cultures that have long given up matchmakers the process of forming relationships remains difficult and complex. Add the difficulties of forming relationships among people from different cultural backgrounds and the complexities are magnified.

The purpose of this chapter is to present some of the results of the committee on relationship development in intercultural contexts that was part of the two-day workshop on intercultural communication sponsored by the Speech Communication Association and held in conjunction with its 1980 convention. In order to provide a coherent state-of-the-art chapter the authors have at many points gone beyond the scope of committee discussion. In this chapter we will do the following: First, we will suggest a metatheoretical framework for the assessment of those theories and perspectives that bear upon the problem of relationship formation. Second, we will discuss some of the perspectives that have ben most frequently advanced for explaining how social bonding operates in intercultural situations. Third, we will discuss our own approaches to the problem area, a cultural values communication approach (Val/Com), and the theory of coordinated management of meaning (CMM). Much of the committee's attention was directed toward these new approaches.

A METATHEORETICAL FRAMEWORK

The study of how persons form interpersonal bonds has intrigued social scientists for many years. This interest is informed by more than the truism "humans are a social animal." Indeed, that truism probably obscures more than it illuminates important issues. Recent scholarship emphasizes the inherent *tension* between autonomy and interdependence. The formation of interpersonal bonds is described by Bochner[1] in terms of dialectical process through which persons work out the competing claims of selfhood and association. The effects of this tension can be clearly seen in those close personal relationships in which partners seem connected by rubber bands—repeatedly pulling and coming together. Case study research by Harris and her associates has identified many instances in which the dynamic of family violence is rooted in the competing claims of self-definition and relational commitment.[2] The tension between selfhood and relationship is explored extensively in Ernest Becker's book *Birth and Death of Meaning*.[3] Becker describes a fundamental paradox of autonomy. The child first learns to give over control of his or her own impulses to an internalized parental voice and thus brings the self under a form of symbolic control. The very young child may be heard instructing the self with such phrases as, "No Billy, don't touch, bad boy Billy." In order to obtain a sense of self one must first surrender aegis over his or her own activity to other persons—and, in the process, obtain others' love, approval, and acceptance. Thus the "I" in Mead's terms is initially developed through interaction as a *representation* of significant others. The "I" takes control of the "me" by first acting as a surrogate other, only later to develop some greater degree of individuation. If Becker's perspective is accepted, we come to see the development of self as in some sense paradoxical. One obtains self-mastery by first surrendering control to others in an intense social bond.

Thus *each person* who attempts to create an adult relationship is the locus of dialectical tension between individual and association. Each person's self is, moreover, the product-in-process of human interaction. For without interaction selfhood could not emerge.

The present chapter specifically focuses on the process of forming social bonds from an intercultural perspective. The foregoing brief discussion of selfhood is meant to frame our chapter in these ways: First, the work of Becker[4] and Bochner[5] illuminates the poverty of mechanistic models of affiliation. The notion of two or more reified selves forming bonds ignores the fact that *each* self is the locus of tension between autonomy and interdependence and that each self emerged as a synthesis of that tension. Second, our analysis points to communication as the locus of those powerful forces through which autonomy, relatedness, and their synthesis are created. The third aspect of our metatheoretical frame is derived from the first two. Namely, that selves and relationships are *dynamic, emergent* concepts, maintained, altered, shattered, and developed through communication in *multiple* social situations.

When these three general principles are applied to the problem of intercultural relationships their importance is further illuminated. Clearly, the synthesis of autonomy and interdependence is not a fixed mathematical outcome but a unique product of persons and the preexisting cultures. We know from anthropological studies that the concept of self which has emerged in the contemporary industrialized West has no duplicate in archaic cultures. Eliade has observed that archaic cultures do not usually produce members who can define the uniqueness of self outside the community role relationships.[6] In these archaic cultures the tension between autonomy and relatedness usually produces a synthesis in which autonomy is given much less emphasis than in more modern cultures.

Contemporary traditional cultures retain some of the same deemphasis of individuated selfhood. Stable communities composed of relatively fixed sets of role relationships tend to produce persons whose identities are virtually defined by that set of relationships in which they participate. It is often very difficult for members of very traditional ethnic groups to define the self in any way other than its situated meaning in traditional forms of social action.[7]

It is also clear that the nature of social relationships varies significantly across and within cultures and that the process of *forming* relationships is clearly different in such countries as Japan or Taiwan compared to middle-class North America.[8] Researchers have found that Eastern cultures have a structured set of interpersonal rules guiding relationship formation that appears to affect such factors as the amount and type of interpersonal disclosure and the frequency and content of interpersonal questions. Similarly, intercultural data indicate, for example, that American blacks and whites gather information significantly differently during the initial stage of relationship formation.[9] Recent research on family relationships in North America suggests that differences in the nature of the preferred *kinds* of close personal relationships produce changes in the nature of the process through which persons form interpersonal bonds. Scanzoni has argued that among middle-class North Americans there has arisen the ideal of a marriage in which "nothing is non-negotiable."[10] If Scanzoni is right then younger persons could be expected to use initial interactions as a kind of testing ground for evaluating the flexibility of the others. This expectation was confirmed in a recent study by Harris, Cronen, and Lesch.[11] Such evidence, while generated within a single cultural milieu, suggests a connection between the kind of relationship sought and the process of interaction through which relationships are formed. The diversity of forms that relationship take across cultures and the varied patterns of talk through which they are created clearly indicate that if we wish to understand relationship formation we must somehow account for the cultural traditions that precede episodes of communication.

Cultural values appear to be a critical cultural construct since they seem to have significant impact on numerous interpersonal factors, including relationship development. Shuter found, for example, that selected friendship patterns appear to be governed by cultural values.[12] Small group process, interpersonal attraction, and self-disclosure also seem to be influenced by cultural values.[13] While cultural values appear to be of central importance, other cultural factors, notably world view and cultural mores, may also have significant impact on relationship development. The need for a sensitivity to cultural traditions constitutes the fourth aspect of the metatheoretical frame for this chapter.

These four principles together form a way of testing the assumptive base of theories that claim to predict and explain the course of relationship development.

THE WELL-TRODDEN GROUND

During the course of workshop discussions participants referred to several well-known theories of relationship develoment—none of which received much enthusiastic support from the majority of participants. The present authors were genuinely surprised not to find ardent supports of exchange, uncertainty reduction, or other mainstream theories. In this section of our chapter we will briefly discuss some of these well-known theories and perspectives applying our metatheoretical frame. Our purpose is not to review extensively these established traditions, for such reviews are available elsewhere. Instead we will attempt to indicate why we think a disenchantment with them seems to have developed.

Exchange Theory

Exchange theory is probably the most frequently employed perspective in sociological studies of family formation and interaction.[14]

They are based upon the economic principle of costs and rewards. This borrowing of a principle of classical economics is open to question on several grounds.

A telling criticism of exchange theory is that it may be impossible to determine a priori what is cost and what is a reward. By ignoring the symbolic character of relationship formation, exchange theory passes over the fact that what is emergent in social action includes the question of what will count as reward or cost. Consider the case of a graduate student forming a close personal relationship with a professor. The graduate student expresses interest in some concept and his or her partner gives a protracted response to the query. Is that response a one-up move—lecturing—a cost? Or is it a sharing of information to create equality—a reward? The problem is not just one of knowing the meaning that particular individuals assign. The most important question is how persons manage the import of this interaction for their particular relationship. How do they work out the meaning of this mini-lecture within the web of other emerging meanings? The important question is how to understand the process by which the significance of messages is created and changed.

Because each person is a locus of tension between autonomy and relatedness, any particular message may be simultaneously both cost and reward. Case studies of troubled relationships have revealed instances in which a particular speech act has positive values for self (e.g., it affirms who I am) but a negative value for the relationship.[15] Specific acts can become simultaneously cost and reward for different aspects of a person's social field. For some persons their perceptions of self and their relationships to others form a reflex loop such that the definition of self depends on the definition of the relationship and vice-versa. For example: "Only in the context of a strong loving relationship can I see myself as a worthwhile person, but if I am not a worthwhile person I could not really be in a strong loving relationship." In this situation a message that rewards the self at the cost of the relationship ultimately strikes a blow at the self concept also.[16]

The metaphor of the marketplace does not seem to capture the subtlety and complexity of human relationships, but that does not mean that persons never think of their relationships in terms of costs and rewards. Doing so, however, entails great risks. If a reward like love is reified, then interactants must utilize a system of clearly discriminable tokens for exchanging units of love; for love (like self-respect, assertiveness, or happiness) is not a material object. To treat it as a material object requires clearly discriminable tokens of the reified abstraction. One can exchange the reified abstraction wealth via material tokens such as coins, chickens, or beads. The question, "Does the coin given to me really carry an increment of wealth?" does not usually come up. But the question "Does bringing home the Friday paycheck really carry with it an increment of love?" does come up. The dereification of the tokens of love receives poignant treatment in the song "Do You Love Me" from *Fiddler on the Roof*. In that song Tevye and Golde deal with the elemental matter of whether darning socks for seventeen years really counts as giving love or only as an obligation enforced by tradition. It is possible that some of the problems that beset the modern American family stem from dereifying the acts that persons perform while continuing to treat love, assertiveness, and self-respect as if they were objects that one could somehow give to a passive receiver.[17]

Finally, exchange theory appears to flow from a Western view of reality and thus may have limited cross-cultural application. The very assumption that social life can be reduced to cost-reward units springs from the West's reverence for categorizing all areas of life experience. The penchant for categorizing runs deep in Western thought. It is most clearly evidenced in Aristotlean logic—a categorical system. In contrast, Eastern philosophies view reality as a process, a gestalt that cannot be readily categorized and thus should be examined as a whole. The conflict between categorical and holistic perspectives of reality—a discontinuity of Eastern and Western thought—places the value of exchange theory in even greater jeopardy.

The foregoing analysis suggests that exchange theory does not provide a universal metalanguage for describing relationship formation in any culture. Rather, it is a particular metaphor that characterizes some relationships and contains its own unique potentiality for interpersonal chaos. For when persons adopt the metaphor of the marketplace they adopt a perspective quite inconsistent with what we know about human development and association.

Uncertainty Reduction Theory

Berger and his associates have set forward a theory of relationship development based upon a single covering law: that the goal of reducing uncertainty about one another governs the processes by which persons form relationships.[18] While the description of relationship development that Berger offers is not very different from that of exchange theorists Altman and Taylor,[19] the causal mechanism is very different.

Recent problems have arisen in the application of uncertainty reduction theory across cultures because the theory is nonspecific about how uncertainty-reducing behaviors could systematically vary across different cultures. Shuter found, for example, that American blacks and whites differ in methods of reducing uncertainty: Whites rely heavily on questions while blacks employ leading statements—a declarative sentence that challenges a communicator to respond.[20] Similarly, Roger Abrahams argues that American blacks and whites discuss different topics in the initial period of interaction.[21]

Communicators in Taiwan attempt to reduce uncertainty by gathering certain demographic data from which they make a rich array of dependable inferences. However, individuals from a low-context culture (i.e., United States) seem to gather different demographic information during initial interaction than do high-context interactants, and they make fewer inferences from the data.[22] It can be argued, therefore, that initial interaction between individuals from low-context and high-context cultures may be fraught with a high degree of misunderstanding since the information each attempts to elicit may be different and the inferential value of those data may vary.

There are also reasons to question the structure of uncertainty reduction theory itself. In its original 1975 statement the theory is presented as firmly grounded in the Durkheimian tradition. Uncertainty reduction is promoted by the maintenance of normative social patterns and talk between homophilous individuals. This perspective has the obvious difficulty of virtually writing creative action out of existence. It also ignores the vital role of weak-ties, which are usually heterophilous ties, in facilitating social change.[23]

A subsequent position statement in 1976 circumvents these problems but presents new ones. Berger et al. argued in 1976 that norm breaking generated information about the other and thus could also reduce uncertainty and facilitate attraction.[24] A similiar argument is made concerning heterophily. The effect of these changes is to make the theory virtually tautological and unfalsifiable.[25] Since any variable manipulation can be interpreted as information, any substantive finding can be interpreted post hoc as support for the uncertainty reduction principle.

Uncertainty reduction does treat relationship development as an emergent process but ignores the dialectical tension inherent in social bonding because it reduces persons to uncertainty-reducing machines. As Kierkegaard so well understood, individual autonomy inherently involves a freedom to create, and total autonomy suggests a "dreadful" freedom.[26] Berger's work does not deal with the problems of working out a synthesis of autonmy and relatedness. Enmeshment in patterns of interaction produce feelings of certainty and predictability, but it is clear from other data that many people in our culture dislike such fixity and that such fixity of pattern is often associated with what Cronen et al. call "unwanted repeated patterns" or URPs.[27].

Humanistic Psychology, Self-Disclosure, and Coorientation

The position of the humanistic psychology movement suggests that if persons of various cultures were to be open with each other, they could then coorient to each other. The ideology of openness is very well reviewed by Parks[28] and, therefore, we shall not treat it extensively here. It is important to observe, however, that maximal disclosure of the self produces anything but autonomy. If all were known about each individual in a collectivity the result would be total immersion in the mass. Such debasement of privacy and separateness is hardly the stuff of creative life. Walter Kaufmann has observed that most creative individuals were in important ways alienated from the larger social order.[29] To see the self as distinct is to see it in distinction from others.

Some adherents of the humanistic tradition emphasize trust, climate, and validation more than sheer openness. Unfortunately, as McNamee notes, this emphasis is often a reductionistic perspective masquerading as systemic theory.[30] The work of Cissna and Sieberg represents a well-elaborated exemplar.[31] Cissna and Sieberg identify criteria by which acts are classified as validating or invalidating. The central contention is that sound relationships are those where more validating acts are performed. However, Harris has reported a case study in which the participants validate each others' reified self-concepts.[32] The effect Harris found is to lock in place a cycle of conflict that neither person wishes to perpetuate. Harris's case study suggests that the function of validating acts depends on the whole web of actions in which they occur. McNamee's nomonthetic study shows that perception of how validating an act is depends on the system of interaction in which it appears.[33] Thus, training persons to be validating does not seem fruitful if conversants are not capable of analyzing larger frames of social action. In practical application to cross-cultural settings, the validating climate emphasis gives us little help in assessing how cultural differences are manifest in validating actions. Indeed it is difficult to know how this perspective would be applied in an Eastern culture where validation of social roles counts more than validation of highly personal aspects of selfhood.

A final aspect of this humanist tradition deserves our attention. Whatever the emphasis—trust, disclosure, or validation—these humanistic approaches share a much older assumption—one that permeates far too many of our basic texts—that successful communication depends on the achievement of coorientation or mutual understanding. In the realm of intercultural contact the coorientational goal suggests that people must understand each other to communicate successfully.

Cushman and Craig[34] and Pearce[35] led the intellectual battle to dislodge the primacy of coorientation. There are data to support clearly the contention that some social episodes work precisely *because* conversants in a close relationship assign different meanings to certain crucial acts. Campbell observes that Eskimo shamans have a very different conception of the rituals they perform than do the celebrants.[36] Shamans often do not take the rituals literally and see the ceremonies as useful for social cohesion, while the celebrants take them much more literally. Would we want to argue that all would be better if the celebrants knew what the shamans' view were?

Ethnography and Desriptive Rules-Based Approaches

Rules-based accounts vary significantly from one another. A number of researchers use the idea of rules in their efforts to give descriptive accounts of how actors form relationships in particular cultural settings. However, when rules are used as descriptors of normative behavior it is difficult to explore how individuals synthesize the tension between relatedness and autonomy. Ethnography is not, nor is it meant to provide, a diagnostic tool for analyzing the dynamics of relationship development in a way that highlights the *uniqueness* of a *particular instance* of couple bonding.

Another problem is inherent in the ethnographic approach. It does not deal with *change* in patterns of bonding that a culture experiences. Anthony Wallace has observed that because societies change, the ethnographic record can never be complete.[37] Thus, ethnographic works that describe rules of relationship formation may become like yesterday's weather report—of historical value only.

Adaptive Approaches

It has been suggested that intercultural communicators develop relationships initially by drawing cultural distinctions—and then adjusting their communicative behavior on the basis of this information.[38] This adjustment, referred to as adaptation by Ellingsworth, may be functional (supportive) or dysfunctional (defensive); therefore, the way intercultural communicators adapt to one another is critical. Ellingsworth's theory of adaptation stops short of identifying the verbal and nonverbal parameters of functional and dysfunctional adaptive styles: With this information, there is no reported research on how communicators draw cultural distinctions; data are needed in this before conclusions can be reached about the power of the approach.

Researchers have also argued that intercultural communicators connect by developing a third culture, a set of communication rules, language patterns, and nonverbal behaviors that are familiar to the interactants.[39] The third culture facilitates the development of a relationship by providing the common ground necessary to move the relationship from a phatic stage to a more personal stage. In developing a third culture, communicators must negotiate a range of interesting issues that, as yet, have not been systematically examined: (1) How do individuals negotiate and select third-culture rules? (2) How are third culture decisions made regarding language and nonverbal behavior? In short, the development of a third culture demands that intercultural communicators establish common communicative ground—how individuals accomplish this certainly warrants close attention. What is needed is a sound theoretical frame for the exploration of this creative process.

The remainder of this chapter is devoted to two approaches that have been advanced as successors to the work discussed above. One is the theory called the Coordinated Management of Meaning and the other is a values-centered approach called Val/Com. Brief presentations of these will be followed by a discussion of how they relate to each other.

COORDINATED MANAGEMENT OF MEANING

The Coordinated Management of Meaning (hereafter CMM) is a general theory of human communication. Cross-cultural and intercultural studies provide a crucial testing ground for a theory like CMM, which purports to be more than a culture-specific explanatory framework. Space does not allow a detailed review of CMM theory in this chapter. (For an overview of CMM theory and research see Pearce and Cronen.)[40] What follows is a brief introduction to CMM theory, with special attention to its relevance for cross-cultural and intercultural studies.

CMM is influenced by certain aspects of action theory, but care has been taken to avoid two errors common to much writing in the action theory tradition. First, CMM theory specifies that although it is best to conceive of what persons do as actions, it does not follow that all acts are predicated on intentions to bring about some subsequent state of affairs. Persons often report that their choice of action is strongly circumscribed by the requirements of context. Von Wright, for example, acknowledges that his practical syllogism does not apply across the whole range of human action, yet he devotes his analysis entirely to those situations in which social actors chose acts to attain specific outcomes.[41] The practical syllogism does not differentiate between the fulfillment of antecedent requirements and attempts to attain a subsequent state. Moreover, the practical syllogism does not separate purposes from functions. An act may indeed elicit a desired consequent but, as Harris has shown, even a consequent like validation of self-concept may function to lock in place a destructive pattern of interpersonal action.[42] Function refers to the effects of events on the systems in which they occur—a concept beyond the scope of action theories like Von Wright's.

A second failing of most action theories is that they assume a discontinuity in the modes of casual explanation. Nomic necessity is ascribed to motion, while practical necessity is ascribed to action. CMM theory rejects this simplistic dichotomy. CMM theorists argue that behavior entails the interplay of multiple modes of necessity: practical, logical, and nomic.[43]

CMM theory avoids the traditional pitfalls of action theory by imbedding purposiveness in a new conception of communication. The central metaphor of coordinated management of meaning is meant to be taken seriously. The fundamental goal of communicating is to achieve coordination. Coordination is *minimally* the perception that the pattern of interaction makes sense, that it appears coherent to participants. This minimal condition does *not* presume that each conversant makes the *same* sense of an interaction, and it is *not* assumed that coherence *always* depends on mutual understanding. Coorientation is one road to coordination but not the only one. Indeed it has been shown that couples may create coherent and mutually satisfying interactions based on inconsistent construals of crucial messages.[44] Management of meaning refers to the process by which meanings are assigned to messages within episodes of interaction.

The central metaphor of CMM suggests a reciprocally causal, morphogenic relationship between patterns of communication and higher orders of context—relationships, self-concepts, even culture itself. Acts create contexts and contexts define acts. The metaphor of

CMM thus illuminates communication as a creative process. The process of creation operates at a variety of contextual levels. While the distinction of Oriental and Occidental cultures is useful, these cultural types are clearly not homogeneous. It can be argued that a relationship or a family may be usefully considered to be a subculture. Relationships develop their own unique ways of knowing and ways of acting—their own logics of social action. Obviously, dyads, families, or social groups have less history, and are more readily altered. However, the difference is more that of degree than of kind.

The primacy of coordination rather than coorientation in the CMM metaphor suggests that interactions can be mutually satisfying—at least coherent—even with imperfect understanding. This suggests that researchers must also avoid the converse assumption that mutual understanding is at work when respondents express satisfaction with episodes of interaction. An obvious implication of this perspective is that one ought not limit one's research to episodes with which conversants express dissatisfaction. Researchers must explore the foundations of successful episodes rather than assume mutual understanding.

Levels of Context in CMM Theory

The meaning upon which persons predicate their choice of acts is represnted as a hierarchy of contextual levels. In prior work CMM researchers have identified six levels of context: (1) context—the verbal/nonverbal behavior available to one's senses; (2) speech acts—the relational level of meaning; (3) episodes—patterns of reciprocal acts perceived as meaningful sequences; (4) relationship—the nature of social bonds between two or more persons; (5) life-scripting—the concept of self in action; and (6) cultural pattern—the essential ways of knowing and acting that define a larger collectivity. These levels of meaning are meant to be heuristically powerful and suggestive—not exhaustive. Persons may develop intermediary levels such as community expectations or subepisodes.

The foregoing set of six contextual levels was presented in the order of part-whole relationship. In social life, however, the organization of hierarchies is not fixed. Cronen and Lannamann have shown that when persons begin evolving a unique relationship, specific episodes may be the context for interpreting the relationship, while an established relationship is most often the context for particular episodes that the couple often enact.[45]

A characteristic of hierarchical systems now receiving increased attention is that they are often not organized into neat levels but instead contain reflexive loops. For example, when a couple discuss the state of their relationship and evolve a new conception of it over the course of conversation, a reflective loop forms between episode and relationship, each contexting the other and each changing over time.

Rules

CMM is often described as a rules theory, yet it has little in common with most rules theories. In CMM rules are not located in social patterns or in collective agreements. Rules in CMM are organizations of meaning in the minds of social actors. They may be highly idiosyncratic to the individuals that hold them. Rules evolve from a person's participation in social action, but particular rules a person evolves may reflect idiosyncratic inferences from social action.

Two kinds of rules are identified in CMM theory: constitutive rules that define meaning and regulative rules that guide action. Both embody a principle that is taken to be a universal of human organization: Actors organize meanings *hierarchically* and *temporally*.[46] For our purpose in this chapter we will focus on the regulative rule to illustrate how CMM research meets the criteria discussed earlier.

The primitive form of a regulative rule is shown in Figure 6.1. In the primitive form there are multiple levels of context within which a person chooses an act. The choice of a particular act is based upon what action preceded it and may be based upon its ability to elicit some particular consequent.

Regulative rules link together to form logics of conversation as each person's act becomes an antecedent condition for the other. Moreover, responsive acts are compared to the consequences desired. For example, it is more likely that the regulative rule above will really elicit another insult rather than the desired apology. The effect may be to generate a spiral of escalating insults. A logic of talk comprised of conjoined regulative rules can be represented as shown in Figure 6.2.

Rule Structure Variables

CMM researchers often study the structure of persons' rules. Regulative rule models isolate a number of variables, each of which is assigned a number in Figure 6.3. Variables 1 through 5 collectively refer

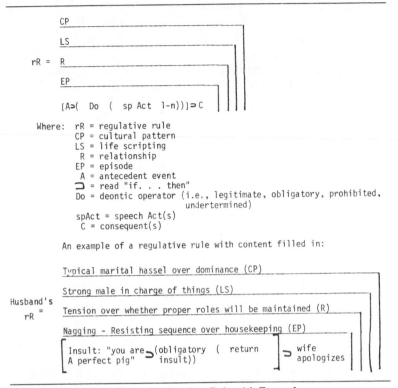

Where: rR = regulative rule
        CP = cultural pattern
        LS = life scripting
         R = relationship
        EP = episode
         A = antecedent event
         ⊃ = read "if. . . then"
        Do = deontic operator (i.e., legitimate, obligatory, prohibited,
                                      undertermined)
      spAct = speech Act(s)
         C = consequent(s)

An example of a regulative rule with content filled in:

Figure 6.1: Primitive Form of a Regulate Rule with Example

to prefigurative force. Each measures the degree to which an aspect of context seems subjectively to require a particular speech act. For example, the life-scripting to speech-act linkage (4) is measured by a Likert-type scale such as this one:

A person like me must respond with this message.

Strongly Agree ____ ____ ____ ____ ____ ____ ____ Strongly Disagree

Variable 6 has been of particular interest. It measures the extent to which a particular act is chosen in order to obtain a particular consequent (C) or is functionally autonomous of consequences. Measurement of this variable allows one to distinguish the extent to which action is felt to be prefigured and the extent to which action is chosen to obtain specific responses.

The use of the functional autonomy variable in conjunction with the prefigurative force variables allows CMM to avoid the unprofitable

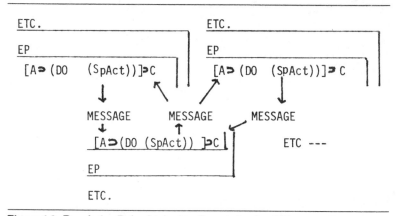

Figure 6.2: Regulative Rules Linked to Form a Logic of Conversation

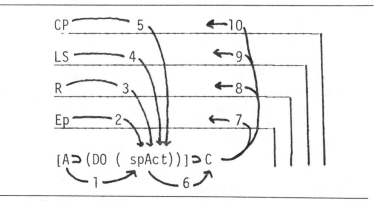

Figure 6.3: Regulative Rule Structure Variables

dispute over whether to model persons as reactive or purposive. The CMM rule models treat reactivity to prefiguring forces and deliberate goal seeking as variables within a unified theoretical frame. This is particularly useful for intercultural studies because persons from different cultures often vary in their feelings about how prefigured—ritualized—some episodes are. In a recent study of relationship development that compared North Americans and Taiwanese persons of comparable age, Alexander et al. found that Taiwanese identified significantly more topics as required by episodes than did the North Americans ($p < .005$), and a near-significant tendency for Taiwanese to identify more topics as prohibited by episodic context ($p < .1$).[47] Consider what is likely to happen when a North American attempts to

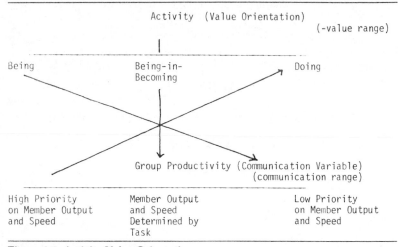

Figure 6.4: Activity-Value Orientation

get acquainted with a Taiwanese. The work of Harris et al.[48] and Scanzoni[49] suggests that college-age North Americans enjoy interactions in which conversants deliberately abandon normative patterns and display their ability to negotiate unique patterns. In an intercultural encounter the Taiwanese individual may work with rules that exhibit very strong prefigurative forces, while the North American's rule might well exhibit weaker prefigurative and stronger practical forces. Thus, Taiwanese attempting to adapt North American norms would look for more stable patterns of interaction and would tend to find what looks to them like chaos.

The final set of rule structure variables, 7 through 10, depicts the relationship of intended consequences to various levels of context. Rather than reifying contextual levels, CMM assumes that conceptions of self, relationship, episode, and so on evolve as conversants examine the successive outcomes of action. A person may feel obliged to perform an act because it expresses his or her relationship with an other. Yet that very act may elicit a response that, when compared to the intended consequent, suggests a different definition of the relationship.

Consider this bind: A male's sense of significance (defined in a certain cultural context) requires him to issue orders to his spouse even though he knows that orders will evoke responses that harm the relationship. Those acts that would elicit responses conducive to a good relationship seem to imply unmanly life-scripting. This predicament would suggest that the male must choose between a particular relationship and a particular self-concept—but the situation might not be so simple.

Suppose that the male in our example does not perceive a neat hierarchical ordering of his life-scripting and relationship. Instead suppose that he perceives these contexts as forming a reflexive □.   In this loop his relationship defines who he is and who he is defines how he sees the relationship. *Now* look at the consequences. Life-scripting requires a particular act. That act elicits a response that indicates a worsening relationship. A worsening relationship implied that his preferred life script is not being enacted. This is the sort of situation likely to produce a realtionship that seems suspended on rubber bands. One partner cannot stay and cannot leave. The foregoing situation is hardly far-fetched. Certain Near-Eastern cultures prize a male self-image that includes a dominant role in the home, while failure to achieve a proper marital relationship is in itself the context for perceiving the self as weak. Now envision a male raised in such a culture attempting to create a family with a liberated North American woman. Our prediction is that for a long period of time he could not stay with her and could not leave her.

Communication Competence: Harris's Systemic Approach

Most models of competence define it as the ability of persons to learn and enact the rules of an extant system. Such models emphasize knowledge of cultural skills like turn taking or topic shifting. Some stress actors' ability to work within the extant meaning of a system through empathy, accurate listening, or understanding others' intentions. Models of competence with these emphases do not address the problems of a reflexive relationship between modes of communication and social systems. They ignore the creative aspect of communication.

CMM theory stresses the idea that modernity in Western industrialized nations has altered the social requirements for communicative ability in ways more fundamental and drastic than has been commonly acknowledged.[50] Specifically, there has been a *structural* change in the relationship between the social order and communication ability, such that *normal* functioning in modern society requires a type of communication ability that is *abnormally* sophisticated in any other society. However, formal educational institutions and informal socialization processes have yet to develop and widely disseminate the communication abilities required by modern societies.

The concept of competence in CMM was developed by Linda M. Harris.[51] Harris defines communication competence as the ability to cocreate and comaintain the social order.[52] This definition clearly focuses on the context-relevance of the skills and attributes of an individual: Any particular skill may be functional or dysfunctional depending upon the requirements of the system. From this perspective, the possession or lack of particular skills is an inappropriate means of differentiating levels of competence. However, individuals can be assessed as more or less competent based on the comparison of their abilities to the requirements imposed by a particular social system. Harris identifies three archetypal levels of competence. *Minimal* competence exists when the individual's abilities are in some way less than required by a particular system, for example, when an individual is lacking in a particular skill or is insufficiently differentiated. Such persons are outside the social system and are unable to move effectively within it. *Satisfactory* competence exists when the individual is enmeshed within the system by a close fit between his or her abilities and the system's requirements. Such persons are well-socialized, and can move comfortably within the system but nct outside it. *Optimal* competence exists when an individual's abilities are greater than and subsume the requirements of a system. These individuals may choose whether to move easily within a system or to act in ways inconsistent with it for their own purposes. For example, Gandhi's tactic of nonviolent noncompliance with legal injunctions was optimally competent because it required a thorough understanding of the social order in British-dominated India, plus an ability to act in noble ways outside the system.

The requisite abilities for participation in a homogeneous social system are acquired by modeling and successful socialization. Satisfactory competence is achieved by enmeshment in the system, and communication or adaptive problems are solved by becoming increasingly enmeshed within or dependent upon the system. In modern society—heterogenous, complex, reflexively self-aware of the human agency of its institutions—the structure of the social systems has changed in such a way that satisfactory competence is impossible. The diversity of family interaction systems forces many couples to negotiate new patterns of interaction and new conceptions of their relationship that are unlike either person's family or origin.[53] The enmeshment of both partners in multiple systems fosters change in the self-concepts and value preferences in both of them. Thus, patterns of interaction that were mutually satisfying at one stage of a close relationship may be unsatisfying to one or both partners at a subsequent time.

The skills required to negotiate new patterns are not simply those required to fit in. Harris has discussed some of the skills of optimal competence. In the domain of assigning meaning to another's messages, minimal competence is reflected in mistaking the meanings of another's messages, and in satisfactory competence in mutual understanding.[54] Optimal competence, however, would entail the ability to treat knowingly a message in a way inconsistent with the other's intent in order to alter a destructive pattern of talk. Another skill Harris discusses is the ability to treat an otherwise serious episode playfully. The ability to introduce an element of play into an otherwise serious episode can help persons distance themselves from the episode and obtain control over it, avoiding overenmeshment in it.

Satisfactory competence is often impossible in modern society. For research and policy, the implications of modernity are that the symptoms of minimal competence should be expected to increase. These include frustrations, confusion, inefficiency, and stress-related pathologies. For pedagogy, the implication is that instruction should be designed to inculcate optimal rather than satisfactory competence.

Summary

CMM research on intercultural communication is still in its early stages. However, it does offer an approach that is consistent with modern insights into the human condition. CMM depicts the actor as unique synthesis of conceptions not only of relationship and selfhood, but also of concepts about culture, episodes, and acts. The illumination of logics of talk via CMM analysis offers a way of exploring the *emergent* quality of relationships. Rule structure variables assess not ony prefiguring forces but also the way social action reflects back on various levels of context, maintaining or altering them.

CMM theory also offers a more useful conception of competence for intercultural studies than those offered by other theorists. Harris's model defines competence in terms of a particular actor's relationship to a system of meaning and action. It broadens the concept of competence beyond fitting in to encompass creative social action. The sensitive reader will of course note that the systemic orientation of Harris's model avoids treating creative action as simply the out-of-step behaviors of a single individual. Indeed, the model suggests conditions under which creative action may be impossible. If, for example, one conversant considers his or her cultural model of a proper relationship sacrosanct, then that conversant may well employ rules that treat all unique forms of interacting behavior as mistakes requiring correction.

Finally, it is useful to note that CMM generates ideographic as well as nomothetic research. It has been used not only to explore that which tends to occur, but also that which transpires in specific episodes of interaction.

VAL/COM:
VALUES/COMMUNICATION APPROACH

In Kluckhohn and Strodtbeck's classic study of cultural values, they argue cogently that value orientations—"complex but definitely patterned principles"—give order and direction to the "ever flowing stream of human acts and thoughts as these relate to the solution of common human problems."[55] Although Kluckhohn and Strodtbeck indicated that value orientations influence the full range of human behavior, which they call the "behavioral sphere," they do not specifically apply value orientations to the communication process. Communication researchers have subsequently tried to apply Kluckhohn's value paradigm to human interaction with the implicit intent of developing principles of intercultural communication that account for cultural variability and similarity in communication.[56] Qualitative in design and implementation, these studies demonstrate that communication *seems* to be significantly influenced by cultural values; however, this research stops short of systematically identifying the specific ways cultural values *can* influence communication variables.

In asking how cultural values can affect communication variables, several assumptions are implicitly raised that have not been addressed by reported research on values and communication. First, the question suggests that a specific cultural value can produce a communicative outcome for an identified communication variable. Second, each communicative outcome can be framed as a hypothesis and systematically tested. And last, tested hypotheses can serve as principles of intercultural communication depending, of course, on the results of communicative studies.

CULTURAL VALUES, COMMUNICATION RANGES, AND HYPOTHESES: A DEVELOPMENTAL PERSPECTIVE

Kluckhohn and Strodtbeck identified five value orientations and the range of cultural variation postulated for each.

(1) What is the character of innate human nature? They divide this orienta tion into three logical divisions (value ranges): Evil, Good and Evil, and Good.

(2) What is the relation of humanity to nature (humanity / nature orientation)? As a three-part range division, this orientation includes subjection to nature, harmony with nature, and mastery over nature.

(3) What is the temporal focus of human life (time orientation)? The range includes past time, present time, and future time.

(4) What is the modality of human activity (activity orientation), which is composed of being, being-in-becoming, and doing?

(5) What is the modality of the individual's relationship to other humans (relational orientation)? This orientation is composed of lineality, collaterality, and individuality.[57]

In theory, each value orientation and the range associated with it can significantly influence human interaction; however, in what specific ways can this occur? To answer this question, it is necessary to develop on a communication level what Kluckhohn and Strodtbeck created for cultural values, that is, postulate a range of communication outcomes for a specific communication variable when a certain value orientation is preeminent. In theory, a communication range for any communication variable can be logically derived from Kluckhohn and Strodtbeck's value orientations.

For example, the activity value orientation and its three-part range can potentially affect any communication variable; in terms of group productivity, the variable selected for illustration, the communication range shown in Figure 6.4, can be postulated.

In developing the preceding communication range, three communication assumptions were used, each of which is logically derived from Kluckhohn and Strodtbeck's value range for activity.

Assumption 1: A culture (doing culture) that values a person for what he or she produces rather than what he or she is may be likely to put a high priority on group member output and speed of task completion.

Assumption 2: A culture (being-in-becoming culture) that emphasizes the kind of activity that has as its goal the development of all aspects of self

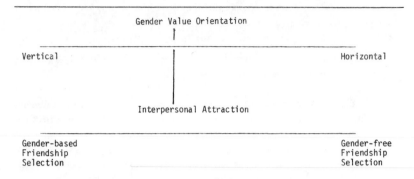

Figure 6.5: Communication Range for Interpersonal Attraction

into an integrated whole may tend to vary productivity norms depending on the relationship of the task to self-growth.

Assumption 3: A culture (being culture) that values spontaneous expression over productivity may place a low priority on group member output and speed and speed of task completion.

The communication range and concomitant assumptions for group productivity can be readily converted into communication hypotheses that postulate communicative outcomes for the doing, being, and being-in-becoming value range.

Hypothesis 1: The more doing-oriented the culture, the more small groups will emphasize member output and speed in task completion.

Hypothesis 2: The more being-in-becoming-oriented the culture, the more small groups will vary productivity norms based on the task's relationships to self-growth.

Hypothesis 3: The more being-oriented the culture, the less small groups will emphasize member output and speed in task completion.

The hypotheses can be tested in appropriate small group studies; in fact, a study of Nigeria (a being culture) and the United States (a doing culture) found that Nigerians work significantly more slowly in small groups than do Americans and, unlike Americans, Nigerians are dissatisfied with central positions in decentralized networks.[58] If these hypotheses are confirmed, they become *principles* of intercultural communication because they establish a tested relationship between values and communication.

Utilizing Kluckhohn and Strodtbeck's value orientations, any communication variable can be selected and a communication range developed, hypotheses generated and tested, and principles of intercultural communication identified. In addition to Kluckhohn and Strodtbeck's value orientations, Condon developed 63 orientations, some of which broaden the scope of Kluckhohn's value orientation on the relationship of "man to other men"—certainly a critical value for communication researchers interested in relationship development.[59]

In identifying other value orientations that influence the "relationship of man to other men," it has been suggested by Condon that cultural values regarding gender influence communication.[60] Condon described a value range for gender including the Western tradition, which essentially "treats women as the weaker sex," and the non-Western tradition, which is based on the premise that "women are supposed to serve men." An interesting value continuum, Condon's value range of Western and non-Western traditions appears to be too limited to explain the existence of matriarchal societies and contextual variations in male/female dominance patterns within Western and non-Western societies.[61]

On close examination of Mead's[62] research on gender, it appears that the cultural range for gender varies from societies that distribute power unequally to men and women, defined as a vertical value in this study, to societies that strive for equal distribution of power to the genders, identified as a horizontal value. It appears, then, that power and its distribution to genders is the bottom line when describing cultural differences in gender orientation.

In a society where a vertical gender value is predominant, either men or women possess more power depending on the context (i.e., family, business). In contrast, a culture emphasizing a horizontal value will strive to equlize power distribution between men and women regardless of context. As with all value orientations, each culture has both vertical and horizontal dimensions; it is the predominance of a particular gender value in a society that accounts for gender difference in power distribution.

Utilizing a power framework it can be argued, for example, that Japan, a vertical culture, distributes power to the sexes unequally, with men possessing more power in the public sector (i.e., business) and women having an edge in the home.[63] While the United States has vertical dimensions, it puts emphasis on a horizontal value and thus struggles, unlike Japan, to equalize the distribution of power to men and women, regardless of context.

It can be postulated that the horizontal and vertical value range for gender can significantly influence communication; accordingly, a range of communicative outcomes can be identified for a selected communication variable, hypotheses generated and tested, and principles of intercultural communication isolated. To explore the relationships of gender values and communication, a cross-culture study was conducted on male same-sex friendship patterns. A brief summary of this study is provided.

The study was conducted in Italy and the United States because available research indicates that these cultures differ significantly in gender values, with Italy possessing more of a vertical gender orientation than the United States.[64] It was speculated that variations in gender values affect same-sex friendship patterns, particularly the extent to which men and women desire to socialize with individuals of the same sex, referred to as interpersonal attraction in this study. Accordingly, the communication range in Figure 6.5 was postulated for interpersonal attraction.

The range suggests that a vertical value results in friendship selection based on gender, while a horizontal value promotes gender-free friendship selection. With regard to friendship selection, the gender is the primary standard for determining interpersonal attraction in a vertical culture; in contrast, gender is not a determining factor for interpersonal attraction in a horizontal culture.

The communication range for interpersonal attraction stems from two assumptions:

Assumption 1: A vertical culture's utilization of gender-based standards in social decision-making (i.e., power distribution) will also be reflected in friendship selection. Hence, in a vertical society it is expected that individuals will choose their friends on the basis of gender, with individuals being most attracted to people with the same degree of social power, namely, interactants of the same sex.

Assumption 2: The value a horizontal culture places on gender-free standards in social decision-making (i.e., power distribution) should be evidenced in friendship selection, with individuals being equally attracted to males and females as friends.

These assumptions provide the foundation for a hypothesis regarding the relationship between gender values and interpersonal attraction.

Hypothesis 1: The more vertically oriented the culture, the more individuals will be attracted to same-sex friendships.

Hypothesis 1a: For the purposes of this study, it is hypothesized that married Italian males are more attracted to male same-sex friendships than are married American males.

To test the hypothesis, a questionnaire was developed on male same-sex friendships and administered to married Italian men living in Rome, Italy, and to married American men in Milwaukee, Wisconsin. The questionnaire developed for this study consisted of 31 items assessing 5 dimensions of interpersonal attraction: (1) frequency individuals see male friends, (2) the need to see male friends more often, (3) the duration of male friendships, (4) the need to have more male friends, (5) the need to socialize with friends in same-sex group.

The data confirmed hypothesis 1a on interpersonal attraction, that is, that Italian men are more attracted to male-sex friendships than are American men. Italians scored significantly higher than Americans on all measures of interpersonal attraction: They see their friends more often than do Americans, a significantly higher proportion of Italians than Americans want to see their friends more often, Italian male friendships appear to last for a longer period of time than do American friendships, a higher proportion of Italians than Americans want more male friends, and more Italians than Americans prefer socializing with male friends in same-sex groups.

The preceding results also provide confirmation for hypothesis 1: The more vertically oriented the culture, the more individuals will be attracted to same-sex friendships. In fact, the cultural value toward gender appears to influence a variety of factors in same-sex friends, obstacles to maintaining these friendships, and the durability of the relationship. Married Italians, for example, report meeting most of their male friends when single; in contrast, married Americans seem to sever ties with friends met before marriage, particularly single friends, and develop new friends at work and through their spouse. Interestingly, while Americans do not indicate why they socialize infrequently with friends met before marriage, Italians report that their spouse is the primary obstacle to maintaining male friends—discouraging them from maintaining old friendships and socializing with their current male friends.

On the strength of the data, it appears that hypothesis 1 may evolve into a principle of intercultural communication, that is, if additional studies on male and famale same-sex friendship patterns in vertical and horizontal societies confirm the trends identified in this investigation. In addition, the results of this study offer support for the theoretical framework presented earlier for developing principles of intercultural communication from cultural values:

(1) A communication range can be postulated for a communication variable on the basis of established cultural values.

(2) Communication hypotheses can be generated from a postulated communication range and the hypothesis systematically tested.

(3) Principle(s) of intercultural communication can be derived from confirmed hypotheses.

Significance of Approach

The significance of a value approach is clearly its transcultural orientation; that is, principles of intercultural communication can be isolated that ought to be applicable to any culture that has a certain value orientation. Of course, this approach requires extensive development and testing in five areas:

(1) the development of instruments for systematically determining central value orientations,

(2) the development of value continuua and the placement of cultures and regions on each continuum,

(3) the development of communication ranges for selected communication variables when a certain value orientation preeminates,

(4) the development of communication hypotheses from a postulated range, and testing these hypotheses.

(5) the development of principles of intercultural communication from tested hypotheses.

With this approach, it may be possible in the future to develop a series of tested principles of intercultural communication that have a high level of predictive value in determining communicative outcomes for selected communication variables when certain cultural values are preeminent.

CONCLUSIONS AND PROSPECTS

What do these two new approaches, CMM and Val/Com, offer to each other? On the first inspection the two seem quite different. CMM emphasizes the hierarchical and temporal organization of meanings while Val/Com emphasizes various continuua of values at the level of culture. CMM is much like a structural-functional theory with equal theoretical interest in the prefiguring role of culture on communication and the creative role of communication as the morphogenic process behind culture. Val/Com is much like a structural theory that describes layers of social organization and examines the transformations by which the higher level of cultural values is made manifest in particular kinds of face-to-face social action.

In spite of such differences, however, the two perspectives offer challenges and insights to one another. The Val/Com approach offers this challenge to CMM work: If two levels of social organization are in a hierarchical relationship such as a life-scripting cultural pattern, by what logic of transformation is a particular life script seen as a manifestation of the cultural pattern, not outside it? Can the heuristic tool of value analysis aid us in uncovering these transforms?

An assumption of Val/Com is that the cultural pattern—an important component of CMM—is reflected in all aspects of communication systems including episodes and regulative rules. In fact, Val/Com suggests that life scripts, relationships, episodes, and rules can be better understood and even predicted if cultural values can be systematically isolated. For example, a series of rule continua can be theoretically developed on the basis of preeminent cultural values. One set of continua could focus on the relationship between values of interdependence/independence and prohibitive/obligatory forms of interaction. It can be argued that as cultures become more interdependent, there is a greater emphasis on prohibitive and obligatory interaction. Conversely, in societies that are less group oriented, conversational prohibitions and obligations may be minimal. These hypotheses spring from the assumption that interdependent cultures protect group relationships by legislating human relationships, that is, by mandating conversational prohibitions and obligations. Support for this theoretical relationship can be found in linguistic data of Eastern and Western cultures that identify a complex of prohibitive and obligatory formalities in the interdependent East and significantly fewer of these linguistic nuances in the more independent West. These hypotheses can be tested, ultimately producing a series of predictive relationships between cultural values (cultural pattern) and regulative rules. There are infinite theoretical relationships that can be posited between cultural pattern and various levels of human interaction, be it life script, episode, or rule. In this way, Val/Com offers CMM the possibility of establishing cultural linkage to seemingly isolated communicative acts. Conversely, CMM offers these challenges to Val/Com: How are cultural patterns of value maintained or altered by social action? What happens when persons create new sorts of relationships that are not direct transforms of extant value?

One of CMM's strengths is its process-orientation—its view that social action and human dynamics are inextricably intertwined. CMM's process view not only helps explain forms of interaction that appear to be outside the paramenters of cultural value, but it also argues for microanalysis of interaction, an analysis that does not always trace interaction to value origins.

Clearly, CMM and Val/Com can either be used together in a research effort or the two approaches can be utilized independently. Regardless of how they are used, the chief strength of both approaches is their primary focus on interaction, be it relationship development or other communication factors. Having returned communication to central importance, cross-cultural researchers can begin examining the impact of culture on human interaction.

NOTES

1. Arthur P. Bochner, "Functions of Communication in Interpersonal Bonding," in *Handbook of Rhetoric and Communication*, ed. C. Arnold and J. Bowers (Boston: Allyn & Bacon, in press). This concept of self has its roots in the earlier work of T. W. Adorno, "Sociology and Psychology," trans. Irving N. Wohlfarth, *New Left Review*, 46 (1967): 78.

2. Linda M. Harris, "Power, Impotence and Physical Violence" (Paper delivered at the Eastern Communication Association Annual Convention, 1980).

3. Ernest Becker, *The Birth and Death of Meaning* (New York: Free Press, 1971).

4. Bochner, "Functions of Communication."

5. Becker, *The Birth and Death of Meaning.*

6. Mircea Eliade, *Myth and Reality* (New York: Harper & Row, 1963).

7. See the case studies reported in Lillian B. Rubin, *World of Pain* (New York: Basic Books, 1976).

8. Dean Barnlund, *The Public and Private Self in Japan and The United States* (Tokyo: Simul Press, 1975).

9. Robert Shuter, "Initial Interaction in Interracial and Intraracial Interactions," *Journal of Social Psychology* (in press).

10. John Scanzoni, "A Historical Perspective on Husband-Wife Bargaining Power and Marital Dissolution," in *Divorce and Separation*, ed. G. Levinger and O. C. Moles (New York: Basic Books, 1979), p. 31.

11. Linda M. Harris, Vernon E. Cronen, and William E. Lesch, "Social Actors and Their Relationship to The Social Order: A Test of Two Theoretical Views" (Paper delivered at the International Communication Association Annual Convention, Acapulco, Mexico, 1980).

12. Robert Shuter, "Values and Communication: A Theoretical Framework For Developing Principles of Intercultural Communication and A Pilot Study" (Paper delivered at the Speech Communication Association Annual Convention, New York, 1980).

13. Robert Shuter, "Cross-Cultural Small Group Research: A Review an Analysis and a Theory," *International Journal of Intercultural Relations* 1 (1977): 90-114.

14. See, for example, Wesley R. Burr, Rubin Hill, F. Ivan Nye, and Ira Reiss, eds., *Contemporary Theories About The Family*, (New York: Free Press, 1979).

15. Linda M. Harris, Vernon E. Cronen, and Sheila McNamee, "An Empirical Case Study of Communication Episodes" (Paper delivered to the Theory and Methodology Workshop, National Council on Family Relations Annual Convention, 1979).

16. Vernon E. Cronen and John Lannamann, "This Is Not the Title: An Empirical Study of Reflexivity in Social Interaction" (Paper delivered to the International Communication Association Annual Convention, Minneapolis, 1981).

17. We are indebted to Professor Linda M. Harris (Human Development and Family Relations Program, University of Connecticut), Professor Alison Alexander (Communication Studies Department, University of Massachusetts), and Mr. Loren Kaplan (School of Education, University of Massachusetts) for their insights that contributed to this analysis of exchange theory.

18. Charles R. Berger and R. Calabrese, "Some Explorations in Initial Interaction and Beyond: Toward A Developmental Theory of Interpersonal Communication," *Human Communication Research* 1 (1975): 99-112.

19. Irwin Altman and Dalmas A. Taylor, *Social Penetration* (New York: Holt, Rinehart & Winston, 1973).

20. Shuter, "Initial Interaction."

21. Roger Abrahams, *Talking Black* (Englewood Cliffs, NJ: Prentice-Hall, 1974).

22. Alison Alexander, Vernon E. Cronen, Kyung-Wha Kang, Benny Tsou, and Jane Banks, "Pattern of Topic Sequencing and Information Gain: A Comparative Study of Relationship Development in Chinese and American Cultures" (Paper delivered at the Speech Communication Association Annual Convention, New York, 1980).

23. Mark S. Granovetter, "The Strength of Weak Ties," *American Journal of Sociology* 78 (1973): 1360-80.

24. Charles R. Berger, Royce R. Gardner, Malcolm R. Parks, Linda Schulman, and Gerald Miller, "Interpersonal Epistemology and Interpersonal Communication," in *Explorations in Interpersonal Communication* (Beverly Hills, CA: Sage, 1976), pp. 149-72.

25. J. J. La Gapia, "Interpersonal Attraction and Social Exchange," in *Theory and Practice In Interpersonal Attraction*, ed. S. Duck (London: Academic Press, 1977).

26. Soren Kierkegaard, *The Concept of Dread*, trans. W. Lowrie (Princeton, NJ: Princeton University Press, 1946).

27. Vernon E. Cronen, W. Barnett Pearce, and Lonna Snavely, "A Theory of Rules Structure and Episode Types, and a Study of Perceived Enmeshment in Unwanted Repetitive Patterns (URPs)," in *Communication Yearbook 3,* ed. D. Nimmo (New Brunswick, NJ: Transaction Books, 1979).

28. Malcolm R. Parks, "Ideology In Interpersonal Communication," in *Communication Yearbook 5*, ed. M. Burgoon (New Brunswick, NJ: Transaction Books, 1981).

29. Walter Kaufmann, *Discovering The Mind*, vol. 2 (New York: McGraw-Hill, 1980).

30. Shiela McNamee, "Structural and Functional Aspects of Interpersonal Systems: A Comparison of Two Perspectives" (M.A. thesis, University of Massachusetts, 1980).

31. K. N. Cissa and E. Sieburg, "Interactional Foundations of Interpersonal Confirmation" (Paper delivered to the International Communication Association Postdoctoral Conference, Asilomar, 1979).

32. Linda M. Harris, "The Maintenance of a Social Reality: A Family Case Study," *Family Process* 19 (1980): 19-33.

33. McNamee, "Structural and Functional Aspects of Interpersonal Systems."

34. Donald P. Cushman and Robert T. Craig, "Communication Systems: Interpersonal Implications," in *Explorations in Interpersonal Communication*, ed. G. Miller (Beverly Hills, CA: Sage, 1976), pp. 37-58.

35. W. Barnett Pearce, "The Coordinated Management of Meaning: A Rules-Based Theory of Interpersonal Communication," in *Explorations in Interpersonal Communication*, ed. G. Miller (Beverly Hills, CA: Sage, 1976), pp. 17-36.

36. Joseph Campbell, *The Masks of God: Vol. 1, Primitive Mythology* (New York: Viking, 1959).

37. Anthony F.C. Wallace, *Culture and Personality* (New York: Random House, 1961), p. 4.

38. W. H. Ellingsworth, "A Theory of Adaptive Intercultural Communication," this volume.

39. William B. Gudykunst, "Toward A Model of Intercultural Relationship Development" (Paper delivered at the Speech Communication Association Annual Convention, 1980).

40. W. Barnett Pearce and Vernon E. Cronen, *Communication, Action, and Meaning: The Creation of Social Realities* (New York: Praeger, 1980).

41. George von Wright, *Explanation and Understanding* (Ithaca, NY: Cornell University Press, 1971).

42. Harris, "The Maintenance of a Social Reality."

43. Vernon E. Cronen and Leslie K. Davis, "Alternative Approaches for the Communication Theorist: Problems in the Laws-Rules-Systems Trichotomy," *Human Communication Research* 4 (1978): 120-218.

44. Harris, Cronen, and McNamee. "An Empirical Case Study of Communication Episodes."

45. Cronen and Lannamann, "This Is Not the Title."

46. Pearce and Cronen, *Communication, Action and Meaning.*

47. Alexander et al., "Pattern of Topic Sequencing and Information Gain.

48. Harris, Cronen, and McNamee, "An Empirical Case Study of Communication Episodes."

49. Scanzoni. "A Historical Perspecive on Husband-Wife Bargaining Power."

50. Pearce and Cronen, *Communication, Action, and Meaning*; Linda M. Harris, "Communication Competence: Empirical Tests of a Systemic Model" (Ph.D. diss., University of Massachusetts, 1979).

51. Harris, "Communication Competence."

52. Harris, "Communication Competence."

53. Salvador Minuchin, *Families and Family Therapy* (Cambridge, MA: Harvard University Press, 1974).

54. Harris, "Communication Competence."

55. F. Kluckhohn and F. Strodtbeck, *Variations in Value Orientation* (Evanston, IL: Row Peterson, 1961), p. 4.

56. John Condon and F. Yosef, *An Introduction to Intercultural Communication* (New York: Bobbs Merrill, 1975); E. Stewart, *American Cultural Patterns* (Chicago: Intercultural Press, 1971).

57. Kluckhohn and Strodtbeck, *Variations in Value Orientation*, p. 12.

58. Robert Shuter, "Cross-Cultural Small Group Research."

59. J. Condon and F. Yousef, *Introduction to Intercultural Communication.*

60. J. Condon and F. Yousef, *Introduction to Intercultural Communication.*

61. M. Mead, *Male and Female: A Study of the Sexes in a Changing World* (New York: William Morrow, 1949).

62. M. Mead, *Male and Female.*

63. F. Gibney, *Japan: The Fragile Superpower* (New York: Meidan, 1979).

64. C. Sforza, *Italy and the Italians* (New York: F. Muller, 1948); L. Sturzo, *Italy and the Coming World* (New York: Roy Publishers, 1945).

7

Returning to Rhetoric

JOLENE KOESTER • *University of Missouri—Columbia*
CARL B. HOLMBERG • *Bowling Green State University*

Because rhetoric can be generally conceptualized in various ways, there are many particular views as to the service rhetoric can perform for theorizing intercultural communication. There are two major positions among them: rhetoric performs a limited function or it performs wide-ranging functions.

Oliver suggests a popular view that there is no rhetoric common to all cultures; instead, there are many rhetorics.[1] However, while rhetorics do vary by culture, the fact that Greek rhetoric began in an intercultural milieu[2] suggests that the possibility of rhetoric for intercultural communication is not limited to a narrowly defined role.

Booth has said,

> It is obvious, for example, that McKeon's hope (which I share) for a "universal architectonic productive art" in a technological age has a good deal more chance for realization if . . . all men speak, in one very real sense, a common language. And if, on the contrary, there are no linguistic "places" that are really common to all men, then I don't see how we are going to find a meeting ground in a new rhetorical world community.[3]

Clearly there are modern rhetoricians who envision an intercultural role quite different than Oliver's.

In pursuing the benefits of rhetoric for intercultural communication, two facets emerge as central: (1) we must discover and analyze rhetorical strategies for intercultural communication used in the past and present, and (2) we must learn to invent new and rhetorical strategies that are not so much based upon past history and current fashion.

In accomplishing this twofold and necessarily ongoing inquiry, the rhetoric of intercultural communication need not be limited to the specific topics of inquiry obtained by other current perspectives on intercultural communication.[4] Koester argues that the rhetorical tradition is currently neglected because intercultural communication scholars turn to the social sciences for research models. She finds evidence in various journals, in the *International and Intercultural Communication Annuals,* and in the description and goals of the 1980 New York City SCA Action Caucus and Seminar on General Theory-Building in Intercultural Communication.[5]

Because of this inclination away from rhetorical perspectives, significant features about intercultural communication can easily be left underdeveloped. For instance, Sarbaugh locates the properties of interculturalness either in characteristics of the situation or in the individuals. However, in elaborating this taxonomy he concentrates on the individuals, largely ignoring situational differences, which many rhetoricians would not do.[6] In contrast, Koester posits that the conscious adaptation of messages to this situational dimension is an additional defining parameter of intercultural communication.

Therefore, one should keep in mind throughout the remainder of this chapter that, while it is necessary for rhetoricians to respond sensitively and sensibly to other intercultural views and interests, we could return to rhetoric for a unique and wide-ranging understanding of intercultural communication. As such, rhetoric suggests its own topics and vantages. By attending to these topics we can add to the body of knowledge about intercultural communication in ways that other perspectives do not—or cannot.

SOME THEORETICAL CONSTRAINTS FOR THEORIZING INTERCULTURAL COMMUNICATION RHETORICALLY

Past practices of rhetoric still suggest new uses for rhetoric in theorizing intercultural communication. Some rhetoricians warn, however, that the unthinking adaptation of extant rhetorical theory may lead to erroneous conclusions. They also point out that this caveat does not mean that rhetoric holds no positive value for theorizing intercultural communication. Instead, it is fundamentally a matter of discerning and applying constraints.

Monfils argues this way when she claims that rhetorical criticism owes its primary debt to Aristotelian rhetoric and, consequently, that the rhetorical critic working interculturally can make detrimental interpretations and evaluations.[7] Despite her critique, she cites some descriptions of the field of rhetorical criticism—by Andrews, Stewart, Scott, and Brock—that *can* serve to inform intercultural communication rhetorically.[8] The basic argument demonstrates that, when rhetorical criticism is sufficiently conceived as universal in scope, it is most suited to include criticism of intercultural discourse.

Methods of rhetorical criticism, Monfils concludes, have not been adequately developed for intercultural criticism. She turns to questions raised by Swanson in a two-article series on the critical process to find appropriate questions to be raised as the traditional rhetorical critic moves to the intercultural domain.[9]

Swanson endorses the reflective stance, which recognizes that criticism is a form of experience, rather than taking objectivity as a basis for criticism. Monfils argues then that any attempts at objectivity in the intercultural rhetorical and critical process are doomed to failure because of the relativity of cultures and their experience. She also considers the problems the rhetorical critic confronts when performing the traditional assessments of criticism: truth-effectiveness and ethical judgment. Her point is that these standards have unique manifestations in differing cultural contexts. Thus, the rhetorical critic must apply standards appropriate to the cultures involved in discourse, and not necessarily standards found only in the Western rhetorical tradition.

Starosta confirms these arguments while demonstrating that intercultural communication has all along been rhetorical.[10] He suggests that cultures exist because people use cultural regularities to govern their behavior. Within this framework, intercultural communication is a coorientation of two culturally unique communicators who are attempting to exchange meanings.

Starosta then directs his attention to the relationships between culture and rhetoric. Emphasizing the intentional quality of rhetoric, he concludes that much rhetoric is actually disguised as culture. That is, culture is often rhetoric *incognito.* According to Starosta, the intercultural rhetorical communication theorist should thus direct attention to the interface of two or more cultures that exert influence upon each other when they attempt to search for repetitive patterns that can promote communication between them.

Starosta introduces the concept of rhetorical interference, which he defines as "the difference in interpretation that is offered by distinctive cultural communication by one or both entities that represents a byproduct of separate cultural projections."[11] This point concurs with Koester and Monfils—and a host of others. In investigating intercultural communication a primary consideration is focusing upon each of the parties and situations involved. It also suggests what may be a starting point for a hermeneutical understanding of cultures and communicating. In sum, rhetoric as a way of getting at intercultural communication is not always something added to the intercultural communication; it is part and parcel of it.

Other ways to consider past rhetorical theory for intercultural communication need to be discovered and developed. Taking Monfils and Starosta as guides, however, we know that splicing former theories and strategies to intercultural communication is not enough. The splicing approach needs to be superseded by the transformation of rhetoric for intercultural communication. This may be done by focusing upon rhetorical criticism for its intercultural promise as well as its promise for the criticism of cultural events. On the other hand, the rhetoric in intercultural communication also needs to be recognized as a new starting point for an intercultural rhetoric. Specifically *how* to keep these constraints operative remains a major goal for investigating intercultural communication.

Stated in the form of rhetorical commonplaces, Monfils and Starosta can be seen as offering two viewpoints that can be merged into one vision of rhetoric for intercultural communication. Monfils would have us concentrate on the relativities and ethics inherent in investigating intercultural communication. Starosta would have us focus on the regularities and thus predictabilities inherent to intercultural communication. An adequate rhetoric of intercultural communication, therefore, must paradoxically account for regularities and irregularities in order to apprehend the full rhetorical domain of intercultural communication.

A NEW RHETORICAL APPROACH

Since former rhetorical approaches are undeveloped for intercultural communication and since the constraints of relativity and regularity beckon auspiciously, it is necessary to discuss the rhetorical methods that are being developed and that meet these concerns. Then topics for further inquiry can be suggested.

Holmberg suggests a new rhetorical method for inquiring intercultural communication that meets the constraints of regularity and relativity. Heuristic matrix theory is a methodology that goes beyond the kernal ideas of McKeon's architectonic productive arts by positing two general procedures.[12] The first general procedure hypothesizes, then demonstrates, that the general architectonic of all intercultural communication involves (1) phenomena, (2) human faculties, and (3) the ecological mesh of faculties and phenomena (including other humans and their faculty deployment).

Each of these three basic principles can be treated as enthymematic commonplaces, which can furthermore flexibly assume other useful meanings. For instance, a "phenomenon" may be conceived as a resource shared interculturally. Since human faculties are developed variously from culture to culture, it may be inquired for how they become the basis of advice for persons in intercultural encounters; that is, faculties and their array may be treated as heuristically generative of information in and of themselves. The ecological mesh may be considered to be the theories, artifacts, and technologies produced when phenomena and faculties enmesh; these may be studied in themselves or used as aids to intercultural communication. Thus phenomena-faculties ecology can become enthymematically transformed for intercultural study to resource-advice-aid. Other such inventive transformations are possible.

Holmberg indicates that theory and theory-building is itself an ecological mesh. Thus heuristic matrix theory may illustratively be conceived as an intercultural ecology that can facilitate the discovery and analysis of significant intercultural data by enabling the inquirer to generate matrices descriptive of those data, either in the threefold form just outlined or in the form of the second general procedure.

The second general procedure calls upon McKeon's architectonic productive arts methods and explains how to generate matrices about any given subject.[13] This invention need not be structured according to Holmberg's threefold nature of intercultural communication described in the first general procedure. The second procedure follows this pattern instead: (1) discover the organizing principle(s) in the subject inquired; (2) discover the architectonic intersection of the principles involved, usually—but not always—expressed in the form of matrices; and (3) discover useful applications of the matrices.

Holmberg generates such a matrix in summarizing a review of the literature about constraints on theory-building for intercultural communication. He discerns five constraints and treats them as enthymematic vectors in a metatheoretical matrix. The vectors must (1) account for structures, (2) be a heuristic system of problem-solving, (3) be a system of communication analysis, (4) be a theory to account for other theories, and (5) be a neutral and variable research instrument. These standards can be applied to heuristic matrix theory and other theories to ascertain their theoretical adequacy for theorizing intercultural communication.

Unlike some theories or methods, heuristic matrix theory is not hopelessly culture bound since a matrix can be fashioned to any cultural form, and not just to the Western rectilinear row and column schemata. Also, the variable terms in a matrix are enthymematic commonplaces and, therefore, can take on a variety of cultures' implications and shades of meaning. Because the variables are symbolic of intercultural relativities, but are arranged in some pattern, the matrices that capture the pattern are empowered to handle the constraint of regularity as well as that of relativity.

In general, this rhetorical method of inquiring intercultural communication can approach its subject with flexible heuristic probes in the form of matrices. Such matrices are advantageous since they may be used to discover new matrices—or strategies—for improving intercultural communication. The procedure inherent in such a methodology also may be incorporated into other approaches to intercultural communication, possibly providing epistomological factors previously unapproachable by that other viewpoint. Once intercultural and cultural data are placed in the form of matrices, those data may be analyzed as a symbolic system. Invention performed on such symbolic systems may stimulate innovations that can be performed in actual intercultural encounters. Such matrices can easily be computerized for facility of analysis.

RETURNING TO RHETORIC FOR THEORIZING INTERCULTURAL COMMUNICATION

The demand for inquiring intercultural communication has been voiced rhetorically for over a decade. The Project Wingspread Conference recommended that "research be undertaken on the nature of invention in non-Western cultures; and further that the interactions between cultures and inventional processes be explored."[14] The Rhetorical Group in the Action Caucus on General Theory-Building in Intercultural Communication at the New York, 1980 SCA Convention supported this view. However, no concrete directions were suggested by the earlier Wingspread Conference or by the Rhetorical Group.

The Project Wingspread Committee on the Nature of Rhetorical Invention did suggest some general directions for inquiry. These may illustrate some directions for the study of intercultural invention. Treated as topics, each may be researched separately or in conjunction with some or all of the others: (1) social resources and conditions available to an inventing person (use), (2) materials and perspectives on facts (hermeneutic), (3) specific persons involved in invention and their unique inclinations to enhance or inhibit invention (personality), (4) deep structures of invention that may be operated at nonconscious levels (methods), and (5) presentational form (style, arrangment).[15]

Some participants in the Rhetorical Group of the Action Caucus advocated the study of invention as a key to understanding the way in which culturally distinct individuals achieve shared meaning. A focus on invention should direct the intercultural communication scholar to explore the strategies and arguments that may also be invented anew to negotiate meaning. The thrust of this major topic concerns what cannot be predicted about speech acts. Perhaps what is most significant in intercultural communication is not what can be predicted, but what *cannot* be predicted; invention as genuine innovation cannot be specifically anticipated. Thus, modern rhetoric can keep us with modern American and European epistemologies of discontinuity in attending to intercultural communication.[16]

The study of the activity of invention creates a significant methodological problem: The empirical investigation of invention and especially of intercultural invention is inhibited by the lack of a single, accepted guide for identifying invention when it happens. Perhaps, then, this hypothesis needs investigation and testing: In intercultural communication, the greater the degree of heterogeneity between the communicators, the greater the probability of a unique invention and presentation of communicative strategies. That is, the greater the difference between communicators, the more likley it will be that they must invent to communicate. How this invention may be characterized and facilitated should be a major goal of our discipline.

The Rhetorical Group also saw potential for the intercultural communication scholar to pursue the study of culturally unique rhetorics that function within a given milieu. In a sense, these participants were arguing for the discovery of intercultural counterparts to something like an Aristotelian system. Second, the group wanted to answer the questions: What functions in each culture for communicative understanding? What functions for understanding how to communicate with persons from another culture, such as for understanding intercultural communication? Other questions need to be addressed: What do other cultures do that Westerners might call rhetoric? How does such a non-Western rhetoric compare to Western rhetoric? What are the advantages of each alone and merged into one system? How might this rhetoric be adequately apprehended? The answer to each of these questions may provide new ideas and methods for theorizing intercultural communication.

Within the framework of the Rhetorical Group's discussions, a consensus was reached that the critical method is particularly appropriate for the study of intercultural communication. Even though many writers have decried the linear, Western orientation of intercultural communication research and have recommended the adoption of *intercultural* research methods,[17] the Rhetorical Group reached a consensus that there was still a strong potential for the possible transformation of rhetorical thoery for intercultural rhetorical theory. In other words, invention and heuristic procedures should be performed upon any rhetorical heritage we can discover, producing theoretical systems geared to a variety of cultures' interpretations of the world, and not just to one interpretation.

Phenomenological inquiries also need to be conducted. To do this the inquirer must go to the act itself and build interpretations, arts, and sciences of intercultural communication upon its phenomenal field. In other words, theory-building in intercultural communication can be innovatively informed by *doing* intercultural investigation for the express purpose of gathering phenomenological data such as experience, structures observed, and other interpretations. These data are themselves based on the act of criticizing and analyzing intercultural communication, and may suggest improvements in the practice of intercultural rhetorical theory.

The Rhetorical Group endorsed the report of the Project Wingspread Conference, which expanded the limits of rhetorical objects away from the traditional speaker-audience situation to include any discourse with suasory potential.[18] A critic or scholar working in the intercultural arena must be open to various interpretations of what functions as a rhetorical object. Quite simply, what has suasory potential in one culture will not always have that capability in another.

The location and study of rhetorical objects in other cultural settings makes two primary contributions to our knowledge: (1) By locating rhetorical objects in different cultures, intercultural communication scholars can gain insight into rhetorical situations as *cultural and intercultural situations.* (2) Once this goal is attained, the study of culturally distinct rhetorical objects may also suggest how *new* cultural contexts are created through intercultural communication, such as countercultures and other dialectical variations in some larger culture. Understanding the rhetoric in cultural and intercultural communication situations can advance the understanding of rhetorical theory itself. In other words, inquiring rhetoric and intercultural communication should bring us closer to finding a genuinely intercultural rhetoric that may be used for the preliminary decoding of any intercultural experience.

The Rhetorical Group also encouraged the study of rhetorical genres.[19] Since genres are sets of rhetorical objects that recur or repeat themselves, but which appear in different cultural and temporal settings, intercultural scholars could derive benefit from studying the modes of their variation. Hence, traditional methodologies may be transformed to study the historical and stylistic interrelation of genres interculturally. The identification of genres in a range of cultures would indicate points of similarity and difference for comparative literature and arts.

"Identification" was also discussed. In the process of the identification of the speaker with the audience, both the rhetor and audience are transformed by participating in that rhetorical process of identification. Understanding identification as an intercultural process may also help typify the way intercultural communicators develop a common but unique set of shared meanings.

The study of illusion was also proposed as an avenue of research. Rhetoric was first accused of being mere illusion by Plato.[20] Nowadays we can inquire into this facet of rhetoric nonpolemically. How do language and other symbol systems create illusions? By examining the way in which rhetorical systems suggest what is real and what is illusion, intercultural communication scholars can learn about how and why people attend to various factors and data in intercultural interactions.

We must face the dearth of rhetorical intercultural communication publications and ask, will rhetoricians exercise their faculties upon intercultural communication? The challenge to modern rhetoric persists: Once the heart of communication study and learning, rhetoric needs to flow to our consciousness as intercultural rhetoric. The powers of rhetoric still remain to be demonstrated for intercultural communication.

NOTES

1. Robert T. Oliver, *Culture and Communication* (Springfield, IL: Charles C Thomas, 1962), p. 155.

2. Carl B. Holmberg, "Dialectical Rhetoric and Rhetorical Rhetoric," *Philosophy and Rhetoric* 10 (Fall 1977): 232-43. Further support for this position may be found in George Kennedy, *Classical Rhetoric and Its Christian and Secular Tradition from Ancient to Modern Times* (Chapel Hill, NC: University of North Carolina Press, 1980), pp. 16, 18.

3. Wayne Booth, "The Scope of Rhetoric Today: A Polemical Excursion," in *The Prospect of Rhetoric,* ed. Lloyd F. Bitzer and Edwin Black (Englewood Cliffs, NJ: Prentice-Hall, 1971), p. 110. McKeon and Booth are joined by a European counterpart; see Chaim Perelman, "The New Rhetoric" also in *The Prospect of Rhetoric,* pp. 115-22; see especially pp. 118ff.

4. In fact, at the Action Caucus on General Theory-Building in Intercultural Communication, which met at the 1980 SCA New York City Convention, a good deal of pressure was placed on the Rhetorical Group to think of intercultural communication mainly from the scientific and socially scientific viewpoint. The Rhetorical Group resisted this bias while opting for a rhetorical view. At the same time they endorsed the value of also rendering rhetoric by scientific modes of inquiry.

5. Jolene Koester, "The Province of Rhetoric: A Neglected Tradition in the Study of Intercultural Communication" (Paper delivered to the Action Caucus on General Theory-Building in Intercultural Communication at the Annual Meeting of the SCA, New York, 1980). For a more complete discussion of the need for communication researchers to utilize both social science and humanistic methods of study, see Ernest G. Bormann, *Communication Theory* (New York: Holt, Rinehart & Winston, 1980) particularly pp. 225-35. For a similar discussion with respect to intercultural communication, see William S. Howell, "Theoretical Directions for Intercultural

Communication," in *Handbook of Intercultural Communication,* ed. Molefi K. Asante, Eileen Newmark, and Cecil A. Blake (Beverly Hills, CA: Sage, 1979), pp. 23-41.

6. L. E. Sarbaugh, *Intercultural Communication* (Rochelle Park, NJ: Hayden, 1979).

7. Barbara S. Monfils, "The Critical Perspective in Intercultural Communication" (Paper delivered to the Action Caucus on General Theory-Building in Intercultural Communication at the Annual Meeting of the SCA, New York, 1980).

8. James R. Andrews, *A Choice of Worlds* (New York: Harper & Row, 1973); Robert L. Scott and Bernard L. Brock, *Methods of Rhetorical Criticism* (New York: Harper & Row, 1972); and Charles J. Stewart, "Historical Survey: Rhetorical Criticism in Twentieth Century America," in *Explorations in Rhetorical Criticism,* ed. G. P. Mohrmann, C. J. Stewart, and D. J. Ochs (University Park, PA: Pennsylvania State University Press, 1973).

9. David L. Swanson, "A Reflective View of the Epistemology of Critical Inquiry," *Communication Monographs* 44 (1977): 207-19 and "The Requirement of Critical Justification," *Communication Monographs* 44 (1977): 306-20.

10. William Starosta, "Intercultural Rhetorical Communication Theory: Some Parameters" (Paper delivered to the Action Caucus on General Theory-Building in Intercultural Communication at the Annual Meeting of the SCA, New York, 1980).

11. Starosta, "Intercultural Rhetorical Communication Theory," p. 9.

12. Carl Holmberg, "Heuristic Matrix Theory for Theory Building in Intercultural Communication" (Paper delivered to the Action Caucus on General Theory-Building in Intercultural Communication at the Annual Meeting of the SCA, New York, 1980).

13. See Richard McKeon, "The Uses of Rhetoric in a Technological Age: Architectonic Productive Arts," *The Prospect of Rhetoric,* ed. Lloyd F. Bitzer and Edwin Black (Englewood Cliffs, NJ: Prentice-Hall, 1971), pp. 44-63. A similar system for rendering specific data is offered in Alfred G. Smith, "Taxonomies for Planning Intercultural Communication," *International and Intercultural Communication Annual* 5 (December 1975): 1-10. It should be noted however that Smith's matrical procedures are mainly to be quantified while McKeon's and Holmberg's procedures are more comprehensive and hence also applicable to discovering and analyzing *qualitative* data. McKeon's and Holmberg's work also focuses on the heuristic generation of data rather than only the sociological generation of data. Both positions represent only two of the possible mathematical topologies for rendering information culturally or interculturally.

14. Robert L. Scott, James R. Andrews, Howard H. Martin, J. Richard McNally, William F. Nelson, Michael M. Osborn, Arthur L. Smith, and Harold Zyskind, "Report of the Committee on the Nature of Rhetorical Invention," *The Prospect of Rhetoric,* ed. L. F. Bitzer and E. Black (Englewood Cliffs, NJ: Prentice-Hall, 1971), p. 235.

15. Scott et al., "Report of the Committee on the Nature of Rhetorical Invention," *The Prospect of Rhetoric,* ed. L. F. Bitzer and E. Black (Englewood Cliffs, NJ: Prentice-Hall, 1971), pp. 231-33.

16. Michel Foucault, *The Archeology of Knowledge,* trans. A. M. Sheridan Smith (New York: Random House, 1972), pp. 4ff. Ernesto Grassi also approaches true invention as discontinuous with the past as he discusses philosophy guided by rhetorical and not scientific auspices, *Rhetoric as Philosophy: The Humanist Tradition* (University Park: Pennsylvania State University Press, 1980), pp. 4-17. McKeon also focuses upon the discontinuities in the history of rhetoric in "Rhetoric in a Technological Age: Architectonic Productive Arts," in *The Prospect of Rhetoric,* ed. L. F. Bitzer and E. Black (Englewood Cliffs, NJ: Prentice-Hall, 1971), pp. 44-53.

17. For example, William S. Howell, "Theoretical Directions for Intercultural Communication," *Handbook of Intercultural Communication,* ed. Molefi K. Asante, Eileen Newmark, and Cecil A. Blake (Beverly Hills, CA: Sage, 1979), pp. 85-94.

18. Thomas O. Sloan, Richard Gregg, Thomas R. Nilsen, Irving J. Hein, Herbert W. Simons, Herman G. Stelzner, and Donald W. Zacharias, "Report of the Committee on the Advancement and Refinement of Rhetorical Criticism," *The Prospect of Rhetoric,* ed. L. F. Bitzer and E. Black (Englewood Cliffs, NJ: Prentice-Hall, 1971), pp. 220-27.

19. See, for example, Karlyn Kohrs Campbell and Kathleen Hall Jamieson, ed., *Form and Genre: Shaping Rhetorical Action* (Falls Church, VA: Speech Communication Association, n.d.).

20. Jacqueline de Romilly, *Magic and Rhetoric in Ancient Greece* (Cambridge, MA: Harvard University Press, 1975).

8

A System-Theoretic View

BRENT D. RUBEN • *Rutgers University*

As with the other chapters in this section of the *Annual*, the system-theoretic perspective was the basis for discussion at the 1980 SCA Intercultural Communication Action Caucus in New York City. And as with the other sessions, a number of individuals participated in the group, each of whom was genuinely in the group's focus—in this case, system theory. Perhaps to a greater extent than in other areas, there were a plethora of approaches and perspectives within the systems' group.

Represented within the group were those who approached the topic in terms of a world view, such as Carley Dodd and Cecile Garmon, who presented a paper entitled "A Scale for the Measurement of World View," and S. Adefemi Sonaike, whose paper was entitled "Intercultural Communication and the Search for a New Information Order." Other papers approached systems theory from the perspective of theory building, metatheory, and methodological concerns. Sharon Ruhly's paper on "Theory Building in Intercultural Communication" and Young Kim's "Applying the Systems Perspective to the Study of Intercultural Communication" fit into this general category, as did Dorothy Pennington's "Issues in Theory-Building." Nemi Jain's "Outline of Cross-Cultural Communication and Systems" emphasized the way in which systems approaches could link various levels of analysis typical to communication research, a facet also mentioned by Young Kim and Sharon Ruhly.

Very early in our discussions it became quite apparent that among those using the terms "systems" in the group there was a considerable lack of agreement on its meaning and on the nature of the systems approach. The differences were perhaps more apparent among those participating in the group who did not prepare papers than among those persons mentioned above.

AUTHOR'S NOTE: *While the motivation for preparing this article should be shared by all those who participated in the systems group at the 1980 SCA InterculturalCommunication Action Caucus—and particularly by Young Kim and Sharon Ruhly—any shortcomings are properly attributed to the author, who is responsible for the substance of the manuscript.*

In this very basic respect, the session underscored the need for the articulation of some of the most basic concepts and terminology of systems theory almost as prerequisite to a useful examination of the import of systems theory for intercultural communication theory. It was in this context that this chapter was prepared. Its aim is to provide a rather fundamental overview of some of the major philosophical roots of systems theory (general systems theory), an explication of basic concepts and terminology, and an exploration of some of the implications of this framework for conceiving of the nature of intercultural communication, culture, and intercultural adaptation.

In the 2500-odd years since the first rudimentary theories of human communication were put forth, a great deal of thought has been directed toward improving our understanding of the phenomenon. One consequence of this intellectual effort has been the emergence, over the years, of a number of metatheoretical frameworks for the field. An approach that has been the object of considerable contemplation and controversy in recent years is *systems theory*.

At least in part, interest and debate regarding systems theory results from the fact that there are a number of different ways in which the term *system* has been used in academic writing and popular discourse. In common parlance, the term *system* is typically used either as a synonym for the establishment, or as a way of referring to a complex technological device such as a stereo system or the tracking system of a guided missile.

In the academic contexts, it has also been used in a number of different ways. In the life sciences, for instance, the *system* is used to refer to biological units and the metabolic processes through which these entities maintain themselves and adapt to the environment.[1] In psychological writings, the term has been used to refer to the collected set of beliefs, attitudes, values, and thoughts of a single individual.[2] In a segment of the literature of therapy and counseling, *system* is used to refer to the family unit, which is seen as crucial to conceiving of, diagnosing, and treating emotional and behavioral disorders.[3]

In political science, sociology, and administrative sciences, *system* commonly refers to the structural-functional definition and interconnections between political, economic, and social institutions within society,[4] while in some philosophical writings the term *system* takes on the global properties of the world or universe.[5]

In other works, *system* is a more general term referring to the common properties of machines, humans, and societies.[6] In a somewhat similar vein are works in which a *system* is viewed even more abstractly, as the basis for a global, macro, and nonreductionist theory.[7]

The view of *systems theory* to be summarized here has its roots in the ideas of writers who have worked in an area called General Systems Theory, where the goal has been to integrate knowledge generated by the specialized disciplines into a broad understanding of the universe and its inhabitants.

The recent history of general systems thinking dates to about 1954, when the Society for General Systems Research emerged. Ludwig von Bertalanffy, credited by his peers as being the father of modern general systems theory, explained the need for systems theory this way:

> Modern science is characterized by its ever-increasing specialization, necessitated by the enormous amount of data, the complexity of techniques, and a breakdown of science as an integrated realm: The physicist, the biologist, the psychologist, and the social scientist are, so to speak, encapsulated in a private universe, and it is difficult to get a word from one cocoon to the other.
>
> There is, however, another remarkable aspect. If we survey the evolution of modern science, as compared to science a few decades ago, we are impressed by the fact that similar general viewpoints and conceptions have appeared in very diverse fields. Problems of organization, or wholeness, of dynamic interaction, are urgent in modern physics, chemistry, physical chemistry, and technology. The same trend is manifest in gestalt theory and other movements as opposed to classical psychology, as well as in modern conceptions of the social sciences. These parallel developments in the various fields are even more dramatic if we consider the fact that they are mutually independent and largely unaware of each other.[8]

Original members of the society articulated specific goals at the time they launched the organization: (1) to study concepts, laws, and models from the various fields in order to see whether they corresponded to one another; (2) to encourage the transfer of ideas from one field to another; (3) to avoid unnecessary duplication of theory development in different fields; (4) to encourage the development of theories and models in fields that lacked them; and (5) to promote the unity of science through improving information exchange among specialists.[9]

GENERAL SYSTEMS THEORY

Systems

The basic building block of General Systems Theory is the system. System is the term used to label *any entity or whole that is made up of interdependent parts in relationship, such that the entity as a whole has properties and functions distinct from those of the separate components.* A simple example of a system is a cake. The ingredients of a typical cake are sugar, flour, salt, eggs, butter, vanilla, and baking soda. When combined and heated, the result is a finished product that is much different than any of the parts by themselves.

The organs of the body are also systems, in that the cells, blood, tissues, and so on all operate together to make that organ a unique, functioning unit capable of performing operations that none of its parts can accomplish independently. An automobile—composed of tires, radiator, alternator, engine, drive train, and so on—is yet another example of a system. The components are interconnected, and the system as a whole has attributes and performs function impossible for any one part alone.

Most systems have physical properties. This is the case, for example, with the solar system, a transportation system, a neurological system, a skeletal system, a stereo system, an exhaust system, an animal, or a cell. The nature of these properties varies greatly, and depending on the particular system, may consist of ingredients like atoms, stars, bones, neurons, genes, muscles, gases, turntables, or mufflers, and so on.[10]

Relationships

Relationships tie the parts of a whole together and thereby define the system. The operation of the automobile, for example, is dependent upon the relationship among the engine, transmission, axle, wheels, and so on. Likewise, the functioning of the home stereo system depends upon the relationship among the turntable, preamplifier, amplifier, cartridge, and speakers. In the same respect, automobiles, stereos, cakes, and families are defined by the relationshion of their parts. In a very obvious sense a cake is, in effect, defined by the ingredients and their interrelationships. And a family system is defined by, and depends for its continued existence on, the relationships among its parts—the individual family members.

Systems, Subsystems, Subsubsystems

Systems are composed of component parts. Often these components are themselves systems, in the sense that they, too, are made up of parts in relationship. The automobile, the stereo system, and the family are each examples. The home stereo unit is composed of parts that are themselves made up of interdependent parts: The amplifier, for example, consists of diodes, capacitors, and resistors, wired together in relationships that are necessary to the operation and definition of the amplifier as a whole. The same is true for a turntable, tape deck, or speakers. Similarly, a family consists of individuals, who are composed of interconnected and interdependent organs, bones, and muscles, and these, in turn, are made up of cells. Most systems are composed of other systems *(subsystems)* which in turn are composed of other smaller and less complex systems *(subsubsystems)*, which are composed of still smaller and less-involved systems *(subsubsubsystems)*, ranging from the largest systems like the astronomical universe on one extreme, to the smallest subsubsub-systems like cells, electrons, or atoms on the other.

Boundaries

Boundaries define the edges of a system and hold the parts together. They protect the system from environmental stresses and exclude or admit substances necessary for the system's continued functioning. In the example of the cake, the pan in which the ingredients are baked serves as a boundary. It holds together the components and allows for the exchange of heat and air. The boundaries of cells are walls; organs have membranes that cover and protect them, while animals have skin, shells, fur, scales, feathers, hair, or external skeletons that keep the parts together and protect the system.

Environment

The term *environment* in systems terminology is the name given to the spatial, temporal, and sometimes symbolic space or set of conditions in which a system operates. The immediate environment of a cake being cooked is the inside of the oven and the heated air contained therein. In a broader sense the environment is everything beyond the outer edges of the pan. One can, therefore, think of environment as the totality of the universe that may be relevant to, but not directly under the influence of, the system one is considering.[11]

Closed and Open Systems

Basically, there are two types of systems: *closed systems* and *open systems*. The idea of closed systems comes from conventional physics and is directly applicable to things in the physical and mechanical realm. Systems are termed closed when they operate in isolation from their environment. An example in physical chemistry is the reaction of several chemicals mixed together in a sealed container. The relationship of the ingredients defining the system is totally a consequence of the reaction of each chemical to the other with no influence from the environment outside the test bottle.

This example points out an interesting characteristic of closed systems: The eventual state of a closed system is always totally predictable since all factors involved are known. In the case of chemicals in a closed container, for example, the final concentrations of the reactants can be calculated precisely from a knowledge of their initial concentrations.[12]

Open systems, on the other hand, are so named because they maintain themselves in a state of equilibrium through a continual give-and-take exchange with their environment. Such systems are influenced by their environment—as might be the chemicals in our previous example, if the vessel were open rather than sealed. Because of this, the eventual condition of open systems is less predictable than that of closed systems.

Living Systems

Living systems are a special instance of open systems and the primary focus of concern for our exploration of the nature of communication in human affairs. All living things grow, develop, and eventually deteriorate through a process of interchange with their environment. This continual give-and-take is necessary to the emergence and survival of all living systems—and the systems that compose them.

The basic process is one of exchange between a system and its environment. A living thing takes in life functions through its permeable boundary, and gives off into the environment other materials as wastes. Plants, for example, make the food they need to grow through an activity called photosynthesis. Necessary to this process is the presence of a number of environmental inputs including sunlight, heat, water, and carbon dioxide. As a byproduct of respiration, plants give off oxygen to the environment.

Most animals, on the other hand, require an intake of the oxygen given off by plants. And, in turn, animals give off carbon dioxide, which is an ingredient essential to the life processes of plants. Additionally, animal metabolism involves the taking in of food from the environment, some of which is plant life. The food is transformed into living tissues and energy by the animal. And, in turn, animals return organic wastes to the environment that serve to fertilize and stimulate the replenishment of the soil and the growth of plants.

Thus, living things take from their physical surroundings those substances necessary to their continued existence and return byproducts or wastes to the environment. These wastes become the substances that other living things utilize for their growth and development. In this very fundamental manner, living things are interlinked and dependent upon one another and their environment for adaptation and survival.

Stress and Adaptation

It is through input and output activities that systems are able to adapt and survive in the environment. Adaptation is a consequence of an ongoing process in which a system strives to adust and readjust itself to challenges, changes, and irritants in environment. The cycle is triggered when discrepancies between the demands of an environment and the capabilities of a system emerge, creating disequilibrium, or *stress*.[13]

Living systems act instinctively to meet the challenge or threat and to restore harmony and balance. Once regained, equilibrium continues until the system is confronted by new environmental demands, or *stressors*, such as extreme temperature changes, high levels of noise, bacteria, the pending attack of a predator, or the pressure of approaching a deadline. The stressors propel the system into disequilibrium and stress, and it again acts to restore harmony. In effect, living systems wage an uphill struggle to adjust. There are always stressors to be dealt with, and the survival of any living system depends upon its capacity for overcoming the threat posed by environmental demands over time. It is as a result of an ongoing stress-adjustment dynamic that living systems grow, maintain themslves for a time, and eventually deteriorate.

LIVING SYSTEM TRANSFORMATIONAL PROCESSES

With plants, the critical environmental exchange involves the transformation of chemicals and other substances necessary to cellular growth and development. As one moves upward on the phylogenetic scale, the nature of the system-environment transactions becomes considerably more complex, requiring the *transformation of information* as well as the *transformation of matter-energy* in order for the system to maintain viability. In contrast to plants, animals have specialized information receptors and information processing centers—nervous systems—that enable them to process and transform information as well as physical matter.

It is to refer to this most basic life process—*the processing and transformation of information by a living system in order to adapt to and adapt its environment*—that we will use the term *communication*. Given this framework, communication is understood to be one of the two basic life processes of all higher-order living systems.[14] A further implication is that communication serves the end of adaptation, to the behavior of all individual and multi-individual systems, and is an ongoing process interrupted only by the death of a system.

HUMAN COMMUNICATION SYSTEMS

In general terms humans have a good deal in common with other animals in this regard. Both adapt to their environments and one another through one or more of the information processing modalities—visual, auditory, olfactory, gustatory, or tactile.

For human systems, however, the nature of the input-transformation-output dynamic is even more complex than for other animals as a consequence of the human capacity and requirements of symbolic language.

Unlike lower-order animals, whose information relationship with their environment is relatively fixed, highly predictable, and often genetically prescribed, humans together must invent and ingest the significance they attach to the elements of the environment through symbolic language.

And, compared with messages created and used by other animals, human messages have far greater permanence and portability.[15] Even the most stable and portable message produced by other animals, such as an odor trail, has a very short life compared to that made possible by the human written symbolic codes. Through symbolic language humans are able to span both space and time with their messages; and by means of various communication technologies, humans are also able to amplify, multiply, transmit, display, store, and retrieve information.

Because of the permanence and portability of symbols and the sophistication of communication technology, humans live in an environment filled not only with physical objects, but also with symbols—some created in the present and others in the past.

In sum, it is the human capacity to create, internalize, permanitize, and intersubjectify symbols and their meanings, as opposed to the limitations of the time-and-space-bound signs of other animals, that most dramatically distinguishes the human from other living systems.

The developmental consequences of human communication are far-reaching from the individual, group, and sociocultural perspectives. As the human infant grows, he or she adapts informationally to an environment composed largely of the symbols and objects whose meaning and significance are the product of the communication activities of other humans. Over time, the individual develops the necessary internalized maps, images, and cognitive rule structure necessary to understand, cope with, and negotiate successfully in his or her physical and social milieu. In so doing, the individual at once adopts, confirms, validates, and diffuses those maps, images, and rule structures.

To put it in a slightly different way, one can say that the individual's ways of acting and reacting on the one hand, and his or her symbolic environment on the other hand, are reciprocally defining and mutually causal. The individual organizes to cope with his or her physical and symbolic environment. As a consequence, he or she is shaped by the environment and in his or her behavior he or she also shapes the environment.

CULTURE AND SYSTEMS

To the extent that members of a social system share particular symbols, meanings, images, rule structures, habits, values, and information processing and transformational patterns they can be said to share a common culture (or subculture).

Individuals are members of a social system—as opposed to a simple social aggregate, when: (1) the unit they are a part of is definitionally distinct from and greater than the sum of the individuals; and (2) the individuals are organized in relationship with one another such that the actions and reactions of one individual will have potential consequences for other individuals and for the social unit as a whole, and vice versa. Thus, members of an orchestra during a performance would be defined as a social system, while individual musicians scattered around a park playing for themselves on a sunny afternoon would be a social aggregate. In the former case the orchestra is defined by the relationship between the musicians and is distinct from and greater than the contributions of the individual musicians. While there is a mutual taking account of one another by members of the orchestra, the park musicians' behaviors are unlikely to be of consequence to one another.

Other more common examples of social systems are friendships, intimate relationships, friendships, small groups, racial groups, families, organizations, and societies.

As social systems emerge and develop, common symbols, meanings, rule structures, and information processing patterns develop concommitantly. Though these dynamics are difficult to describe in static terms, they are perhaps clearest in two- or three-person systems. In relations between very close friends, roommates, or lovers, for instance, each individual adapts to the maps and communication patterns of the other. In this process a number of relation patterns develop, along with a common language, a body of rules, standardized meanings, greeting forms, and a host of other habits, many of which are unique to the relationship. In effect, each such relationship has its own culture—probably better termed subculture, which results from the negotiated creation, shared use, and mutual validation of symbols, meanings, and communication rules and patterns.

The same processes are operative in social systems involving larger numbers of people. Subcultures are created in families, clubs, prison communities, social clubs, educational institutions, and business organizations. For each, characteristic and distinguishing symbols, rules, meanings, language usages, conventions of dress, and greetings evolve over a time as a consequence of evolving communication patterns and the mutual adaptation of the individuals involved.

Societies represent the largest, most complex social systems of concern to the social-behavioral scientist. The cultures of societal systems are composed not only of a range of shared symbols—language, currency, flags, heroes—but also of common patterns for greeting one another, expressing affection and hostility, standing while conversing, dressing, gesturing, comprehending one's role in the universe, rearing children, conceiving of courtship and marriage, eating, defining gender roles differentially, valuing the objects in the environment and deeds of others, and so on, and so on.

For the individual seeking admission to one of the many social systems in which participation is either mandatory or voluntary, the culture of that system represents the primary source of objectified reality to which the person must adapt. Like the adaptation living systems make to the atmosphere in which they exist, individuals adjust, often unknowingly, to the cultures and cultural realities confronting them. Most of the learning occurs through natural and inevitable processes; one would learn to speak the language and learn the nonverbal gestures of a culture, for example, without ever being *taught* them.

As individuals organize themselves with the various cultural and subcultural realities, the resulting behavior contributes to the objectification of the subculture and cultural reality to which others in the social system are adapted. To take a simplistic example, each individual who enters an elevator, walks to the rear, and turns to face the front does so without much conscious thought because he or she has internalized the cultural standards associated with elevator riding. Yet in carrying out these behaviors, each person at the same time contributes to validation and perpetuation of these standards by his or her actions.

CULTURE AND COMMUNICATION

Culture is directly and indirectly the product of communication. Were it not for the capacity of human systems to create and use symbolic language, the creation of common symbols and meaning would be impossible. And, without communication, the information generated in one place and time could not be preserved or transmitted from one place to another, a capability that allows for the accumulation and transmission of culture from one generation to the next and from one geographic locale to another. It is also through information processing and transformation that humans become aware of and are able to adapt to the many distinctive standards, customs, rules, and conventions that characterize the cultures and subcultures.

While it is a logical implication of the foregoing discussion to conclude that cultures and subcultures are defined, shaped, and transmitted through communication, the reverse is also apparent. That is, the maps, images, and cognitive rule structures, and communication patterns, individuals acquire are largely a consequence of having adapted to the demands of the various social systems—relationship groups, organizations, and societies—of which they have been a part. In effect, then, there is a reciprocally causal and mutually defining relationship between human communication and culture; culture is the product of communication, and human communication processes and outcomes are the result of culture.

INTERCULTURAL COMMUNICATION AND ADAPTATION

In a circumstance where the behavior of individuals, (whose images, maps, and rule structures developed in one cultural milieu) takes note of or is taken note of by an individual (whose images, maps, and rule structures are developed in another culturl milieu), *intercultural communication* has taken place.

It is an implication of this perspective that interpersonal situations are intercultural to the extent that no two individuals carry precisely the same cultural and subcultural baggage. As in other interpersonal situations, the nature and outcomes of intercultural events will depend upon a number of factors, including the goals of the individuals, the natures of the subcultures and cultures to which each has adapted, the extent to which the symbols, meanings, and rule structures of those cultures and subcultures are similar, and so on.

Implicit in this perspective, also, is the notion that intercultural communication generally involves some degree of stress and readjustment, as the individual strives to organize meaningfully with the persons who reflect differing subcultural and cultural orientations. The extent of this adjustment depends upon the prior degree of congruence between the communication patterns characteristic of the two individuals.

Cultural adaptation takes place when an individual with maps, images, cognitive rule structures, and communication patterns developed in response to one set of cultural and subcultural realities is placed in a physical and symbolic environment where he or she must contend with distinctive cultural and subcultural realities. In such circumstances, stress results as the individual endeavors to adapt to the demands and opportunities of the environment.

This phenomenon is often labeled and discussed under the heading of "culture shock." Much of the discussion has viewed this phenomenon in limited non-systemic, negatively oriented terms, as an ailment, disability, weakness, or *unavoidable problem* to be overcome. Viewed in systems terms, culture shock is seen as a manifestation of a generic process that, as noted earlier, occurs whenever the capabilities of a living system are not totally adequate to the demands of the environment.[16]

Further, culture shock—and the generic stress phenomenon—are conceived of as part-and-parcel of the stress-adaptation cycle. Thus, to the extend that stress is said to be responsible for pain, suffering, frustration, and anxiety, so must it then be credited as an impetus for personal growth, learning, change, and creativity for the individual, and change, development, and progress for the social systems of which those individuals are a part. In this framework stress and change are regarded as defining characteristics of living systems, and are particularly evident in intercultural circumstances where change and difference are endemic.

SUMMARY

The attempt has been to provide an introduction to the fundamental concepts of general systems theory, an exploration of role-afforded communication in activities of living systems, and an overview of implications of this perspective for conceptualizing the nature of human communication, culture, intercultural communication, and intercultural adjustment.

Based on this discussion the following propositions may be useful as a summary of the major premises of the system-theoretic perspective as it relates to intercultural communication.

(1) A *system* is any entity or whole made up of interdependent parts in relationship, such that the entity as a whole has properties and functions distinct from those of the separate components.

(2) Living systems are organisms that maintain their form and function through continual transactions with the environment.

(3) With higher-order living systems, the nature of the system environment transactions necessarily involves both (a) the transformation of matter-energy, and (b) the transformation of information.

(4) *Communication* can be defined as the processing and transformation of information by a living system in order to adapt to and adapt its environment.

(5) While human and animal systems have a good deal in common with regard to communication, human communication is more complex by virtue of the capacity and requirements of symbolic language, and the potential for permanence and portability of symbols.

(6) For the human individual, the process of adaptation to the environment involves adjusting informationally to the symbols and objects whose meaning and significance are the product of the communication activities of other humans.

(7) *Culture* can be defined as those symbols, meanings, images, rule structures, habits, values, and information processing and transformation patterns and conventions that are shared in common by members of a particular social system or group.

(8) Cultures result from the negotiated creation, shared use, and mutual validation of symbols, meanings, and communication rules and patterns.

(9) Cultures (and subcultures) are concomitant with the emergence and development of all social systems—intimate relationships, friendships, families, small groups, ethnic or gender groups, organizations, and societies.

(10) Cultures and subcultures confront the individual with an objectified reality to which he or she must adapt in order to participate in the obligatory and optional social systems in the environment.

(11) Culture is the product of communication, and human communication processes and outcomes are largely the result of culture.

(12) Intercultural communication occurs when the behavior of an individual whose images, maps, and rule structure, developed in one cultural milieu, takes note of or is taken note of by an individual whose images, maps, and rule structures are developed in another cultural milieu.

(13) All intercultural communiction involves some degree of stress and adjustment as the individuals strive to organize meaningfully with one another's subcultural and cultural organizations.

(14) *Cultural adaptation* occurs when an individual with maps, images, cognitive rule structures, and communication patterns developed in response to one set of cultural and subcultural realities is placed in a physical and symbolic environment where he or she must contend with distinctive cultural and subcultural realities.

(15) *Stress*, generally termed culture shock—occurs when an individual whose images, maps, rule structure—developed in one cultural milieu— is forced to contend with a second distinctive cultural and subcultural milieu to which his or her maps, images, and rules are not well adapted.

(16) The experiencing and resolution of stress—characteristic of many situations of concern for intercultural communication practitioners and researchers—are inevitable aspects of the adaptation process, essential for growth and change, necessary defining qualities of all living systems.

NOTES

1. See Ludwig von Bertalanffy, *General Systems Theory: Foundations, Developments, Applictions* (New York: Braziller, 1968); Chester A. Lawson, "Language, Communication, and Biological Organization," *General Systems*, 8 (1963); and James G. Miller, "Living Systems," *Behavioral Science*, 10 (1965).

2. See R. R. Grinker, Sr., ed., *Toward a Unified Theory of Human Behavior* (New York: Basic Books, 1967); William Gray, Fredrick J. Duhl, and Nicholas D. Rizzo, *General Systems Theory and Psychiatry* (Boston: Little, Brown, 1969); Jurgen Ruesch and Gregory Bateson, *Communication: The Social Matrix of Society* (New York: W. W. Norton, 1968); Geoffrey Vickers, *Value Systems and Social Process* (New York: Basic Books, 1968).

3. See Gray, Duhl, and Rizzo, *General Systems Theory and Psychiatry;* Ruesch and Bateson, *Communication;* Paul Watzlawick, Janet H. Beavin, and Don D. Jackson, *Pragmatics of Human Communication* (New York: W.W. Norton, 1967).

4. See Kenneth F. Berrien, *General and Social Systems* (New Brunswick, NJ: Rutgers University Press, 1969); Walter Buckley, *Sociology and Modern Systems Theory* (Englewood Cliffs, NJ: Prentice—hall, 1967); Joseph H. Monane, *A Sociology of Human Systems* (New York: Appleton-Century-Crofts, 1967); Odd Ramsoy, *Social Group as System and Subsystem* (New York: Free Press, 1963).

5. See Ervin Laszlo, *The Systems View of the World* (New York: Braziller, 1973).

6. See Gregory Bateson, "Cybernetic Explanation," *American Behavioral Scientist* 10 (1967); J. H. Milsum, "Technosphere, Biosphere, and Sociosphere," *General Systems* 13 (1968); Norbert Wiener, *Cybernetics* (New York: John Wiley, 1948); Norbert Wiener, *The Human Use of Human Beings* (New York: Avon, 1950).

7. See W. Ross Ashby, "General Systems Theory as a New Discipline," *General Systems* 3 (1958); Ludwig von Bertanlanffy, "General System Theory," *General Systems* 1 (1956); Kenneth Boulding, "General Systems Theory—The Skeleton of Science," *Management Science* 2 (1956).

8. Von Bertalanffy, *General System Theory,* p. 1.

9. Von Bertalanffy, *General systems Theory,* p. 15.

10. A. D. Hall and R. W. Fagen, "Definition of System," *General Systems* 1 (1956): 18.

11. C. West Churchman, *The Systems Approach* (New York: Delacorte, 1968), p. 63.

12. A more detailed discussion of closed versus open systems is provided in Brent D. Ruben, "General System Theory," in *Interdisciplinary Approaches to Human Communication,* ed. Richard W. Budd and Brent D. Ruben, (Rochelle Park, NJ: Hayden, 1979).

13. See Hans Selye, *The Stress of Life* (New York: McGraw-Hill, 1956); Kenneth R. Pelletier, *Mind as Healer, Mind as Slayer* (New York: Delacorte, 1977).

14. This significant point was first made by James G. Miller, "Living Systems," *Behavioral Science* 10 (1965): 338. The implications of this perspective have been discussed extensively in the subsequent works of Lee Thayer, *Communication and Communication Systems* (Homewood, IL: Irwin, 1968), p. 17; and Brent D. Ruben, "Intrapersonal, Interpersonal, and Mass Communication Process in Individual and Multi-Person Systems," in *Human Communication and General Systems Theory,* ed. Brent Ruben and John Y. Kim (Rochelle Park, NJ: Hayden, 1975).

15. A point discussed in considerable detail in Brent D. Ruben, "The Symbol-Using Animal," in *Communication in Human Behavior* (New York: Macmillan, 1982).

16. See Brent D. Ruben, "Communication and Conflict: A System-Theoretic Perspective," *Quarterly Journal of Speech* 64 (1978).

III

NEW THEORETICAL DEVELOPMENTS

9

Mass Media and Culture
Toward an Integrated Theory

HAMID MOWLANA • *American University*

Several important concepts, problems, and processes of communication and culture have been receiving overwhelming attention in the work of mass media theorists. This has been especially true during the last decade. A larger proportion of the literature falls normally under the headings of mass culture, mass media and society, cultural integrity, communication and cultural domination, cultural dependency, and cultural pluralism.

At the same time, these subjects are assuming great importance in the broader disciplines of sociology, economics, political science, and anthropology, as well as in the areas of development and regional studies. As a result, interdisciplinary approaches have become more frequent. As the phenomena under examination are highly complex and cover a wide spectrum of social reality, any attempt at a global interpretation necessarily transcends the limits of a given discipline. Consequently, the study of mass media and culture has preface to cross-disciplinary frontiers, making a holistic as opposed to a specialized, compartmentalized approach to social science imperative.

The emphasis of this chapter is on the theoretical and analytical bases focused on the phenomena of mass media and culture. After an examination of the range and definition of phenomena, an attempt is made to lay a foundation for an identification, classification, and critical evaluation of major approaches, theories, concepts, and propositions, paying particular attention to problems of analytical integration within the field of study and to problems of interdisciplinary contributions and coherence. Finally, a framework of analysis called "toward an integrative theory of mass media and culture" is outlined.

There is a considerable body of speculation and generalization concerning the relationship of the mass media of communication to culture. While there is a wide variety of assertions on this topic, there are three positions or approaches of prominence that approximate some provocative, if not necessarily clear, "theoretical" statements. The word "theoretical" is placed in quotation marks to indicate that the statements of the proponents do not in fact constitute a set of interrelated propositions of sufficient coherence to justify the label of a theory. Nevertheless, the following theoretical positions must, by virtue of their popularity, provocativeness, the articulateness of their supporters, and their prevalence among the students of mass media, be taken as the point of departure in the discussion of mass media and culture.

THE TRIPLE M THEORY

Perhaps the most discussed of these three schools of thought in the Western world is the so-called theory of mass society. Its articulation by the students of mass media and culture has created a triangle labeled "triple M theory"—mass society, mass media, and mass culture. The essentials of the theory are rather familiar.[1] *Society* refers to a relational system of interaction between individuals or groups, and *culture* to the pattern of values, norms, ideas, and other symbols that shape the individual's behavior. Thus, *mass society* refers to a type of society in which the relations between individuals have assumed a mass character. As the mass of the population has become incorporated into society, the central institutions and the central value systems guiding and legitimating these institutions have extended their boundaries. Mass society, furthermore, is an industrial society. The division of labor has made its members more interdependent than before. Mores and morals are in constant flux; relations between individuals are tangential and compartmentalized rather than organic. With successive technological advances, especially in the field of communication, the economics of mass media and the polity of such societies demand that a successively broader audience be reached and, hence, the level of performance be directed more and more toward a common denominator of taste. One result of this process, as the proponents of this theory assert, is the hint of mass culture or popular culture. As the individuals lose a coherent sense of self in such societies, their anxieties increase. They search for new faiths to provide anchors.

Mass culture represents the cultural correlates of mass society and mass media.[2] With the rise of industrialization and urbanization, the traditional monopoly of culture on the part of the aristocracy is broken. Whereas folk culture was the outcome of community and is centered around community, mass culture emerges when the community—that is the different groups and individuals linked to each other by concrete

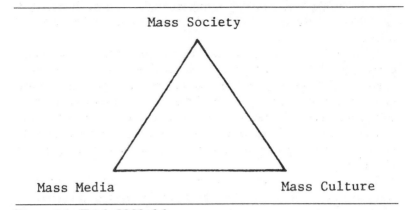

Figure 9.1   Triple M Model

values and interests—is eroded. Mass culture is distinguished thus by its standard mass production and marketability.

Culture under the triple M theory has often been divided into a series of discriminatory categories such as high culture and popular culture, highbrow and lowbrow, avante-garde and kitsch. The term mass culture is often used to mark a distinction between authentic, long-lasting art and mass-produced commodity culture such as popular music and the soap opera.

In its early days, the growth of mass culture, or what has been termed commodity culture by the critics of capitalism, led to strong dissent movements and a wide appeal in the industrialized West for discrimination and taste. Some of its best-known critics included Mathew Arnold[3] in England, Nietzsche[4] and Karl Mannheim[5] in Germany, Baudelaire[6] in France, Ortega y Gasset[7] in Spain, and C. Wright Mills[8] in the United States.

Following the early elitist critics came those who not only confined themselves to denunciation of the mass media but attempted to explain the division of cultures into various categories. There are considerable differences—moral, political, scientific—between these writers, but all came from the Western industrial-capitalist economy, especially the United States and England, where features of mass society and mass media were well developed. Among them were sociologists such as Ernest van den Haag,[9] Daniel Bell,[10] David Reisman,[11] Bernard Rosenberg,[12] Edward Shils,[13] and many others; the social scientists and philosophers of the Frankfurt school such as Theodore Adorno,[14] Leo Lowenthal,[15] Walter Benjamin,[16] Herbert Marcuse,[17] and Max Horkheimer;[18] and finally, culturalist and media critics such as T. S.

Eliot,[19] Dwight MacDonald,[20] Irving Howe, [21] Clement Greenberg, [22] Q. D. Leavis, [23] Raymond Williams, [24] Denys Thompson,[25] and a host of others.[26]

Rejection or dispute over mass culture and mass media implies concern for the cultural deprivation suffered by individuals and not a rejection of the masses. Perhaps the only common ground for those involved in the debate over the role of mass media and the merits of mass culture is the general consensus that the major concern is with the artists and individuals and their relationship to the society and culture. It is the business of defining what relationship is and should be that generates disagreement.

The debate falls into two very broad, and often overlapping, categories of opinion. It involves those who discern something positive in the development of mass culture and those who do not. Within these categories, of course, there are differing hypotheses, qualifications, and projections. Critics on both sides may have similar insights in the structures of their viewpoints but differ radically in their conclusions.

TECHNOLOGICAL DETERMINISM

A second set of propositions attempting to understand the phenomenom of mass media and culture is the view of technological determinism. It is one of the most popular and now largely orthodox views of the nature of social and cultural change: Modern civilization is the history of new technological inventions. The steam engine, printing press, television, and the automobile have created for modern humanity these new conditions. Research and development, which have set conditions for modern technology and thus for cultural and social change, are self-generating. One of its most quoted advocates, Harold Innis,[27] suggested that historically, fundamental breakthroughs in technology are first applied to the process of communication. The printing press created the age of mechanics and the telegraph opened to us the age of electronics. The forms of social organization and the stages of society and the characteristics of culture were all determined by the medium of the time. In fact, the development of Western civilization can be best analyzed and understood in terms of a competition for dominance between media of communication.

In his work Innis argued that any given medium will bias social organization. Time and space took cultural meaning. In cultural terms, time meant the sacred, the moral emphasis upon religion and hierarchy; space meant the present and future emphasis upon state, technical, and

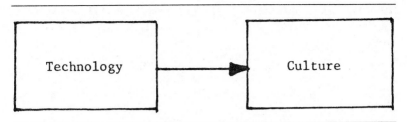

Figure 9.2   Technological Determinism Model

secular development. The bias of media of communication in favor of one institution meant the assurance of cultural characteristics of that institution. On the cultural level, this principal contrast could be seen between oral and written traditions. Whereas oral culture tended to be time-binding with limited capacity for technical change, written tradition led to space-binding and consequently favored the growth of political authority.

In the debate over the mass media and culture, this technological determinist school of thought made its popular appearance in the writings of Marshall McLuhan[28] in the 1960s—first in North America and then in Western Europe. Extending on the work of Innis, McLuhan argued that "the things on which words were written down count more than the words themselves." He sharpened Innis's thesis; that is, the medium is the message. Whereas Innis and McLuhan assumed the centrality of communication media in their argument, they differed in the way the medium affects the individual and its culture. Whereas Innis saw the medium of communication principally affecting social organization, McLuhan found its principal effect on sensory organization and thought. Art and technology become extensions of humanity: stone axe for hand, wheel for foot, glasses for eyes, radio for voice and ears, and money for storing energy. His theme throughout his writing is that the West has lost its balance primarily because with writing and then with print it allowed sight to take precedence over the other senses. On the other hand, the tribal people, that is the non-Westerners who rely on speech more than anything else, live in a more vivid world, using more of their sensoriae than the West, and therefore are in balance with their environment. In terms of the media of communication, radio thus becomes a hot medium and the telephone cool—movies are hot and the television cool. Hot media extend one single sense in high definition, the state of being well-filled with data.

The technological determinist school of mass media and culture, especially the ideas and methodologies associated with Marshall

McLuhan, has come under attack and criticism by both culturalist and media theorists in the West and the neo-Marxists elsewhere.

Less determinist than the pure technological determinist school is the view of symptomatic technology. Emphasizing other causal factors in social change, it views particular technologies as symptoms of change of some other kind, but like pure technological determinism it assumes that research and development are self-steering, except in a more marginal way. This margin, however, is being used in the total service of the system.

The theory of technological determinism, as it relates to the mass media and culture, suffers from two inherent weaknesses. First, it views only one aspect of a medium—its material or technological form—as its essential defining and determining characteristic. In short, theory can be seen to depend on the isolation of technology, that the dominant technology of communication increasingly shapes the rest of the culture. Or to put it simply, it does not really matter how and to what purpose the medium is used, just that it *is* used. From this point of view, to diversify video necessitates only an expansion in the number of channels and a further expansion and proliferation of the technology. Second, much of the technological determinist view of mass media and culture is based on the historical evidence with no dynamic of its own and also entirely on Western experience. The generalization begins to suffer.

POLITICAL ECONOMY THEORY

The third theory of mass media and culture is a political economy theory. Among the many proponents of this theory are new Marxists, the New Left, or just simply those with socialist views of society. In essence, the political economy theory is a socialist strategy in a general sense. But like the students of the mass society theory and technological determinism school of thought, the writers of this tradition, too, have their own varieties.

In the triple M theory the triangle-circle of mass culture, mass media, and mass society is closed; the media of mass communication are the parent of mass culture, mass culture is the child of the mass communication, mass media were born out of mass society. The political economy theory questions the cognitive sense of closing this circle and substantiates the supposition that the media of mass communications are not so much a cause of mass culture as a tool to shape it. They serve as channels to convey cultural contents, which have already filled—and independently of those media—the cells of a social structure that has assumed a "mass" character. As the Polish scholar Zygmunt Baumann[29] writes, "for culture to become 'mass' it is not enough to set up a television station." Certain conditions of life and social situations first become standardized, providing the right chemistry and the right conditions for the reception of uniform mass media messages. The following are the components involved in this process: Component one is *dependence on the market* "where a man placed in the macro-social situation of the circulation of commodities is exposed to the culture-forming influence of the market." Component two is *dependence on organization* that "is supra-personal rather than non-personal— absolutely and without exception." And finally, component three is *dependence on technology*. Dependence on technology generates disorientations and anxiety and humanity cannot bypass it in the complex modern society it has generated. But how can we strive to end the isolation of the individual participants from the social learning and production process so entangled by the three dependent factors just outlined? This is the political core of the question of the media and culture in the political-economy theory. It is over this point that socialist concepts differ from the triple M theorists and technological determinists.

If the image of mass society, that the triple M theorists portray is drawn from the laissez-faire doctrine of economics (if not totally from the Protestant view of society), the political economy theorists draw most of their ideas from the Marxist view of production.[30] By and large, the triple M theory of the media and culture is a theory of social control from above even though it is premised on the necessity for making concessions to mass tastes in order that the masses be controlled most effectively. The political economy theorists view the process from below where, through an elaborate feedback of political and economic machinery, the masses can participate in the production and distribution of cultural messages. Furthermore, whereas the so-called theory of mass society is a statement of alienation from the contemporary society, the political economy theory views the process on a more positive ground.

Most proponents of this school of thought assume that humanity is essentially good and that social forces are responsible for its corruption. From this point of view cultural standards are not seen as problematical but as epiphenomena of social conditions. If favorable social conditions and the right economic and political institutions are created, desirable cultural standards will spring into efflorescence. Erich Fromm,[31] as one of the leading spokesman of this school, has argued that because of the unfavorable conditions of a mass society, humanity becomes so

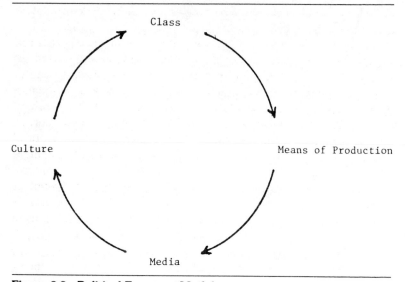

Figure 9.3 Political Economy Model

alienated that it is unable to resist mass culture. It loses its consumer sovereignty and is compelled to buy whatever supply of culture is at hand. Here Dwight MacDonald's metaphor of Gresham's law gives support to the theorists of political economy. For him the market is purely one of runaway inflation that cannot be checked because standards are continually falling. Low-grade demand stimulates low-grade supply and vice versa.

One of the first political-economic analyses of the media and culture within the total context of capitalist society was made by the Frankfurt school. This group included Walter Benjamin, who studied the interconnection between technological advances and culture forms, Leo Lowenthal, who examined the popular literary cultures, Theodore Adorno, who wrote on radio music and jazz, and Herbert Marcuse, whose theory of the effect of the rationalizing process of capitalism on language and culture became the basic assumption of many media and culture critics, especially those of the New Left in the 1960s and 1970s. Like the triple M theorists, here too there were both optimistic and pessimistic views.

For example, whereas Henri Lefebvre[32] emphasized the disappearance of a general code of communication and the conversion of daily life into a spectacle, and Jean Baudrillard[33] spoke of the implication of this change where objects are transformed to signs, Hans Magnus Enzensberger[34] took a more optimistic view, arguing that the new media of socialism could democratize culture, once it has been taken out of the hands of the bourgeois intellectuals.

During the past decade, a growing number of media theorists and writers taking another view of political economy, have analyzed the specific conditions of cultural production in colonial and dependent countries. Such writers as Ludovico Silvo,[35] Antonio Pasquali,[36] Evelina Dagnino,[37] Armand Mattelart,[38] Herbert Schiller,[39] and others, drawing their ideas heavily from the studies of the dependency theorists, have advanced the notion of cultural imperialism and cultural domination to show how media have been used to homogenize culture and create a market mentality.

To summarize, the political economy theorists base their analysis of the media and culture on the notion that the dominant ideas in a society are those of the dominant class and that the class which is the dominant material power of the society is also the dominant cultural and spiritual power. Thus, they concentrate on the basic structural and economic foundations of society. It is in these that the political economy determinists perceive the fundamental reasons for the increasing preponderance of those elements in the culture of the entire society, which have become macrosocial universals over those that are still subject to subcultural diversification.

TOWARD AN INTEGRATIVE THEORY

One of the most fundamental fallacies underlying tha biases of the triple M theory is the assumption of mass society as an atomized system where the relations of one individual to another have become increasingly amorphous. The technological determinists fall in the same trap as well when they view Western society as being print oriented, linear, and when they attempt to contrast that with non-Western society. However, the rise of ethnicity around the world and the development of political, social, and economic subcultures both in the Western and non-Western worlds, as well as in other global regions, are only recent examples of some of the pluralist societies in which— through the course of structural differentiation—an increasing variety of solidarities has been developing.

Most of the theories and discussion of the mass media and culture reviewed in the previous pages are historically biased. For example, in the triple M theory, since the effort is directed at preserving the standards of the past, continual references to these standards usually accompany the debate. What is needed is a dynamic paradigm that can take the social, economic, political, and structural variables into account. Such a model must make a distinction between production and distribution of cultural messages.

There is a need for a shift in emphasis in the analysis of communication systems, especially mass communication systems, from an exclusive concern with the source and content of messages to analysis of the message-distribution process.[40] Control of the distribution process is the most important index of the way in which power and values are distributed in a communication system, which may be the global community, a country, or some smaller cultural unit.[41] To prepare a documentary television program of one kind or another that will be viewed by ten persons requires no more effort from producers and artists than to prepare one for ten million people. The nexus is between the economics and politics of distribution and quality, not quantity.

The mass media system is viewed here as a rather complex social system consisting of actions carried out within the context of external social conditions of the community and the society in which it operates. The operation of no one part of the mass media system and process can be fully understood without reference to the way in which the whole itself operates; or to put it more succinctly, no part of the mass media canvas stands alone, but each is related to both the *formation* (production) and *distribution* processes of its messages.

To distinguish a mass communication system from other social systems, we need to identify its main units in order to map the boundaries that usually separate it from elements outside the system. The boundaries of a mass communication system can be defined as all those actions more or less directly related to the formation and distribution of its messages in a society.

Although "the fabric of popular culture that relates the elements of existence to one another and shapes the common consciousness of what is, what is important, what is right and what is related to what else, is now largely a manufactured product,"[42] the research on mass communication has made little effort to apply economic principles and concepts to this "manufactured product." The distribution sequence of the mass media has been one of the most neglected areas of communication research; yet this very distribution sequence has become the most critical, vital, and controversial aspect of the total mass media system.[43]

Our traditional preoccupation with the rights of individuals and groups to *produce* and *formulate* their desired messages rather than the right to *distribute* and *receive* has been one reason for this neglect. Our assumptive framework of communication research, with emphasis on producers and consumers of messages, and the consequent social effects have been another. Yet, the growth of communication technology, the expanding national and international market, and the creation of institutional policies and reglations all have made distribution the most important sequence in the chains of mass communication.

Mass communication, in economic terminology, is a form of indirect exchange, and the problem involved is the transfer for manufactured products or messages from the producer of form or utility to the ultimate consumer. Owing to the great size and complications of our modern means of mass communication, this transfer is sometimes a very involved process and requires the assistance of a number of intermediate agents.

A good deal has been written in recent years, mostly by economists, about the high cost of distributing mass communication messages to the consumers.[44] It is easy enough to see that the journalists are productive agents. It is more difficult to give full credit to the telecommunication machinery that hauls their written messages and the local distributor who sells them over the counter—simply because they are not creators of messages.

But the promptness and convience with which one may secure a news item or a newspaper depend upon the services rendered by the distributor—be it Intelsat, RCA, or a given post office—as much as upon the productive efforts of the journalist.

In analyzing the mass media and culture, the structural changes occurring in the media must be taken into account for they produce expansion, differentiation, and domination.

One major consequence of national development is the expansion of and accessibility to cultural content by a large segment of the population. In the new societies and especially in the so-called Third World countries, the most conspicuous example of this has been the expansion of education.

The second aspect of change is that of differentiation. The term "mass" media itself has been misleading, suggestion both undifferentiated content and undifferentiated audience. Although the intention here is not to discuss the definition of mass media, it is important to emphasize that it is difficult by any standard to find a modern mass media directed at or used by the entire population. Rather, a preponderance of mass media is explicitly directed at differentiated segments of the population. In fact, the trend in some highly industrialized countries like the United States is toward specialized and class media.[45] Henceforth, then, the term "mass" media should be redefined to include those impersonal channels—old and new—that are intended for, and made available to, anyone who is a potential user of these channels within distributive limits.[46]

The third aspect of change is domination. Here, with differentiation and specialization, functional capacity in the communication system increases with the consequences of domination. Not only can one medium become dominant over another, but it can also lead to changes in content. One system's method and content can become dominant over the other. The consequence of this interaction will determine the cultural level of that society or that system.

Another aspect of the integrative theory of the mass media and culture is the concept and phenomenon of cultural pluralism.[47] While the notions of cultural pluralism and multiculturalism are recent, the phenomenon they express is not. The birth of nations during the last two decades, the upheavals and changes occurring in the old nations, are not simply the result of drastic changes in demographic or economic sectors. They also indicate an important development on the intellectual level. Advances in communications and transportation have helped to lessen cultural isolationism. These advances in technology also tend to increase the cultural awareness of minorities by making them more conscious of the distinctions between themselves and other groups. The individual becomes more aware of alien ethnic groups as well as those who share his or her identity. Communications plays a pervasive role not only in social mobility and nation building but also in strengthening ethnic consciousness.[48]

Previous theories of communication and culture fail to explain both the historical incidence of ethnic states and solidarities outside the context of social and economic modernization (such as the Germanic states and the medieval political community of Western Europe), and instances in which societies emerge from the experience of modernization without an ethnically defined political identity and are unable to assume a dual identity. This identity is dependent upon the distribution of ethnic and cultural characteristics, and a congruity among such components as language, religion, cultural heritage, and physical proximity. Where this congruity exists a particularistic identity and pattern of solidarity is also likely to exist. Conversely, where there are significant incongruities in these components, the mobilized individual will opt for an ethnically neutral, univeralistic political identity. When cultural consciousness precedes political consciousness and presupposes an awareness of other cultures, increased antagonisms are likely to occur. Assimilation is even more of a natural foe to self-determination than the multinational state due to the emotional power of ethnic consciousness.

Thus, significant diversification of the mass media requires not only better and varied technologies, but also new conceptions of cultural functions as well as new patterns of initiation and audience. "However much [TV] may be contributing to social stability and unity in American society," John C. Cawelti[49] of the University of Chicago has demonstrated that "the medium of commercial television is not contributing much to enhance the pluralism of American society." He suggests that "initiators would have to be responsible to the traditions of the subculture rather than to their success in getting more undifferentiated people to watch their programming." Expounding on the concept of the new media, Cawelti downplays the elements of the "the vehicle (representing the technology or craft which is employed in the transaction)" and "the conventions (representing the genres or symbol systems involved in the process)," but emphasizes two remaining elements in the communication process: the initiator (generally, the sender of the message) and the audience:

> In this medium, the initiator would be a particular subcultural group and the audience would be defined as members of various other subcultural groups. The genres of this medium would grow out of the purpose of enabling one subculture to project its values, styles, and traditions to other groups, or conversely enabling members of a particular subculture to see themselves as other groups see them.[50]

Finally, central to the integrative theory of the mass media and culture is the role of the state, with its own special and unique image of itself and the role it perceives it should play.[51] This is one of the most neglected aspects of the media and culture phenomenon as often discussed by the triple M theory and the technological determinism theorists. A centralized system of mass communication tends to emphasize the instrumental use of the media more than the authentic side of the arts and culture. Such a central system, whether capitalist or socialist, reinforces and reproduces existing relations of production and distribution. The main task of the media becomes the programming of ideology in forms of mass culture, popular culture, and people's culture.

Writing on radio and television as art forms in the Soviet Union, Nikolai Shanin considers successful programs as those that "tend toward the journalistic style and belong to the 'document-art' genre." It stems, he continues, "from the specific nature of television art which is permeated with documentary and journalistic aspects that create a *feeling of immediacy of experience*" (italics are mine).

> On account of its immense audience appeal, television art is the most democratic vehicle to carry out the ideological tasks assigned to it. It

enters television programs during the peak evening hours, in the actual leisure time of the working-man.[52]

The similarity of perception on the role of mass media, especially television, vis-à-vis the mass or working man between the capitalist and certain socialist countries has not gone unnoticed. Hans Magnus Enzensberger has advanced the line of left-wing criticism from the point where the mass society theorists left off:

> A socialist perspective which does not go beyond attacking existing property relationships is limited. The expropriation of Springer is a desirable goal but it would be good to know to whom the media should be handed over. The Party? To judge by all experience of that solution, it is not a possible alternative. It is perhaps no accident that the Left has not yet produced an analysis of the pattern of manipulation in countries with socialist regimes.[53]

The following is a summary of the factors underlying the urgency for an integrative theory of the media and culture:

(1) emergence of a universal superculture based on science and technology,
(2) development of world economy,
(3) revival of ethnicity,
(4) appearance of transnational actors, and
(5) the role of nation-states in national development.

Such a theory will encompass the following major variables:

(1) technology,
(2) production process,
(3) distribution process,
(4) cultural message,
(5) political and economic system, and
(6) cultural and value system.

The relations between the mass media and culture and the dissemination of cultural messages in a national system, when the above distinction is made, may then be presented in rudimentary terms as in Figure 9.4, which depicts the media and culture cycle at work. Stage A, representing production and technology lines, is the core of the media hardware; the production of radio and TV sets would be an example of the associated technologies. Stage B represents the distribution capability of the system in terms of both telecommunication and communication infrastructure. Stage C, sharing the distribution and cultural content lines, represents the marketing and management side of

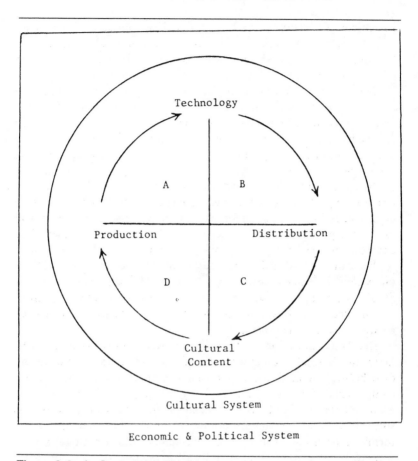

Figure 9.4 An Integrative Model

the process. Finally, stage D would include the programming and actual program production, completing the cycle. The process of production and reproduction of these cultural messages in all four stages is controlled by two factors: (1) cultural and value systems, and (2) political and economic systems.

The communication act, in societal, national, or international levels, then, can be explained as follows:[54] (1) *Who produces* and (2) *who distributes* (3) *what* to (4) *whom* in which (5) *channel* under what (6) *conditions* (values), with what (7) *intention* (purpose) under what (8) *political economy* and with what (9) *effect?*

Here we can see that external interference has the ability to play a decisive role in shaping the cultural content of any system if the sovereignty in each or a combination of these four stages is lost to an outside system. This aspect of cultural dependencey can be illustrated by looking at the media and culture cycle represented in Figure 9.4 in terms of the quadrants created by the communications technology axes. The type of communications technology that has been most frequently transferred from industrial to nonindustrial countries falls in the upper and lower right-hand quadrants designated as stages A, B, and C, such as media hardware, television programs, and marketing. The implications of this pattern of technology and program transfer become clear when the diagram is seen as representing the components of control in a communication system, absolute control over which occurs only to the possessor of all four components. In the absence of a single actor controlling all four components, effective control of a system will fall to the possessor of certain of the components before others. For example, in the instance at hand, a country may have the most sophisticated broadcasting apparatus imaginable and the technical know-how to disseminate messages through it. But unless this country is also producing its own messages, its control over the total communication process is lost to the outsider, and hence its dependency on the outside system increases.

The Americanization of world culture, so often discussed, might be better understood as the interaction of such a message-producing and distributing system vis-à-vis the media technology and cultural content components of the diagram. If American pop culture is successful around the world—and it is—it becomes so by this circular process. The software aspect of communication technology, for example, in the forms of programs, shows, and film enters, into a national system seeking to reflect some popular cultural tastes; the product in turn feeds back into the system and reinforces that which has already been found popular.

In the interaction of two cultural systems it is clear that external links and relationships have exercised a fundamental influence on the shaping of the structure of mass media and cultural systems, and, therefore, on their functioning and outcome, as well as on the process of structural transformation. Nevertheless, the importance attached to these external links should not lead us to underestimate the existence of structures of underdevelopment internal to the system.

It is here that the pure theory of the so-called free flow of information ignores the inherent weaknesses in many dependent areas of the globe and the total lack of the structures that would seek to instill a counteracting discriminatory capacity in their citizens faced by a bombardment of messages originating in the outside system.

However, unfurling the banner of an open door policy, the commercialist insists that the removal of all impediments—by both the strong and the weak—will contribute to the development of world culture and redound to the benefit of all concerned. Though this even-handed judgment seems admirable and even attractive in the abstract, it ignores the experience of four centuries during which the powerful imposed Ricardian free-flow trade principles on the weak, while themselves violating those principles to protect favored sectors of their economies. The irony is well-captured by economist and historian Carlo Cippola:

> It was fortunate for England that no Indian Ricardo arose to convince the English people that, according to the law of comparative cost, it would be advantageous for them to turn into shepherds and to import from India all the textiles that were needed. Instead, England passed a series of acts designed to prevent importation of Indian textiles and some "good results" were achieved.[55]

CONCLUSION

Because of the growing awareness of the importance of "culture" in national and international relations, the media and developmental theorists and policy makers have had to deal more and more frequently with questions of a cultural nature. Faced on one hand with the considerable complexitiy of the subject, and on the other hand with the inconsistencies and imbalances of this phenomenon in the cultural program of nations, the relations of mass media and culture have occupied a prominent and crucial role in the relations among and between nations. The integrative theory presented here is an attempt to show the complexity and the process of this phenomenon with the hope that it might suggest certain guidelines for the students and practitioners of the mass media and culture as well as for those in policy-making positions.

The need for a new conceptual framework stems from the explicit regcognition that some of the major theoretical explanations analyzed in this chapter were concerned primarily with Western historical experience—a parochialism reflected in some of the concepts employed. Such phenomena as the multiplicity of nation-states, the rise of ethnicity, the diversity of national developmental goals and needs, the incredible diffusion of technology by national and transnational actors, and the simultaneous entry of many nations into the industrial-technological as well as communication and information age have not been taken into consideration by the past theories. It is for this reason that such models of mass media and culture have proved inadequate for understanding new communication problems that have come into being during the last two decades; they are even less appropriate for the study of mass media systems in new nations.

In the light of the integrative theory of mass media and culture, it is evident that the developing countries must develop their own national communication policies, striving for more control over all sectors so as to further their developmental goals and to reassert their cultural sovereignty and protect their cultural heritage.

Any mass media system striving to integrate itself into a national cultural system must have its policies clear in regard to the following areas:

(1) cultural heritage and group tradition,
(2) individual and human rights,
(3) development policy and spread of culture,
(4) cultural exchange and enrichment in the field of international communication,
(5) cultural pluralism,
(6) intelligent discrimination in the selection of communication technology (especially in regard to its hardware aspect) and the media.

For example, what are the rights of a minority group that wants to protect and develop its own cultural identity in a national or international system? Can the kind of cultural situation prevailing in the relationships between the developed and less developed countries be called, to use the popular term, "interdependent"? In the promotion of culture, worldwide, what are to be the components of an international cultural program? What should be the role of mass media in helping to articulate and give identity to the various biological (age-group), psychological, and aesthetic groupings that have begun to emerge as a result of the decline of traditional groupings in modern societies?

The old theories of mass media and culture usually took a one-way view of the process—that of the impact of the media on culture. They also dismiss the factors of culture and value systems in this process by either basing their argument on political and economic systems or technological and mass phenomena. The integrative view, by contrast, introduces such variables as culture and value systems and attempts to assess the impact of culture on the media. In short, the integrative theory can have explanatory power as to why such countries as the Soviet Union, the People's Republic of China, Cuba, Yugoslavia, and

Tanzania might pursue different and varied media systems due to their cultural differences, though they all speak of a socialist strategy. How should we take into account, in a country like Lebanon, the differences among the various groups playing roles in Lebanon's political structure? What will be the relationship between the Indian caste system and the conception and reception of mass media? How about the Scandinavian countries, where there exist almost two principles that the triple M theorists consider quite contradictory: stringent economic control and a degree of political freedom and autonomy?

A given mass media system might not be able immediately to find answers to these and similar questions, but taking an integrative approach will enhance that system's ability to minimize and manage them better, because under this theory it becomes evident that no one system operates in isolation. By becoming aware of all the components, a given system can evolve policies to increase its effectiveness and carry out its policy objectives. Whereas the triple M theory is too narrow in scope and the political economy theory presents a monolithic picture ignoring the importance of different cultural variables and the rise of new phenomena on the world stage, the integrative theory attempts to take a broad overview while not avoiding the importance of micro-level components.

NOTES

1. Daniel Bell, "The Theory of Mass Society," *Commentary* 22 (July 1956): 75-83; and *The End of Idology* (New York: Collier Books, 1961); also, W. Kornhauser, *The Politics of Mass Society* (London: Routledge & Kegan Paul, 1960).

2. Bernard Rosenberg and David Manning White, eds., *Mass Culture* (New York: Free Press, 1957), and R. A. Bauer and Alice Bauer, "America, Mass Society, and Mass Media," *Journal of Social Issues* 16 (1960): 3-6.

3. Mathew Arnold, *Culture and Anarchy* (Cambridge: Cambridge University Press, 1960).

4. Friedrich Nietzsche, *The Will to Power*, in *Complete Works* (London, 1910), 2: 265-66; and *Human All-Too-Human: A Book for Free Spirits*, vol. 7: 277.

5. Karl Mannheim, *Essays on the Sociology of Culture* (London: Routledge & Kegan Paul, 1956); and *Man and Society in an Age of Reconstruction* (London: Kegan Paul, Trench & Trubner, 1940).

6. Charles Baudelaire, *A Lyric Poet in the Era of High Capitalism* (London: New Left Books, 1973).

7. Jose Ortega y Gasset, *The Revolt of the Masses* (London: Unwin Books, 1932).

8. C. Wright Mills, *The Power Elite* (New York: Oxford University Press, 1956); and *White Collar: The American Middle Classes* (New York: Oxford Univeristy Press, 1951).

9. Ernest Van den Haag, "Of Happiness and of Despair We Have no Measure," in Rosenberg and Manning White, eds., *Mass Culture*, pp. 504-36.

10. Daniel Bell, "The Theory of Mass Society." See also his recent work, *The Coming of Post Industrial Society* (New York: Basic Books, 1973).

11. David Riesman, "Listening to Popular Music," *American Quarterly* 2 (1950): 359-71; and his *The Lonely Crowd* (New Haven : Yale University Press, 1950); also David Riesman and Michael Maccaby, "The American Crisis," *Commentary* 29 (June 1960): 461-72.

12. Bernard Rosenberg, "Mass Culture in America," in Rosenberg and Manning White, eds., *Mass Culture*, pp. 3-12.

13. Edward Shils, "Mass Society and Its Culture," in *Culture for the Millions?* ed. Norman Jacobs (Boston: Beacon Press, 1964), pp. 1-27.

14. Theodore W. Adorno, "Television and the Patterns of Mass Culture," in Rosenberg and Manning White, eds., *Mass Culture*, pp. 474-88.

15. Leo Lowenthal, "Historical Perspectives of Popular Culture," *American Journal of Sociology* 55 (1950): 323-32; and *Literature, Popular Culture and Society* (New York, Prentice-Hall, 1961); also "An Historical Preface to the Popular Culture Debate," in Jacobs, ed., *Culture for the Millions?* pp. 28-42.

16. Walter Benjamin, "The Work of Art in the Age of Mechanical Reproduction," in ed. Hannah Arendt, *Illumination* (London: Jonathan Cape, 1970), pp. 219-53.

17. Herbert Marcuse, *One Dimensional Man* (Boston: Beacon Press, 1962); and *Counterrevolution and Revolt* (Boston: Beacon Press, 1972).

18. Max Horkheimer, "Art and Mass Culture," *Studies in Philosophy and Social Science* 9 (1941).

19. T. S. Eliot, *Notes Toward a Definition of Culture* (London: Faber & Faber, 1948).

20. Dwight Mac Donald, "A Theory of Mass Culture,"*Diogenes* 3 (Summer 1953): 1-7. Reprinted in Rosenberg and Manning White, eds., *Mass Culture*, pp. 59-73. See also his "Masscult and Midcult," *Partisan Review* 27 (Spring 1960): 203-33.

21. Irving Howe, "Notes on Mass Culture," in Rosenberg and Manning White, eds., *Mass Culture*, pp. 496-503.

22. Clement Greenberg, "Avant-Garde and Kitsch," in Rosenberg and Manning White, eds., *Mass Culture*, pp. 98-107; see also his *Art and Culture* (Boston: Beacon Press, 1961), pp. 3-21.

23. Q. D. Leavis, *Fiction and the Reading Public* (London: Chatto & Windus, 1932), and *Mass Civilization and Minority Culture* (Cambridge: Minority Press, 1930).

24. Raymond Williams, *Culture and Society* (London: Penguin, 1963); and his *Television: Technology and Cultural Form* (London: Fontana, 1974).

25. Denys Thompson, ed., *Discrimination and Popular Culture* (London: Penguin, 1964).

26. For a broad discussion of Culture see A. L. Kroeber and Clyde Kluchohn, *Culture: A Critical Review of Concepts and Definition* (New York: Vintage Press, 1952); and Louis Schneider and Charles Bonjean, eds., *The Idea of Culture in the Social Sciences* (New York: Cambridge University Press, 1973), see especially chapters by Talcott Parsons, Kenneth Boulding, and Lucien Pye.

27. Harold Innis, *The Bias of Communication* (Oxford: Oxford University Press, 1950).

28. Marshall McLuhan, *Understanding Media* (New York: McGraw-Hill, 1964).

29. Zygmunt Baumann, "A Note on Mass Culture: An Infrastructure," in Denis McQuail, ed., *Sociology of Mass Communication* (London: Penguin, 1972), pp. 61-74.

30. Karl Marx, *Capital*, 3 vols. (Moscow: Foreign Language Publishing House, 1961); see also *Marxism and the Mass Media: Towards a Basic Bibliography* (New York: International Mass Media Center, 1974).

31. Erich Fromm, *The Sane Society* (London: Routledge & Kegan Paul, 1956); also his *Escape from Freedom* (London: Kegan Paul, 1942); and *Man for Himself* (New York: Rinehart, 1947).

32. Henri Lefebvre, *Critique de la vie quotidienne* (Paris: Gallimard, 1970).

33. Jean Baudrillard, *La Societe de Consommation* (Paris: Gallimard, 1970).

34. Hans Magnus Enzensberger, "Constituents of a Theory of the Media," *New Left Review* 64 (1970): 13-36.

35. Ludovico Silva, *Theoria y Practica de la Ideologia* (Caracas: Nuestro Tiempo, 1971).

36. Antonio Pasquali, *Communicacion y Cultura de Masos* (Caracas: Monte Avila, 1972).

37. Evelina Dagino, "Cultural and Ideological Dependence: Building a Theoretical Framework," in *Structures of Dependency*, ed. Frank Bonita and R. Girling, (Stanford: Stanford University Press, 1973).

38. Armand Mattelart, "The Nature of Communications Practice in a Dependent Society," *Latin American Perspectives* 5 (Winter 1978): 13-34; see also his *La Cultura como Eurpresa Multinacional* (Mexico City: Editorial ERA, 1974); *Mass Media, ideologies et mouvement revolutionnaire* (Paris: Anthropos, 1974).

39. Herbert I. Schiller, *Communication and Cultural Domination* (White Plains, NY: International Arts and Sciences Press, 1976); also his *Mass Communication and American Empire* (New York: Kelley, 1969); *The Mind Managers* (Boston: Beacon Press, 1973).

40. Hamid Mowlana, "A Paradigm for Comparative Mass Media Analysis," in *International and Intercultural Communication,* ed. Heinz-Dietrich Fischer and John C. Merrill (New York: Hastings House, 1970) pp. 474-84.

41. Hamid Mowlana, "A Paradigm for Source Analysis in Events Data Research: Mass Media and the Problems of Validity," *International Interactions* 2 (1975): 33-44.

42. George Gerbner, "Communication and Social Environment," *Scientific American* (1972): 152-62.

43. Hamid Mowlana, "Political and Social Implications of Communications Satellite Applications in Developed and Developing Countries," in *Economic and Policy Problems in Satellite Communications*, ed. Joseph N. Pelton and Marcellus S. Snow, (New York: Praeger, 1977), pp. 124-42.

44. Roger Nall, *Economic Aspects of TV Regulations* (Washington, DC: Brookings Institution, 1973).

45. Hamid Mowlana, "Mass Media and the 1976 Presidential Election, *Intellect* 106 (February 1977): 244-45.

46. Hamid Mowlana, "Mass Communication, Elites and National Systems in the Middle East," in *Der Anteil der Massenmedien bei der Herausbildung des Bewubtseins in der sich Wandelnden Welt* (Leipzig: International Association for Mass Communication Research, IX Scientific Congress, 1974), vol. 1: 55-69.

47. Jerzy A. Wojciechowski, "Cultural Pluralism and National Identity," *Cultures* 4 (1977): 50-54.

48. Hamid Mowlana and Ann Elizabeth Robinson, "Ethnic Mobilization and Communication Theory," in *Ethnicity in an International Context*, ed. A. A. Said and L. R. Simmons, (New Brunswick, NJ: Transaction Books, 1976), pp. 48-63.

49. John C. Cawelti, "Cultural Pluralism and the Media of the Future: A View from America," *Cultures* 4 (1977): 56-82.

50. John C. Cawelti, "Cultural Pluralism and the Media of the Future," 70.

51. Hamid Mowlana, "Toward a Theory of Communication Systems: A Developmental Approach," *Gazette: International Journal of Mass Communication* 17 (1971): 17-28. For the role of various states in national communication policies see George Gerbner, ed., *Mass Media Policies in Changing Cultures* (New York: John Wiley, 1977); and M. Teheranian, F. Hakimzadeh, and M. L. Vidale, eds., *Communications Policy for National Development: A Comparative Perspective* (London: Routledge & Kegan Paul, 1977).

52. Nikolai Shanin, "Radio and Television as Art Forms in the Soviet Union," *Cultures* 4 (1977): 83-92.

53. Hans Magnus Enzensberger, "Constituents of a Theory of the Media," in McQuail, ed., *Sociology of Mass Communication*, p. 104.

54. This is a modification of Harold Lasswell's formula—"Who Says What in Which Channel to Whom with What Effect?" in the *Communication of Ideas*, ed. Lyman Bryson (New York: Harper & Brothers, 1948), p. 37.

55. Quoted in Mark Selden, "Dollars and Dependence: Blue Prints for Southeast Asia," *The Nation* (April 23, 1973): 522; for a critical commentary on culture and imperialism see Julianne Burton and Jean Franco, "Culture and Imperialism," *Latin American Perspectives* 5 (Winter 1978): 2-12.

10

Cultural Convergence
A Mathematical Theory

GEORGE A. BARNETT • *State University of New York at Buffalo*
D. LAWRENCE KINCAID • *East-West Communication Institute*

Central to the examination of intercultural communication are the theoretical notions of culture, the differences between the cultures of different social systems, and the effects of these dissimilarities on the accuracy of information exchange between members of different cultures. Also important, but less often addressed, are the effects of communication among different cultures on the cultures themselves. This chapter will focus on the second issue. It will begin with a theoretical discussion of culture and cultural differences, and a discussion of the effects of communication on cultural differences using the convergence model of communication. Once this background has been provided, the chapter will shift to a theoretical discussion of the methodological issues in the measurement of these concepts. Finally, a mathematical theory will be presented that will provide for the precise prediction of the rates of convergence among cultures as a result of intercultural communication.

THE PROBLEMS OF
INTERCULTURAL COMMUNICATION

Definitions of culture center upon extrinsic factors such as the artifacts that are produced by society (clothing, food, technology, etc.), and intrinsic factors such as the beliefs, attitudes, perceptions, and values of a society. Murdock emphasizes that culture consists of habits

AUTHORS' NOTE: *The authors would like to thank Joseph Woelfel for his insightful comments on earlier drafts of this chapter. Dr. Barnett's portion of the chapter was written while he was on a research fellowship at the East-West Center, Honolulu, Hawaii during the summer of 1979. An earlier version was presented to the Intercultural Division of the International Communication Association at their annual meeting in Acapulco, Mexico, May 1980.*

and tendencies to act in a certain way, not the actions themselves.[1] In his definition of culture, Prosser emphasizes language patterns, values, attitudes, beliefs, customs, and thought patterning.[2] The notion of thought patterning and expectation has become prevalent in the most recent definitions of culture. For example, Goodenough says that culture is not things or behavior, but rather "the forms of things that people have in mind, their models for perceiving, relating, and otherwise interpreting them." Geertz treats culture as an ordered system of meanings and of symbols, in terms of which social interaction takes place and develops.[4] And finally, Nieburg defines culture as socially shared activities, and therefore the property of groups rather than individuals.[5]

By treating culture as an organized system of significant symbols (following Geertz), and as a property of groups rather than individuals (following Nieburg), the field of intercultural communication research can avoid needless discussions about whether or not intercultural communication exists as a special phenomenon for study. In a sense, communication occurs—and is made possible—because of the differences that exist among people. Were there no differences among people there would certainly be no need to communicate. This assumption turns most discussions of intercultural communication to the *degree* of difference that exists.

Martin, for example, concludes that communication can be effective regardless of how great the differences are between people, therefore "there is no such thing as cross-cultural communication."[6] Kluckhohn argues that when people from two groups "share enough basic assumptions so that they can communicate in the broadest sense of that term—comfortably, then their cultures are only variants of a single culture."[7] The problem with both of these approaches, of course, is that the important criteria—effectiveness and comfort—are applied as categorical rather than as continuous terms. If all degrees of effectiveness and comfort are considered acceptable, then there is no intercultural communication. If no degree of effectiveness and comfort are satisfactory, then all communication is intercultural. Sarbaugh suggests that since all communication is intercultural to a certain degree, then the heterogeneity and homogeneity of the participants can be used to discern the degree of "interculturalness."[8] Degree calls for precise definitions of difference and precise methods of measurement.

From this brief discussion it becomes clear that the fields of intercultural communication would develop further by treating culture as a property of groups rather than individuals, by creating a more precise definition of culture as the organization of significant symbols, and by creating a method of measurement precise enough to discern the degree of differences that exist between groups as well as within groups.

The study of intercultural communication research should focus on communication between groups in which the differences in organization patterns of thought are greater between groups than within each group. This is an important phenomenon to study today for several reasons. Such differences create a greater potential for communication breakdown, misunderstanding, disagreement, and conflict at a time in history when the frequency of communication and the amount of interdependency among cultures is high and increasing very rapidly. Under such circumstances the need for mutual understanding, cooperation, and collective action across large cultural gaps is greater than ever before. The main purpose of intercultural communication theory should be to describe, to explain, and to predict changes in these cultural differences—the degree and direction of cultural convergence and divergence—that occur over time as a result of communication among different cultural groups.

COMMUNICATION AND CULTURAL CONVERGENCE

The approach that we have taken toward intercultural communication is not compatible with most conventional models, which treat communication as basically a linear, or one-way, act of persuasion. The basic problem of intercultural communication as we have defined it is the change in the differences of collective representations or patterns of thought that occur over time as a result of communication. This perspective calls for a model of communication that focuses on the mutual relationship between participants rather than what one participant does to another.

The convergence model of communication satisfies this basic requirement.[9] Communication is defined as a process of convergence in which two or more participants share information in order to reach a better mutual understanding of each other and the world in which they live. Meaning is not treated like a physical object that can be transmitted. Only information can be transmitted. Information is a difference in matter-energy that affects uncertainty in a situation where a choice exists among a set of alternatives. Differences in matter-energy, such as the words on a written page, do not "contain" meaning to be released or received by others. Information is given meaning by those who perceive such differences when they apply concepts available to them to interpret and to understand them.

On a psychological level of analysis, meaning is a choice or decision-making process involving the application of concepts, which affects the level of uncertainty that exists prior to their application. At the physical level of reality, there is a unity of information and action. Information (as a physical difference) is created by action; action (and its physical trace) is information, and is available—potentially, at least—for interpretation and understanding with whatever concepts are available from past experience or can be created.

An understanding of how another participant understands shared information can only be reached by the sharing of additional information or what is commonly known as feedback. Several cycles of such information exchange are often required to correct for initial divergence of understanding. Effective feedback observed over more than one cycle of information exchange leads to "a series of diminishing mistakes—a dwindling series of under-and-over corrections coverging on the goal."[10] When feedback is not adequate to its task, "the mistakes may become greater; the network may be 'hunting' over a cyclical or widening range of tentative and 'incorrect' responses ending in a breakdown."[11]

Thus, communication is not just an information-transmitting process; it is much more. Communication is a convergence process, in which two or more participants share information to reach a better mutual understanding. Convergence is a tendency to move toward one point or toward one another, to come together and unite in a common interest or focus. Divergence is moving away or apart. Each term implies the other: As two or more persons or groups move closer to one another in terms of their interpretations and understanding, they may simultaneously move away from others. Both terms are easily applied to human communication as a dynamic, social process.

Once the interpretation and understanding of information is raised to the level of shared interpretations and mutual understanding, what once could be considered only as individual information processing becomes a social process: communication among two or more persons who hold the common purpose—if only for a brief moment—of understanding one another. Whether or not the participants converge or diverge—reach a mutual understanding—is a question for further theoretical development for empirical research. Once the participants reach some level of mutual understanding they may or may not agree with one another's respective points of view. Increased mutual understanding, as a matter of fact, can lead to greater disagreement. By simply dichotomizing mutual understanding and agreement, we can conceive of four possible outcomes of communication: (1) mutual understanding with agreement, (2) mutual understanding with disagreement, (3) mutual misunderstanding with agreement, and (4) mutual misunder-standing with disagreement. Each of these states may also be conceptualized and measured as a continuous variable.

The convergence model represents human communication as a dynamic, cyclical process over time, characterized by mutual causation rather than one-way causation, and emphasizing the interdependent relationship of the participants. The analysis of the communication process on three levels—the physical, the psychological, and the social—raises the social aspects of communication to a position that is at least equal to the psychological and the physical aspects of communication. Mutual understanding becomes the primary function of the communication process, and a prerequisite for collective action and the successful achievement of other types of human purposes or goals.

The laws of thermodynamics predict that all participants in a closed system will converge over time on the mean collective pattern of thought if communication is allowed to continue indefinitely.[12] Thus, unlimited communication between subcultures would lead to the homogenization of the total system, with the equilibrium value tending toward the collective mean. The cultural convergence resulting from such communication can only be delayed or reversed by the introduction of new information from outside the system and/or by the formation of boundaries restricting the flow of information. Relatively bounded, isolated subcultures would be predicted to experience more convergence toward their own local subsystem means than toward the mean of the larger intercultural system, even though the net homogenization of the whole system would continue to increase.

It is not difficult to find examples of the convergence or assimilation of two or more different cultures into one common culture showing elements of both. The pluralistic American society is one such example. Many different immigrant groups came to this country, each with their own attitudes, values, and beliefs, that is, subjective cultures. Together, they made up the American culture, with each group retaining their own culture. The within-group cultural variances were considerably less than the overall between-groups differences. Over time, as these immigrant groups interacted, certain elements were borrowed from one group and shared by all. The overall differences among these cultures became smaller and smaller. An uniquely American culture emerged with the between-ethnic group differences approaching the variance of the culture within any single group.

Another example of cultural convergence that readily comes to mind, is the formation of the English culture from the native Anglo-Saxons and the conquering Normans. The English culture, which took over two hundred years to emerge following the Norman invasion in 1066, contained elements of both cultures. The clearest aspect of this can be found in the English language. Certain words were borrowed from the French (Norman) and other lexical items from the Anglo-Saxon. Together, they merged to form Middle English. Dietary terms may serve as an example. The French words beef, veal, and pork were added to the English words cow, calf, and swine to produce a richer and more varied language. The following mathematical model is designed to described this process of cultural convergence.

THE MEASUREMENT OF CULTURAL PROCESSES

The organized patterns of thought of a cultural group can be precisely measured following Woelfel and Barnett's procedures for measuring collective consciousness:

> That aggregate psychological configuration which constitutes the culture of a society and toward which individual beliefs may seem to tend, may be represented accurately as the average matrix $\overline{S}$, where any entry $\overline{S}_{ij}$ is the arithmetic mean conception of the distance or dissimilarity between objects i and j as seen by all members of a culture.[13]

These objects may be abstract aspects of belief, attitude, ritual, and patterned activity, including such things as a society's institutions (family, education, economic), its language, religion, or nation-state. Typically, they are defined in relation to the self, the individual members of the social system. It is this representation of culture that will be used as the theoretical basis for the measurement of culture and culture differences.

In a sense, culture may be taken to be the collective cognitive state of a social system's members, what Durkheim called the "collective consciousness."[14] But, because society is in a continual state of flux, changing as certain individual members die and new members enter the on-going system (through immigration or birth), society has an existence apart from any single individual. It is more than simply the sum of the individual's representations. Society has emergent properties as a whole. One of these is its culture. This emergent property is made possible through the interactive processes of society's members. The members' interactions curtail deviate conceptualizations and provide the impetus toward the central, shared zeigeist that constitutes a society's culture.

The processual nature of culture may be represented by a series of matrices, mean s_{t_0}, mean s_{t_1}, mean s_{t_2}, ..., mean s_{t_n}, whose elements are consistent across time. Cultural change may be simply the difference between mean s_{t_i}, and mean s_{t_j}, . With sufficiently frequent measures, it becomes possible to describe precisely cultural processes by calculating the velocities and accelerations of the individual elements of culture (mean s_i) as well as the overall cultural change over time. The velocities and accelerations are necessary for any discussion of cultural processes and, as will be discussed later, they are necessary to describe the convergence among a number of different subcultures toward the mean, collective culture; or, for that matter, the convergence of different world cultures toward a global mean.

This conceptualization may also be applied to compare a number of different societies at one point in time, each with its own culture. The difference between two cultures mean s_1 and mean s_2, at any one point in time is simply the degree of discrepancy mean s_{i1} - mean s_{i2}. This assumes, of course, that mean s_1 and mean s_2 are composed of the same or linguistically equivalent elements (cultural objects). While back-translation procedures can generally handle the linguistic problems, complications may arise when the second culture does not have a concept equivalent to the first.

Any size group or social system, whether with as few members as a small task group or as many as the entire Chinese society, possesses a culture. Work groups may develop their own patterns of acivity, language, and relationships to the objects in their environment. These may differ considerably from other task groups within the same parent organization. Likewise, entire societies develop their culture from interactional patterns of their members. While the theory presented here is directly applicable to all of these organizations, the pragmatics of studying intercultural communication processes compels us to observe situations where the differences in these collective representations are great. That is, situations where the *potential* for misunderstanding as a result of communication is highly probable and the *potential* for change in the collective representations as a function of future interactions among members of different social systems is also great. Further, it may be suggested that in these situations a great deal of energy will be required for these cultures to converge upon a common set of representations necessary for greater mutual understanding.

While all groups, and even single individuals to a certain extent, may possess an unique culture due to divergent patterns of socialization and personalized histories, it is more useful to view culture *only* as an emergent property of social systems. Thus, it seems less tenable to argue that single individuals may be viewed as entire *social* systems with a personal culture. Inndividuals within societies are products of unique past experiences, rendering all cultures heterogenous. While culture may be best represented by a measure of central tendency (the mean dissimilarity estimate among a set of cultural objects), there may be considerable variance about this average. *In intercultural communication we are interested in those cases where information is exchanged among groups whose cultures differ greatly.* Thus, the potential for misunderstanding and for cultural change resulting from future changes is great.

In a statistical sense, we are interested in only those cases where the between-group differences greatly exceed the within-group variance. This is not to suggest that there might not be a degree of overlap in cultural patterns between the two societies; only that the cultural averages are significantly different between the groups. By examining only those situations of extreme differences, this research can be placed more in line with the traditional anthropological notion of culture and what current communication researchers label as intercultural communication.

It is worth noting that this conceptualization of culture is dynamic and multidimensional. It allows for the simultaneous interactions among the various components constituting culture and describes the ongoing flow of ideas among societies. Societies, then, may not be labeled as modern or traditional, only has having this set of cultural relations at some point in time. These relations are contingent on the historical patterns of interaction both internal and external to the system. Thus, pejorative attributions about a society's culture are then avoided. Messages cannot be considered as isolated entities designed in one culture to change only a single isolated component of another society. Rather, cultural differences exist for historial reasons. Thus, the Western-linear model of the role of communication and sociocultural change is abandoned for one allowing for the simultaneous exchange of information and the holistic notion of cultural change resulting from intercultural interaction.

The dynamic nature of a society's value system and the over-time effects of communication may be measured through a variant of metric multidimensional scaling—GALILEO$_{tm}$.[15] Briefly summarizing, their argument goes as follows. The meaning of any set of concepts may be represented by an $N \times N$ dissimilarity (distance) matrix. Each row (vector) of the matrix describes the definition of a concept that is defined as the symbol's relationship to all the other concepts. These data are generally gathered by a series of direct magnitude estimates of the dissimilarity of pairs of concepts, using a criterion standard (unit of measure) of some length against which these estimates can be made. This distance matrix provides a static picture of the interrelationships among a set of concepts possessed by a single individual. The collective consciousness, that aggregate psychological configuration constituting culture, may be represented as the average distance matrix generated from a representative sample of the population of the society under investigation.[16] Process can be recorded in successive matrices at known time intervals and the changes between the matrices calculated.[17]

While these matrices provide accurate representations of a social system's culture, they are somewhat cumbersome due to their size. In order to reduce the data to usable proportions, the eigenvalues of the matrix's scalar products matrix are calculated. Mathematical models exist that provide an interpretation of these matrices in terms of Riemannian geometry.[18] The concepts are treated as points in a non-Euclidean manifold and techniques are available within $GALILEO_{tm}$[19] to obtain the dimensionality of this space as well as the location of the particular concepts on these dimensions.[20] This process is mathematically identical to converting a matrix of distances among cities to a graphic representation such as a map. In that special case, an $N \times N$ table of cities may be described with little loss of information in a reduced two-dimensional Euclidean space. In the case of culture and cognitive states, the spatial manifold may contain up to $N - 1$ dimensions, some of which will be imaginary (the eigenvalues for those dimensions will be negative). After a series of Riemann spaces have been generated at separate points in time (or among a set of groups), they may be rotated to a solution minimizing the squared distance between the theoretically stable concepts.[21] Then, it becomes possible to concentrate on the motion of particular dynamic cultural concepts. The differences between cultures may then be determined simply by subtracting the loadings between spaces and change over time within a single culture may also be determined in this manner. A computer program, $GALILEO_{tm}$[22] performs all the calculations necessary to perform the procedures described.[23]

These procedures have been applied with great success to members of a variety of different cultures and languages. Among them, French and English Canada;[24] Mexico (Spanish);[25] South Africa (English);[26] Australia (English), Micronesia (English), Israel (Hebrew);[27] New Zealand (English);[28] the Ivory Coast (French);[29] Philippines (Ikelano);[30] Korea (Korean)[31]; and Japan (Japanese),[32] as well as quite frequently and in a variety of differnt circumstances in the United States.

THE MATHEMATICAL THEORY OF
CULTURAL CONVERGENCE

Mathematically,[33] the simplest case to describe convergence would be the scalar, with one point (concept) on a single dimension with only one group displaced from the equilibrium position. It is simply,

$$m\ddot{x} + C_x x + K_x \dot{x} = o \qquad [1.0]$$

where

    m = the concept's (object's) mass,
    C = a velocity dependent linear dampening force,
    K = a linear restoring force,
    x = the coordinate value or displacement from convergence,
    $\dot{x}, \ddot{x}$ = the first and second derivatives with respect to time of the deplacement
        respectively.

This equation is in the homogeneous form (equal to zero). It represents a closed system, with no forces acting upon the converging system and may be treated as the mechanical analogy with a particle (oscillator) (m) attached to spring (K) and a dashpot (C) that has been set into motion.

In the case where one must assume an open or nonconservative system—one with additional forces altering the patterns toward convergence—the differential equation becomes

$$m\ddot{x} + C_x \dot{x} + K_x x = F_x \qquad [2.0]$$

where
    F_x represents the impressed force.
Thus, these additional forces would operate to prevent the convergence of an element of a group's culture with the equilibrium position. These forces would be such things that would prevent the unrestricted (random) exchange of information among a set of cultures, such as a well-defined social structure or geographically isolated groups. Another class of variables which would prevent cultural convergence would be information from sources external to the system. That is, immigration or mass media might prevent the process of homogenizing the overall culture.

This formulation is the most general. It includes four terms, the first- and second-order derivatives, the linear term, and the generalized residual (F_x). In specific cases where these terms become zero or constant, they maybe dropped from the equation without loss of information. Equation 2.0 is useful in stochastic situations, with unknown forces operating to prevent the return to equilibrium.

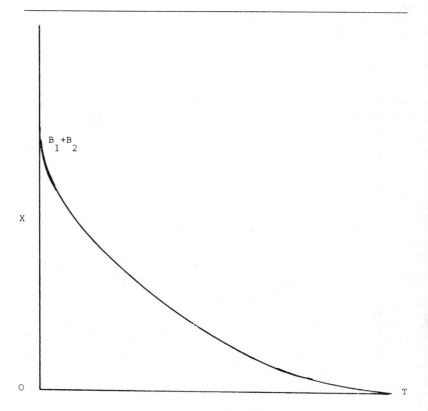

B_1, B_2 are the positive roots of the exponential parameters of the system derived through the integral of the displacement.

$$X = e^{pt}, P = \pm \sqrt{\frac{\alpha_3}{\alpha_1}} = \pm B$$

Figure 10.1   Exponential Decay to Convergence

Three cases are of special interest because under these conditions the system will return to equilibrium convergence. They are:

1. $\left(\frac{c_x}{2m}\right)^2 > \frac{k_x}{m}$

[3.1]

This is the case of exponential decay. When this condition occurs the system is overdamped and the level of displacement will not oscillate over time. It is graphically displayed in Figure 10.1.

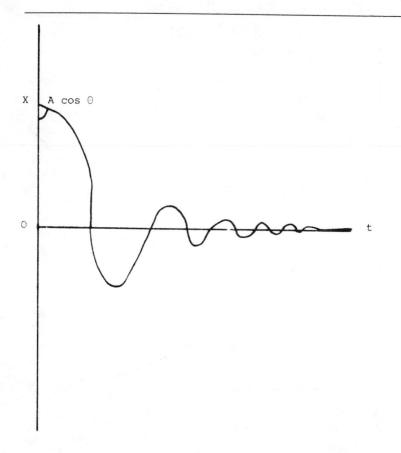

A is the constant magnitude vector from origin determined by the phase angle θ.

Figure 10.2   Damped Oscillation to Convergence

The second case is:

2. $\left(\dfrac{c_x}{2m}\right)^2 < \dfrac{k_x}{m}$

[3.2]

In this case, the system will oscillate in accordance with cos Θ, the phase angle of the curve produced by the function of the displacement over time. It is said to be underdamped and the deviation from equilibrim (amplitude of $_dx/dt$) will decrease exponentially with time. This case is graphically displayed in Figure 10.2.

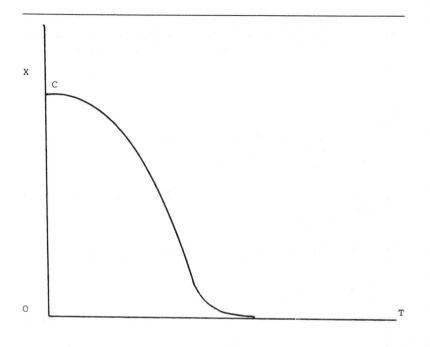

C is the constant linear dampening force.

Figure 10.3   Critically Damped Decay to Convergence

The third case is,

3. $\left(\dfrac{c_x}{2m}\right)^2 = \dfrac{k_x}{m}$ or   [3.3]

   $c = 2\sqrt{k_x m}$ [3.31]

In this case, the system is critically damped. After a short time interval, x will decrease more rapidly than in 3.1 and convergence will be more rapid. This is shown in Figure 10.3.

The case presented in this chapter requires a more general situation. There are many points (concepts), a multidimensional manifold, and a number of different cultures each converging over time on a common equilibrium.

To describe a single cultural system there are equations required ρn equations required for ρ dimensions and n concepts. The equilibrium case may be described with the more general indicial notion,

$$m_{ij}\ddot{Q}_j^k + c_{ij}\dot{Q}_j^k + k_{ij}Q_j^k = o \qquad [4.0]$$

where

> m_{ij} = a matrix of the products of the masses of concepts i and j,
> c_{ij}^k = a matrix of linear damping forces,
> k_{ij}^k = a matrix of linear restoring forces,
> Q_j^k = a matrix of linear damping forces,
> $\dot{Q}_j$, $\ddot{Q}_j$ = the first and second derivatives of Q_j respectively (i, j = 1,2,...,n) points or concepts,
> (k = 1,2,...,ρ) dimensions.

In most general cases, with outside forces acting upon the cultural system,

$$m_{ij}\ddot{Q}_j^k + c_{ij}^k\dot{Q}_j^k + k_{ij}^kQ_j^k = F_i^k \quad \text{or,} \qquad [4.1]$$

$$m_{ij}\ddot{Q}_j^k + c_{ij}^k\dot{Q}_j^k + k_{ij}^kQ_j^k - F_i^k = o \qquad [4.1a]$$

However, since each cultural system is the impressed force for the other, the two culture situation may be represented as follows.

$$m_{ij}\ddot{Q}_j^k + c_{ij}\dot{Q}_j^k + k_j^kQ_j^k - (\hat{m}_{ij}^k\hat{\ddot{Q}}_j^k + \hat{c}_{ij}^k\hat{\dot{Q}}_j^k + \hat{k}_{ij}^k\hat{Q}_j^k) = o \qquad [4.2]$$

Equation 4.2 assumes that these two cultures exist in a closed system with no residual forces acting upon them. The same operation may be performed as in 4.1 to include these external forces.

$$m_{ij}\ddot{Q}_j^k + c_{ij}^k\dot{Q}_j^k + \hat{k}_j^k\hat{Q}_j^k - (\hat{m}_{ij}^k\hat{\ddot{Q}}_j^k + \hat{c}_{ij}^k\hat{\dot{Q}}_j^k + \hat{k}_{ij}^k\hat{Q}_j^k) = F_i^k \qquad [4.3]$$

Again, these external forces represent additional cultural systems. They may be added to 4.3 by replacing F_i^k without limit, until the entire suprasystem is closed. This is the equilibrum state of cultural convergence.

Equation 4.3 may be simplified somewhat if it is assumed that

$$c_{ij}^k = f(Q_j^k) = \text{constant, and} \qquad [4.4a]$$

$$k_{ij}^k = f(Q_j^k) = \text{constant} \qquad [4.4b]$$

$$m_{ij}\ddot{Q}_j^k + c\dot{Q}_j^k + kQ_j^k - (\hat{m}_{ij}\hat{\ddot{Q}}_j^k + \hat{c}\hat{\dot{Q}}_j^k + \hat{k}\hat{Q}^k) = F_i^k \qquad [4.5]$$

In this case it is assumed that the viscosity of the cultural manifolds are homogeneous and that all the particles (concepts) have the same total drag. Equation 4.5 may be further simplified if one assumes that all the concepts are of equal mass, ($m_i = m_j$, i,j = 1,2, . . . ,n).

$$m\ddot{Q}_j^k + c\dot{Q}_j^k + kQ_j^k - (\hat{m}\ddot{\hat{Q}}_j^k + \hat{c}\dot{\hat{Q}}_j^k + \hat{k}\hat{Q}_j^k) = F_i^*$$ [4.6]

In order to predict the rates of convergence for the groups as described in this chapter, one must assume that the overall composite culture represents a closed or conservative system with no forces from outside the system to impinge upon the individual groups. One must also assume (for the given data) that all the value concepts are of equal mass across the set of cultural groups ($m_{i1} = m_{i2}$). This assumption makes it possible to *estimate* final equilibrium manifold. It will be an aggregate multidimensional space formed from each group's mean dissimilarity matrix (mean D_1) weighted by that group's proportion of the total population (p_i) as indicated by formula 5.0.

$$p_1(\text{mean } D_1) + p_2 (\text{mean } D_2) + ... + p_n (\text{mean } D_n) = \Sigma_i^n = 1^{p_i} \text{mean} ^{D_i}$$ [5.0]

In order to determine the discrepancies among a series of cultures, samples from those societies may be compared in the following manner. The spatial manifolds from all the sample cultures are rotated to a least-square congruence as if each data set represented a different point in time. Since the researchers may have no additional information with regard to the relative stability of the concepts across cultural boundaries, all concepts should be treated equally and included in the least-square solution. This is done for all possible pairs of subcultures resulting in a $(K + 1) \times (K + 1) \times n$ matrix of the dissimilarity among the subcultures (K) and for the artificial composite culture (+1), for each concept (n). This is then reduced to a $(K + 1) \times (K + 1) \times n$ matrix by averaging across the concepts. The resultant matrix could then be treated like any other square symmetrical matrix of discrepancies. The data are orthogonally decomposed. In a sense, this is a multidimensional analysis of the residual variance unexplained by the least-square best-fit rotation. That is, after the maximal shared variance accounted for by the measured cultural concepts are removed, the subcultures are again compared. The proportion of variance explained by the residual intercultural matrix is compared to the sum of the traces of the individual subcultural matrices. The residual variance may then be scaled to reveal the dimensions unaccounted for by the previous analysis.

With the degree of discrepancy for each subculture from the common culture described only at one point in time, it is not possible to determine the *rate* of convergence. Additional measurements are required to calculate the velocities ($\dot{Q}$) and accelerations ($\ddot{Q}$) of the individual concepts and overall cultural systems.

The masses of concepts (M) must also be determined. This may be done by setting one concept to a unit mass and then determining the others as ratios to that concept's mass. At this point, a theory or empirical measurement is needed to determine the masses of other concepts. Woelfel and Saltiel point out that the mass of a concept is its resistance to change when impacted by a message (external force), such that the greater a concept's mass the greater its resistance to change.[35] Barnett proposes using the frequency of occurrence of a concept in natural language as an indicator of mass.[36] The greater its occurrence, the greater a concept's mass will be. Barnett's procedure probably cannot be used because there may be no indicators of frequency of occurrence of words in some cultures. Thus, empirical measures are called for.

The empirical measures may take either of two forms, experimental manipulation of the system by inserting a number of messages into a sample of the culture, or by carefully monitoring the messages that naturally impinge upon the members of the social system through content analysis and the resultant changes in the cultural configuration. The latter alternative is probably too costly and time consuming for actual implementation. The same experimental procedures are necessary in order to determine the linear dampening forces and the linear restoring forces. In this way, the differential equation 4.6 may be solved and provide an accurate prediction of cultural convergence.

The potential energy resulting from the displacement from convergence may be derived from equation 1.0. Ignoring the damping forces, for a conservative or closed system,

$$m_l\ddot{x} + K_x x = 0 \text{ or, for an open system,} \tag{6.0}$$

$$m_1\ddot{x} + K_x x = F_x \tag{6.1}$$

Thus, the potential energy, or the energy that will result from the return of a single particle to equilibrium will be:

$$V_x = \frac{K_x x^2}{2} \tag{7.0}$$

or the integral of 6.1. The potential energy is a function of the linear restoring forces (constant) and the total displacement. The kinetic energy, or the energy resulting from the return of the particle to equilibrium will be:

$$T_x = \frac{m_1 \ddot{x}^2}{2} \qquad [8.0]$$

It is also derived from the integral of 6.1. It is a function of the mass and the acceleration of the particle.

In the case presented here, there are many points (concepts), dimensions, and cultures. In the case, the potential energy in equation 7.0 would become:

$$V = 1/2 \, K_{lm} q_l q_m \qquad [9.0]$$

where

K_{lm} = a matrix of real constants (linear restoration) obtained from evaluating,

$$K_{lm} = \frac{\partial^2 V}{\partial q_l \partial q_m} \qquad [9.1]$$

at the coordinates q_{ql} and q_{qm}.

l = m = a vector of length equal to the number of dimensions times the number of particles (concepts) minus the constraints equations

$$l = m = (i)\,(j) - c \qquad [9.2]$$

q_l, q_m = vectors of displacement l or m elements long.

While different in form, this formulation of the potential energy between two cultural systems is identical to Woelfel and Fink.[37] They write that the total magnitude of discrepancy among two cultural systems may be given by the trace of the scalar products matrix S" in equation 10.0 and 10.1.

$$AT = B + E \qquad [10.0]$$
$$S" = E(E) \qquad [10.1]$$

where

A = the coordinate system (spatial manifold) for system A,
B = the coordinate system for system B,
T = a linear operator which minimizes the trace of S".

The operator T includes the set of rotations and translations required to eliminate artifactual differences in the coordinate loadings and minimize the overall difference between the manifolds. This has been discussed, earlier in this chapter and in greater depth by Woelfel and his associates.[38]

When the columns (dimensions) in A and B are orthogonal (independent), as in the GALILEO System, the partial derivatives (∂) vanish.[39] Also, since K is a constant, it may be set such that the potential energy produced by the interaction of two divergent cultures becomes equal to the total discrepancy from convergence between the systems.

Historically, the argument has been made that human systems cannot be modeled according to the laws of mechanics. By treating the culture of a society as an elastic-solid body, something "human" will be lost. However, rather than considering the quantification of cognitive and social attributes as reductionistic, the authors feel that one should view the mathematization of experience in a manner similar to the Pythagoreans, not as an impoverishment, but as an enrichment. Numbers were sacred, the purest of ideas permitting mental operations without reference to the world of senses.[40] Indeed, for the construction of intercultural theory, mathematics is the ideal form for describing such processes. It is a universal and abstract symbol system that makes no reference to any given culture or specific point in time. From a scientific viewpoint, it allows for precise theory construction, testable in any society, yet abstract enough to take into account specific cultural variation. Further, it is universally understood regardless of the host culture.

Models of this sort have been shown to be quite useful in the prediction of collective experience.[41] Barnett and associates have shown that a mechanical model provides utility in the description and prediction of political processes.[42] Indeed, a number of cases have been reported where an elastic-solid model seems appropriate. That is, a force or powerful communication message causes displacement from an equilibrium point for a culture, followed by a return to that position for the collective attitudes. Barnett described this pattern concerning attitudes toward the "most serious national problem" with measures before, during, and after campus riots in response to action during the war in Vietnam and an assassination attempt on George Wallace.[43] Barnett found a return to an equilibrium position following the 1976 Presidential campaign for political attitudes.[44] The campaign events caused a departure from the equilibrium. In his study of the attitude change of collectivity, Woelfel found an elastic-solid model described by a set of second-degree differential equations accurately described the process.[45]

Differential equation models are becoming more common throughout intercultural research. Barnett has used them to describe the diffusion process.[46] Doreian developed a differential model to describe the communication patterns between the People's Republic of China and the Republic of India between 1954 and 1964.[47] The model estimated the reciprocal communication behavior of the two nations and allowed for the interpretation of their relations. The comunication system became unstable just prior to the onset of war between the two nations and the model was used to distinguish a situation that did lead to war from another that did not.

It would be a serious mistake to conclude that the approach to communication taken in this chapter treats human beings as mechanical objects, or that the mathematical theory applies directly to human beings per se. The mathematical theory is applied at a much higher level of abstraction. What we have done in this chapter is to apply the mathematics developed for the prediction of motion in spatio-temporal continuum to the prediction of the motion of the collective conceptual representations of cultural groups in multidimensional space. We consider it a worthwhile goal of science to discover the degree to which cultural change, as it is conceived and measured in this manner, can be predicted by the mathematical theory developed in this chapter.

EPILOGUE

This manuscript was first written in October 1979. Since that time, there has been an initial empirical test of the proposed theoretical model. The results are encouraging, suggesting support for the model. They will be briefly described here to help clarify this approach to the study of intercultural processes. These preliminary findings were reported to the mathematical modeling study group of SCA's Action Caucus on Intercultural Theory, in New York, November 1980. A complete report of these findings was presented at the International Communication Association's meetings in Minneapolis, May 1981.[48]

GALILEO$_{tm}$ data were gathered during 1978 under the direction of D. L. Kincaid and June Ock Yum at the East-West Communication Institute, Honolulu. Randomly selected samples of five ethnic groups (Caucasians, Japanese, Filipinos, Koreans, and Samoans) on the island of Oahu were asked to complete a questionnaire that included a series of direct pair comparisons among the following 14 concepts:

(1) Success	(8) Sense of Authority
(2) Happiness	(9) Family
(3) American	(10) Children
(4) The Ethnic Group	(11) Divorce
(5) Me	(12) Friendship
(6) Individual Freedom	(13) Hate
(7) Saving Face	(14) Love

These concepts were chosen because it was expected that clear differences among the ethnic groups' subjective culture would result. Also included with the pair comparisons were questions on media use, interpersonal interaction, language use, and a series of demographic items. One of these asked for length of residence on Oahu. These items would help to identify those factors that facilitate cultural convergence or restrict the free flow of information.

The mean responses to the GALILEO$_{tm}$ items for each ethnic group were combined to form an equilibrium multidimensional manifold according to formula 5.0. That is, the mean value for each estimate of each ethnic group was weighted by the group's proportion of the population. These means may be taken to be the operationalized subjective culture for each ethnic group. The equilibrium or converged culture is the weighted grand mean of the five ethnic groups. Excluded from the equilibrium manifold were Love, Hate, and the Ethnic Group. Love and Hate were the criterion pair and relationships with the ethnic group were expected to be unique for each group. This weighted distance matrix was next transformed into a multidimensional space.

Next, the Korean portion of the sample (N = 325) was separated by length of residence on Oahu, and multidimensional spaces formed for each year. For example, all Korean immigrants with less than one year were combined and a space formed for that group. Those individuals with between one and two years of residence were aggregated, and so on. The spaces for each year were rotated to a least-squares congruence with the equilibrium manifold and the discrepancies of each annual group from the equilibrium calculated.

While the range of residence on Oahu was 75 years, only the first 15 years were included in the analysis because the later years had so few representatives. The first 15 years included 293 immigrants, or 90% of the Korean sample.

The mean discrepancies (differences) for the first 15 years were entered into a nonlinear curve fitting program, SSQFIT, at Rensselaer Polytechnic Institute. Output for the underdamped, critically damped, and overdamped cases were generated. These models explain between 28% (underdamped) and 34% (critically damped) of the variance in the empirical data.

These results are encouraging considering that there are only 15 points in time included in the analysis. This is far too few to precisely fit a curve. Also, each single point in time may contain measurement error because the later points were aggregated from only two or three sets of individual estimates. This is far too few to estimate the subjective culture of a group, the unit of analysis suggested by the theory.

Future research is planned using the individual's communication (mass media and interpersonal inteaction) as well as social economic factors in a causal model to predict the individual's discrepancy from the equilibrium. In this way, the factors restricting the free flow of information to the individual and preventing cultural convergence between different groups can be examined.

NOTES

1. G. P. Murdock, "How Culture Changes," in *Man, Culture, and Society*, ed. H. L. Shapiro (New York: Oxford University Press, 1956), p. 249.

2. M. H. Prosser, *The Cultural Dialogue* (Boston: Houghton Mifflin, 1978), p. 153.

3. W. H. Goodenough, "Cultural Anthropology and Linguistics," in *Language in Culture and Society*, ed. D. Hymes (New York: Harper & Row, 1964), p. 36.

4. C. Geertz, *The Interpretation of Cultures* (New York: Basic Books, 1973).

5. Harold L. Nieburg, *Cultural Storm: Politics and the Ritual Order* (New York: St. Martin's Press, 1973).

6. L. J. Martin, "The Contradiction of Intercultural Communication," in *International and Intercultural Communication*, ed. H. D. Fisher and J. C. Merrill (New York: Hastings House, 1976), p. 432.

7. C. Kluckhohn, *Culture and Behavior* (New York: Free Press, 1962), p. 65.

8. L. E. Sarbaugh, *Intercultural Communication* (Rochelle Park, NJ: Hayden, 1979).

9. See D. L. Kincaid, "The Convergence Model of Communication" (East-West Communication Institute Paper Series, Honolulu, Hawaii, 1979) 18; D. L. Kincaid with W. Schramm, *Fundamental Human Communication*, Module text (Honolulu: East-West Communication Institute, 1975); E. M. Rogers and D. L. Kincaid, *Communication Networks: A New Paradigm for Research* (New York: Free Press, forthcoming).

10. K. W. Deutsch, "Toward a Cybernetic Model of Man and Society," in *Modern Systems Research for the Behavioral Scientist*, ed. W. Buckley (Chicago: Aldine, 1968), p. 390.

11. K. W. Deutsch, "Toward a Cybernetic Model of Man," p. 390.

12. J. Woelfel and E. L. Fink, *The Galileo System: A Theory of Social Measurement and Its Application* (New York: Academic, 1980).

13. J. Woelfel and G. A. Barnett, "A paradigm for mass communication research" (Paper delivered at the annual meeting of the International Communication Association, New Orleans, April 1974), pp. 6-7.

14. E. Durkheim, *Suicide: A Study of Sociology*, trans. G. Simpson (Glencoe, IL: Free Press, 1951).

15. See J. Woelfel, "Metric Measurement of Cultural Processes" (Paper delivered at the annual meeting of the Speech Communication Association, Chicago, December 1974): G. A. Barnett, "Social System Homophily as a Function of Communication" (Paper delivered at the annual meeting of the International Communication Association, New Orleans, April 1974); G. A. Barnett, "An Association Model for the Diffusion of Complex Innovations" (Paper delivered at the annual meeting of the International Communication Association, Chicago, April 1978); J. Woelfel and G. A. Barnett, "A Paradigm for Mass Communication Research"; R. T. Wigand and G. A. Barnett, "Multidimensional Scaling of Cultural Processes: The Case of Mexico, South Africa and the United States," *International-Intercultural Annual 3* (Falls Church, VA: Speech Communication Association, 1976); T. L. McPhail and G. A. Barnett, *Broadcasting, Culture and Self: A Multidimensional Pilot Study* (Report to the Ministry of the Secretary of State, Canada, November 1977); G. A. Barnett, "Spatial Modeling of Social Networks: With Applications to the Diffusion Process" (Paper delivered at the annual meeting of the International Communication Association, Philadelphia, May 1979); G. A. Barnett, "On the Nature of Synonyms: And This Little Piggie. . ." (Paper delivered at the annual meeting of the Eastern Communication Association, Philadelphia, May 1979).

16. Durkheim, *Suicide*.

17. G. A. Barnett and J. Woelfel, "On the Dimensionality of Psychological Processes," *Quality and Quantity* 13 (1979): 215-32.

18. J. Woelfel, G. A. Barnett, and J. W. Dinkelacker, "Metric Multidimensional Scaling in Riemann Space" (Paper delivered at the annual meeting of the Psychometric Society, Hamilton, Ontario, August 1978); J. Woelfel and J. Saltiel, "Cognitive Processes as Motions in a Multidimensional Space," in *International and Intercultural Communication*, ed. F. Casmir (New York: Oxford University Press, 1978); Barnett, "Spatial Modeling of Social Networks."

19. J. Woelfel, R. Holmes, and D. L. Kincaid, "Rotation to Congruence for General Riemann Surfaces Under Theoretical Constraints" (Paper delivered at the annual meeting of the Intercultural Communication Association, Philadelphia, May 1979).

20. Woelfel and Fink, *The Galileo System*.

21 See J. Woelfel, J. Saltiel, R. McPhee, J. Danes, M. Cody, G. A. Barnett, and K. B. Serota, "Orthogonal Rotation to Theoretical Criteria: Comparison of Multidimensional Spaces" (Paper delivered at the annual meeting of the Mathematical Psychological Association, West Lafayette, IN, August 1975); Woelfel, "Metrical Measurement of Cultural Processes."

22. J. Woelfel, E. L. Fink, K. B. Serota, G. A. Barnett, R. Holmes, M. J. Cody, J. Saltiel, J. Marlier, and J. R. Gillham, *Galileo—A Program for Metric Multidimensional Scaling* (Honolulu: East-West Communication Institute, 1976).

23. The GALILEO$_{tm}$ computer program may be obtained for a small fee by writing George Barnett. It is currently available at over 20 universities.

24. G. A. Barnett, "Linguistic relativity: the role of the bilingual," in *Communication Yearbook 1*, ed. B. Ruben (New Brunswick, NJ: Transaction Books, 1977); G. A. Barnett, "Bilingual Semantic Organization: A Multidimensional Analysis," *Journal of Cross-Cultural Psychology* 8(1977): 315-30 (1977); McPhail and Barnett, *Broadcasting, Culture and Self.*

25. Wigand and Barnett, "Multidimensional Scaling of Cultural Processes."

26. Ibid.

27. Barnett and Woelfel, "On the Dimensionality of Psychological Processes."

28. D. Steward, "Communication and Innovation Amongst Farmers in Otago" (Ph.D. diss., Dunedin, New Zealand: University of Otago, 1979).

29. M. N. Adams, "Media Forum Impact on National Integration in a Rural Ivorien Community: A Cultural Approach Using the Multidimensional Scaling Method" (Ph.D. diss., Florida State University, 1978).

30. C. Fajardo, "Television and Sex Roles in the Philippines" (Paper delivered at Television and Sex Roles Workshop, East-West Communication Institute, Honolulu, July 1979).

31. H. S. Park "Television and Sex Roles in Korea" (Paper delivered at Television and Sex Roles Workshop, East-West Communication Institute, Honolulu, July 1979).

32. S. Maramatsu, "Television and Sex Roles in Japan" (Paper delivered at Television and Sex Roles Workshop, East-West Communication Institute, Honolulu, July 1979).

33. This section of the chapter is largely derived from Triffert (1968). For an indepth discussion of the elastic-solid model and an indepth derivation and explanation of these equations see Triffert (1968).

34. Equation 5.0 assumes that all groups contribute to the equilibrium culture in proportion to their population. It further assumes that unrestricted exchange of information occurs among the different cultures. That is, certain groups are not isolated by the social structure and that the mass media does not restrict the process of communication.

35. J. Woelfel and J. Saltiel, "Cognitive processes as motions in a multidimensional space," in *International and Intercultural Communication*, ed. F. Casmir (New York: Oxford University Press, 1978).

36. Barnett, "On the Nature of Synonyms."

37. Woelfel and Fink, *The Galileo System.*

38. Woelfel et al., "Orthogonal Rotation to Theoretical Criteria"; Woelfel, "Metric Measurement of Cultural Processes"; Woelfel et al., "Rotation to Congruence."

39. Woelfel and Fink, *The Galileo System.*

40. A. Koestler, *The Sleepwalkers* (New York: Grosset and Dunlap, 1963).

41. Woelfel and Fink, *The Galileo System.*

42. G. A. Barnett, K. B. Serota, and J. A. Taylor, "A Method for Political Communication Research" (Paper delivered at the annual meeting of the Association for Education in Journalism, San Diego, August 1974); G. A. Barnett, K. B. Serota and J. A. Taylor, "Campaign Communication and Attitude Change: A Multidimensional Analysis," *Human Communication Research* 2 (1976): 227-44; K. B. Serota, M. J. Cody, G. A. Barnett, and J. A. Taylor, "Precise Procedures for Optimizing Campaign Communication," in *Communication Yearbook 1*, ed. B. Ruben (New Brunswick, NJ: Transaction Books, 1977); G. A. Barnett, "A Multidimensional Analysis of the 1976 Presidential Campaign" (Paper delivered at the annual meeting of the International Communication Association, Chicago, April 1978).

43. Barnett, "Social System Homophily."

44. Barnett, "A Multidimensional Analysis of the 1976 Presidential Campaign."

45. Joseph Woelfel, personal correspondence.

46. G. A. Barnett, "The Diffusion of Complex Innovations" (Unpublished, East Lansing, Michigan State University, 1975); G. A. Barnett, "Association Model for Diffusion of Complex Innovations."

47. P. Doreian, "A Dynamic Model of Sino-Indian Relations" (Unpublished, University of Pittsburgh, 1979).

48. D. L. Kincaid, J. O. Yum, T. Woelfel, G. A. Barnett, "The Cultural Convergence of Korean Immigrants in Hawaii: An Empirical Test of a Mathematical Theory." *Quality and Quantity*, forthcoming.

11

Adaptive Intercultural Communication

HUBER W. ELLINGSWORTH • *University of Tulsa*

In a recent ICA *Yearbook* essay the author asserted that intercultural communication study as it had emerged between 1960 and 1976 was based on five major propositions, which were then stated and analyzed. A revised perspective was proposed, leading to the conclusion that cultural variability is present in almost all communication behavior and that scholarly concern for it might be better expressed through an expanded examination of cultural variables in interpersonal communication, rather than by the creation of a separate area of study.[1]

Publication of this somewhat iconoclastic view produced neither discernible public discussion nor observable alternation in the pattern of study, to judge from academic course descriptions, published research, and conference programs. Lack of response may be attributable to indifference, to passive acceptance or rejection, or more probably to the institutionalization that intercultural communication study has undergone during almost two decades. Radical change is unlikely so long as interest and support continue, yet few advocates appear satisfied with the current state of development. It is noteworthy that the field so far has been spearheaded by teaching, training, and conferences, with a relatively small body of clearly identifiable research, much of it descriptive or single variable in nature, and characterized by disparity in definition and methodology.[2] Publication of theories inductively derived from research has been even more limited, perhaps because of the fragmentary nature of the research base.[3] Yet activities such as theory building are clearly needed to focus the field and point up areas of agreement and disagreement among scholars. If research-derived theory is not yet very possible, an alternative is rational generation of theory in a form that is subject to empirical examination. This chapter is an attempt to specify a real-time, task-oriented dyadic theory of intercultural communication, which is perceived as interpersonal communication with some distinguishing characteristics.

METHODS AND PROCEDURES

A useful methodology of theory building is provided by Robert Dubin.[4] Dubin stresses the joint importance of rational and empirical contributions to theory construction and is concerned with both description and prediction to further the scientific goal of understanding. Dubin's methodology is complex and comprehensive, but an abstracting of key elements—units, laws, propositions, and system state—provides a suitable basis for producing a focused theory of adaptive intercultural communication.

In Dubin's system the basic element is the *unit,* "a property of a thing." A unit is a repeated event or behavior capable of being assigned a value, which at a given time ranges from absent to present in some degree, or can be described as changed or unchanged. At least two units are necessary for a theory, and the chosen number will depend on the complexity of the system being theorized about. Units are connected by *laws of interaction* specifying how the units are related. Laws are not predictive, but arbitrarily describe the ongoing relationships of units. Within these relationships occur possibilities for predictive, correlative combinations of unit values relationships labeled "more," "less," and "the same." Thus, propositions predict "the more . . . the less," "the less . . . the more," "the less . . . the same," and so on. Because it is not situation-based, a proposition is not directly testable by empirical methods, but can be analyzed into two or more testable hypotheses phrased according to the problem being investigated.

One additional concept, *system state,* is employed to describe the constellation of unit values as they persist at a particular time. Given this abridged apparatus of theory building, the other requisite is a statement defining and describing the system to which the concepts are to be applied.

System Definitions

A number of technical terms are employed that are first defined and then presented in the system description:

(1) *Foreignness* is a concept central to the identification of intercultural interaction. It is the initial perception by one participant that the other is from a background different from his or hers, based on superficial observation of physical appearance, name, manner of speaking, dress or adornment, and other external tokens of cultural identity. Interaction

will reinforce or mitigate the initial perception of degree of foreignness. The term is entirely relative and nonprejudicial. It focuses on one person's perception of the other as culturally different.

(2) *Communication style* describes the individual's accustomed behavior in symbolic interaction, including verbal pattern (ranging from voice quality, vocal volume, and articulation through word choice and statement structure to accustomed use of a particular dialect or language) and nonverbal behavior (kinesic and proxemic mode and contact rituals).

(3) *Beliefs* in this description are defined by Milton Rokeach as "any simple proposition, conscious or unconscious, inferred from what a person says or does, capable of being preceded by the phrase 'I believe that. . . . ' "[5] Cognitive beliefs represent a person's knowledge and the degree of agreement or disagreement with that knowledge. Affective beliefs underlie degree of arousal about an object or concept. Behavioral beliefs predispose to action. The three are inseparable and interactive. As Rokeach describes it, the belief system is the total cognitive universe of a person's beliefs about the social world and his or her self.

In the description being presented, beliefs are asserted to have a cultural base growing out of nurture and conditioning.[6] It is not assumed that each person from a particular culture has identical beliefs, but rather that similarity of beliefs is one of the things shared by members of a culture. When individuals from different cultures interact, they may become aware that some of the beliefs invoked by the other are drawn from a culture-based belief system different from their own and are not simply a matter of individual difference.

(4) *Adaptive behavior* is an attempt to accommodate to the perceived foreignness of the other participant, both through altering communication style and by adjusting to invoked difference in belief. Some attempts at adaptation will be regarded by the other as complimentary and supportive and are labeled "functional." Others may be perceived as gauche, compromising, or even insulting, and are nonfunctional.[7]

(5) *Participants* are those who join in a task-oriented dyad. Because the encounter is not casual or fortuitous, one individual will have been the initiator of the contact and the other the respondent.

(6) *Intercultural communication* must be defined formally and also operationally with enough detail to identify cases for study. A simple and useful starting point is: "An interpersonal encounter may be designated as intercultural when the participants act as though they believe it is intercultural." Using prior accustomed intracultural communication style as a baseline, if a participant now alters communication style slightly (such as speaking more loudly and clearly) to markedly (such as switching to another dialect or language) he or she is indicating that the other individual appears "foreign" and that some adjustment in accustomed style is necessary in order for contact to be made. If the other also shows efforts at adaptive behavior, then the necessary condition for initiation of intercultural communication has occurred. Descriptive research is

needed to determine what it is that cues adaptive behavior and the extent to which cueing is normative or idiosyncratic. If cueing can be specified, then the more sophisticated question occurs of whether perceived degree of foreignness is correlated with magnitude of adaptive behavior. With this discussion, the definition may be more precisely stated as: "An interpersonal encounter is intercultural while the participants are undertaking adaptive behavior based on their estimates of the foreignness of the other." If mutual adaptive behavior persists during the real-time encounter, then the interaction is classifiable as intercultural. If the participants discover that they share a communication style that is not foreign to either, the situation will not become intercultural except as culture-based differences in belief arise and are adapted to. If adaptation in style and beliefs is needed, but one or both cease to make the effort, the situation is no longer within the bounds of intercultural communication.

System Description

The key elements of an interpersonal communication system are participants, setting, purpose, process, and outcomes. These are the "things," in Dubin's terms, from which events arise and can be specified as units. It is particular characteristics of these things in some situations that make them potentially intercultural.

Participants. An individual can only be foreign relative to someone else. The two must appear to one another as sufficiently different for a mutual cueing of foreignness. In addition, the participants will share some linguistic code at a level sufficient to make symbolic interaction possible. The definition does not include translated or mediated situations, which require their own description and theory. The effects of using a shared language, which is primary to one and secondary or tertiary to the other, will be discussed as part of the setting.

While such things as appearance and manner of speaking are observable tokens of cultural identity, intercultural communication is clearly more than a mutual alteration of style, because of the possibility of misunderstanding and disagreement arising from latent belief systems of the participants. If purposeful interpersonal communication is the acknowledgment of similarities and differences, and the symbolic negotiation of differences related to the agenda of purposes, the same is also true of intercultural contacts. But in the latter case, predictability is sharply lessened when culture-based beliefs are invoked. Sources of ambiguity include possible erroneous identification of the kind of foreigner, incomplete or inaccurate knowledge of the cultural stereotype with which the other has been correctly identified, and the extent to which the individual actually conforms to the cultural stereotype. When the association is ongoing, there is a repeated opportunity for learning, and uncertainty about the other's style and beliefs will decline. The description presented here focuses on first-time encounters, which are less predictable and whose outcomes determine in part whether contact will be renewed. With a first-time encounter, adaptation will include a sensitive verbal probing of beliefs related to task or purpose to identify areas of commonality and disagreement before they become manifest problems.

To summarize the discussion of participants, the intercultural system is composed of two persons, mutually perceptable as foreign, whose communication styles signal underlying belief systems drawn from differing cultures.

Setting. Participants in intercultural communication come together in an environment that is both physical and social. Ideally they would meet as true peers, devoid of social role differences and power inequity, and at cultural parity to achieve mutually developed equitable purposes. The contact would happen in a location neutral to both and be conducted in a nonfirst language. If such settings do occur, they are probably rare enough not to be useful as a basis for theory. Most cases of intercultural communication occur in settings that contribute to inequity between participants, growing out of social role differences, language of choice, perceived power and influence, and locale. Disparity will probably be present when the language of choice is primary to one and secondary or tertiary to the other, and when one is physically on home ground and the other is a visitor. The net effect of disparities will tip the balance of the relationship from equity toward hierarchy and influence both the process and its outcomes.

Purpose. This theory is about purpose-related encounters, rather than fortuitous or casual encounters. Consequently, purpose exists for one or both participants before the encounter. The fact of cultural or national difference will often be a factor in initiating the encounter. Purposes arise from needs for information, cooperation, participation, or agreement in such areas as commerce, manufacturing, defense, education, science, technology, politics, agriculture, medicine, the arts, or scholarly research. As with interpersonal communication generally, the initiator will have in mind a purpose for seeking contact and the respondent a reason for agreeing to participate. In intercultural communication, purpose and setting are interactive elements. If the initiator has an advantage in status or the potential for exercising power, he or she may be able to summon the other, state his or her purpose as a directive, and thus place the burden of adaptation on the respondent. If a potential respondent has a resource badly needed by the initiator, the respondent is in a power position and may impose the major obligation of adaptation on the initiator. If each has something the other needs, if their goals are separate and noncontradictory, or if there is a commonality of purpose that must be jointly pursued, adaptive responsibility will approach parity, and the most manifest cases of intercultural communication will occur.

Process. The process (or in Dubin's term, the system state at any particular time) of intercultural communication centers around adaptation. When things are going well—when style adaptation is functional and work is proceeding—latent belief differences are less likely to be manifest. Nonfunctional style adaptations may be followed by the invocation of belief-based disagreement. Another dynamic dimension of the system state is the use of communication strategies growing out of relative congruence of purpose. When the parties agree that their interests are mutual or noncontradictory, cooperative strategies of work and adaptation will appear. When one needs somethng the other is reluctant to supply, persuasive strategies will appear, accompanied by an adaptation shift to the persuader. When there is considerable disparity in status or power, the strategy may become coercive and the burden of adaptation may shift from the stronger to the weaker to the point that intercultural communication is no longer occurring.

Outcomes. Interpersonal communication has both purposeful and personal outcomes. Some are related to the achievement, modification, or thwarting of original purposes, and some to the effect of the experience on the participants. In intercultural communication the latter has special dimensions. Participants have been responding not only to the other as an individual, but also to prior beliefs about what that group of foreigners is like. Thus an important outcome will be reinforcement or modification of prior cultural stereotypes and this learning will become a part of the cognitive resources for future encounters. Whether the learning later proves to be functional or nonfunctional will depend on the extent to which the next such foreigner conforms to the stereotype. Thus experience does not necessarily increase competence in intercultural communication, though it has the potential for doing so. Another important outcome of intercultural interaction is self-examination. Adaptation involves confronting not only the other, but also one's self. In the process, the personal cultural stereotype is reinforced or modified, and this learning also becomes a part of the background of future intercultural encounters.

Purposeful outcomes where cultural difference is present do not differ significantly from interpersonal ones in general, but their achievement may require more time and energy because of the requirement for adaptive behavior.

THEORY DEVELOPMENT

The theoretic model presented here consists of eight units, eight laws of interaction, and ten propositions. The units, or properties of things, are drawn from the prior description of things labeled participants, purposes, setting, process, and outcomes. Units are linked by laws of interaction from which propositions are derived.

Units

Participant-Related Units. The properties of individual participant behavior specified as units are adaptation of communication style and adaptation to invoked culture-based beliefs of the other.

Purpose-Related Units. Two of these are dyadic: mutual purpose and noncontradictory purposes. Two are individual: persuasive purpose and coercive purpose.

Process-Related Unit. This is, in Dubin's term, a collective unit encompassing the values of adaptation, purpose, and setting at any given time and thus monitoring the state of the system, as well as examining whether or how the system has changed over time.

Outcome-Related Unit. This is a unit of change in the individual culture-based belief system as a consequence of adaptation to the foreignness of another.

Laws of Interaction

The purpose of laws is to state the ongoing relationships by which units affect one another. While more than eight are possible, the following specify the major relationships:

(1) Adaptation of communication style affects achievement of purpose.

(2) Adaptation of communication style affects invocation of culture-based belief differences.

(3) The burden of adaptive behavior is distributed relative to the nature of individual and dyadic purposes.

(4) The burden of adaptive behavior is affected by the extent to which setting favors one or the other participant.

(5) Individual strategy is affected by relative equity, noncontradiction, or inequity of purpose.

(6) The burden of adaptive behavior is affected by relative equity or inequity of status or power.

(7) Individual strategy is affected by relative equity or inequity of the setting.

(8) Amount of change in the culture-based values of participants is relative to the amount of adaptive behavior engaged in.

Propositions

Specification of eight units and eight laws of interaction logically provides for deriving a large number of propositions. The following list is not exhaustive, but identifies the major possibilities:

(1) An increase in functional communication style adaptation will be accompanied by accelerated progress toward task completion.

(2) A shift toward equity in adaptation will accelerate progress toward completion of mutually rewarding tasks.

(3) When nonfunctional adaptive behavior occurs, it will be followed by invocation of culture-based belief differences.

(4) When nonfunctional adaptive behavior occurs, rate of progress toward task completion will be slowed.

(5) When participants share a purpose requiring equitable cooperation, they will display equity in communication style adaptation.

(6) When a participant invokes a persuasive strategy, he or she will then increase efforts at communication-style adaptation.

(7) When the setting favors one participant, the less-favored will display more adaptive behavior than the more-favored.

(8) When the initiator of a contact has an advantage in status and/or power, the respondent will assume the greater burden of adaptive behavior.

(9) When the respondent has an advantage in potential power or control, the initiator will assume the greater burden of adaptive behavior.

(10) The more functional adaptive behavior an individual engages in, the more change will occur in his or her culture-based beliefs.

SUMMARY

In an attempt to contribute to focus and development, I have presented a rationally derived, task-oriented dyadic theory based on Dubin's methodology. Intercultural communication is viewed as occurring under conditions often characterized by disparity of purpose, inequality in status and power, and advantage related to setting. Mutual adaptation of communication style is proposed as the necessary condition for intercultural communication to occur and continue. When equity is not present, the burden of adaptation is predicted to shift toward the less advantaged. When equity is present, adaptive behavior will be shared. The theory also predicts that adaptation will result in alteration of the individual's culture-based beliefs.

DISCUSSION

It may be validly argued that limitations imposed on the adaptive theory exclude some of what is normally regarded as intercultural communication. Among the interactions that fall outside the parameters are casual, fortuitous, and recreational encounters. These are excluded because they are hard to simulate under controlled conditions and difficult to observe empirically in natural settings. Also excluded are language-translated interchanges in formal settings, which are observable, but have a different dynamic because the presence of the translator screens or excludes some of the adaptation that occurs in two-person systems. Group interactions are not included because of the complexities of adaptation, especially in multicultural groups. Perhaps the most important exclusion is of "third-culture" interactions.[8] In this perspective, adaptation is accomplished at the affective, rather than behavioral, level by developing an attitudinal frame of reference for dealing with persons from other cultures. The third-culture concept has been praised since its publication in 1963, but development of its rich possibilities is still limited. Until a third-culture theory of effects is better developed, a behavioral theory of adaptation at least offers a testable and trainable alternative.

With its self-imposed limitations, the proposed adaptive theory provides focus, relative simplicity, refutability, and applicability to a wide variety of task-oriented encounters.

NOTES

1. Huber W. Ellingsworth, "Conceptualizing Intercultural Communication," in *Communication Yearbook 1*, ed. Brent Ruben (New Brunswick, NJ: Transaction Books, 1977), pp. 99-106.

2. Tulsi Saral, "Intercultural Communication Theory and Research: An Overview," in Ruben, *Communication Yearbook 1*, pp. 389-95.

3. In a comprehensive current survey of communication theory, Stephen W. Littlejohn, *Theories of Human Communication* (Columbus, OH: Charles E. Merrill, 1978) makes no reference to the existence of intercultural communication theory. Yet some theorizing has been undertaken, for example, William B. Gudykunst, Richard L. Wiseman, and Mitchell R. Hammer, "Determinants of the Sojourner's Attitudinal Satisfaction: A Path Model," in Ruben, *Communication Yearbook 1*, pp. 415-25. This article is a sophisticated, theory-related investigation of sojourner attitudes.

4. Robert Dubin, *Theory-Building* (New York: Free Press, 1969).

5. Milton Rokeach, *Beliefs, Attitudes and Values: A Theory of Organization and Change* (San Francisco: Jossey-Bass, 1969), pp. 121-25.

6. Milton Rokeach, *The Nature of Human Values* (New York: Free Press, 1973).

7. The author's experience in task-related contact with a large number of foreign sojourners in the United States and also as a foreign sojourner in Latin America and Southeast Asia leads to the conclusion that sincere efforts at adaptation are vital, but that there is not high predictability that they will prove functional. His use of inelegant but workable host-country language was often countered by requests to proceed in English, even when the host's competence in it was even more limited. Some persons perceived the visitor's initiative in using their language as a perjorative reflection on their competence in English; still others were pleased at the adaptive effort. Whether at home or abroad, the desire to practice a secondary language appears widespread. The most consistently appreciated social adaptation was the sojourner's acceptance and enjoyment of local food and drink. The most challenging adaptation was consumption of a *balut*, or fertile duck egg just short of hatching. The hosts believed that only a "true Filipino" could eat and enjoy *balut*. Another adaptation perceived as functional has been acknowledged of and expression of interest in historical and cultural sites not known as obvious tourist attractions.

8. For what is generally regarded as the original presentation of the third-culture concept see John Useem et al., "Man in the Middle of the Third Culture," *Human Organization* 22 (1963): 169-79. Evidence that it is still regarded as a viable idea is found in Gudykunst, Wiseman, and Hammer, "Determinants of the Sojourner's Attitudinal Satisfaction."

12

The Roots of Conflict
A Theory and Typology

DENNIS W. TAFOYA • University of Massachusetts

The relationship between academe and the public is not linear. For example, one communication-related product of the 1960s was the public's increased desire to expand their communication effectiveness beyond the traditional public speaking context; there appeared a need to communicate more effectively with each other on a face-to-face or interpersonal level.

Various disciplines moved to meet this need by developing courses and areas of study for the individual, groups, organizations, or cultures and by writing papers or designing studies with direct appeal and utility. Academe's response proved fruitful, for the public not only accepted and encouraged further publication and study of relevant materials and issues, but incorporated and/or created vocabulary to describe what was happening (relating, identifying), or why it did not happen (a generation gap or communication breakdown).

Innovation seldom has a single effect and two problems developed with communication researchers' and the lay public's attempts to describe communication phenomena. The first problem dealt with accuracy. Communication researchers were not simply trying to answer questions or provide solutions; they were also offering a new way to view problems and difficulties associated with human interaction; they were interested in educating an interested public that communication is best viewed as a process and not as a linear event.[1] Gibb's article on "defensive communication" neatly illustrates this twofold—information with education—approach in his introduction:

> One way to understand communication is to view it as a people process rather than as a language process. If one is to make fundamental improvement in communication, he must make changes in interpersonal relationships. One possible type of alteration—and the one with which this paper is concerned—is that of reducing the degree of defensiveness.[2]

AUTHOR'S NOTE: *I would like to thank Robert Norton and Bill Gudykunst for comments on earlier drafts of this chapter.*

The link apparently did not set. Ten years later Smith worked to clarify the problem associated with the use of terms and vocabularies designed for convenience and not accuracy. In his paper, "The Fallacy of the Communication Breakdown," he argued that the use of at least one convenient term, communication breakdown, was not "consonant with the view of communication as a process."[3] "This term," wrote Smith,

> perhaps more than any other, reflects a view of communication as a directional, linear event that may break down. The very word breakdown implies a disruption or a malfunctioning of an element or part of a mechanical system. . . . While the term communication breakdown has been useful in populating a communication-oriented approach to the study of speech in the classroom, the term is highly misleading. Students who are introduced to the concept equip themselves to go into the world to locate communication breakdowns, repair them, and leave the world a better place.[4]

Determining whether the development and use of such terms was initiated in academe or by the public as a means for describing phenomena or dealing with jargon is not important. Smith's observation that misconceptions may arise from the indiscriminant use of such terms seems valid. Yet the terms were not popularized without reason. They did and still do fill the need to describe or account for the fact that most individuals have recognized a difficulty in, or reluctance to engage, in conversation with another person or group of people.

Heider[5] claimed that people try to account for human behavior by attributing causality to another's behavior. According to Heider, the individual seeking to account for another's behavior does so by isolating and determining the strengths associated with internal (person-specific) or external (enviromentally specific) causes. But what do these internal or external causes look like and how are they percieved by the individual?

Attempting to answer those and related questions illustrates a second problem associated with attempts to define elements interfering with communication effectiveness—lack of standardization. We have already illustrated typical conventional terms and phrases used to describe an inhibited process, but as Smith pointed out, attempts to describe the ideal communication process are "incomplete, inaccurate, and contradictory."[6] The following typologies illustrate Smith's position. They evolved over a twenty-year period. They are important to present here for they reflect the attempts of researchers—generally semanticists and psychologists—to classify and categorize sources of communication "breakdown."

EARLY TYPOLOGIES OF
COMMUNICATION BREAKDOWNS

The Semanticists

Early semanticists tended to view humanity's interaction with its environment as dependent upon its ability to reason from the specific to the general. This process, abstraction, is defined as the moving "from the infinite numbers of submicroscopic characteristics of the event [to] a large but finite number of macroscopic characteristics."[7] It is also around this process that the first typology described communication difficulties. Johnson[8] reasoned that

> There is something to be gained by high-lighting the fact that what is common to the various aspects of communication, to speaking, writing, listening, and reading is to be seen precisely in the process of abstracting. This means that the defects and inefficiencies that so often affect these language functions are to be understood to an important degree as disorders of abstraction.[9]

Johnson saw the "disorders of abstraction" as falling, "rather definitely," into three categories:

(1) Disorders of abstracting, in the speaker and in the listener (or writer or reader);
(2) Disorders of overt expression (speech defects and impaired bodily action due to paralyses, etc.); and
(3) Disorders of sensory reception (mainly visual deficiency and hearing loss).[10]

As is generally apparent, the emphasis of this schema is on the physical or mechanical aspects of human communication. Additionally, the focus is more specific to the individual rather than the dyadic or multipersonal setting. Finally, no psychological items are included nor is there an effort to discuss the relationship between items included and possible psychological factors related to them, as in the case of stuttering, for example. Given the focus on the abstraction process, the noninclusion of the above dimensions is defensible. However, failure to include these dimensions does tend to limit the scope and potential usefulness of the typology.

Later typologies, as disciplines broadened their perspectives, generally remedied these deficiencies. By the 1960s, for example, Hayakawa,[11] described semantics as "an intellectual method to enable us to apply scientific ways of thinking to everyday life, to problems of social interaction, to problems of decision in practical affairs, as well to the critical analysis of problems in science scholarship."[12]

Nearly ten years earlier Irving Lee[13] called for a multidisciplinary approach to the application and study of communication. Lee's goal was specific. He wanted a "joint consideration of the barriers and breakdowns in the very process of communication itself."

Lee saw barriers,[14] breakdowns,[15] and obstacles[16] as synonymous terms describing the situation that "comes not from a misunderstanding of what was said but from a failure to understand how another could with good reason say that."[17] Yet Lee does not offer a typology descriptive of his definition of communication breakdown.

Rather, he developed a "catalogue of expressions of dissent" that was both interpersonal and psychological in content. More important, it represents an exploration of a potential communication barrier—disagreement. The five patterns appearing most frequently as expressions of dissent for Lee were

(1) The inquiring-investigative attitude, in which one states his positions and shows that he is willing to listen some more;

(2) The air of incredulity, in which the speaker does not invite further explanation but in which he doesn't refuse it either;

(3) The inclination to laughter, in which one lets everybody know in a good-natured manner that what the other person proposes just doesn't deserve mature consideration;

(4) The expression of suspicion or distrust, in which we hear a note of resentment; and

(5) The mood of dismissal, in which a man makes it clear that he wishes to go no farther, to talk no more about something which is to him impossible, unthinkable, wrong, unnecessary, or just plain out of the question.[18]

Lee's work makes a shift from the more scientific approach of the general semanticist to that of current communication theorist. His typology differs most from Johnson's in that its scope includes possible psychological characteristics and that Lee, neither in the typology nor in his definition, considers possible physical barriers or obstacles to communication.

The Psychologists

The shift in emphasis from the physical to the more psychological may have been influenced in part by changing attitudes regarding the value of interdisciplinary approaches to questions and also by general studies and reports then being published in psychology. By the early 1950s the discipline of social psychology was generally established and its investigation of personality, motivation, and perception was influencing many academic areas, including communication. The earlier typologies developed by the social psychologists were similar in perspective to early typologies of the semanticists. That is, they tended to be narrower in scope than those of later periods. Katz's[19] typology, published a year after Johnson's, is illustrative of the thinking of some early psychologists. He began his article by stating: "Physical barriers to communication are rapidly disappearing, but the psychological obstacles remain."[20]

Like the general semanticists, Katz was principally concerned with the nature of language as a contributor of barriers or obstacles to communication. He recognized the semanticists as contributing "to exposing the inaccuracies and weakness in language," but went on to point out that the imperfection of language is not due solely to the weakness of its representational quality. "Language as it exists is not the product of the scientist trying an exact set of symbols; it is the product of the arena of everyday life, in which people are concerned with expressing their emotional and psychological wants."[21] Further, he felt that the psychological nature of language, its "emotional loadings, polar words, and fictitious concepts," were the "background against which more specific difficulties in communication can be understood."[22]

Katz outlined the following "specific obstacles" to communication between people:

(1) the failure to refer language to experience and reality;
(2) the inability to transcend personal experience in intergroup communication;
(3) stereotypes: the assimilation of material to familiar frames of reference; and
(4) the confusion of percept and concept: reification and personification.[23]

As with others discussed, Katz omits potential categories for the study of communication interaction—in this case the possibility of physical characteristics. Similarly, Ruesch[24] generally does not include physical characteristics in his typology of communication disorders, but does view them as critical in his discussion of "conditions which interfere with successful communication." Ruesch stated that

conditions which interfere with successful communication may be divided into two groups: those located within the individual and determined by his physical and psychological structure, and those beyond an individual's control and related to interference with the free flow of messages. The later disturbance is located between people, and the participants per se may be healthy people who are capable of rational behavior. But because they cannot exchange messages with each other—for example, because of language difficulties—then an interpersonal or group disturbance of communication develops.[25]

Ruesch's typology contains twelve items; it is the largest typology developed. Threatening content and the timing of messages, information overload, and "the value judgment as a disruptive reply" are among the items in this group.[26] Despite the fact that physical factors are among the conditions that interfere with successful communication as defined, they do not appear in the typology. The general focus of the items is on the nature of the message vis-à-vis the participants. Three years later, Haney,[27] a professor of business and former student of Lee, offered five other barriers that had the same, or a similar, orientation to Ruesch's. This list included the inference-observation confusion, allness, indiscrimination, polarization, and intensional orientation. Finally, Parry,[28] acknowledging that "there is no suggestion that the headings [of his typology] represent the outcome of systematic research or statistical analysis,"[29] provides us with the last of the typologies to be reviewed. This typology includes

(1) limitations of a receiver's capacity;
(2) distraction,
(3) the unstated assumption,
(4) incompatability of schemes,
(5) intrusion of unconscious or partly conscious mechanisms,
(6) confused presentation, and
(7) the absence of communication facilities.[30]

Since Parry, no other typologies have been developed in either communication or psychology discussing the problems of communication between individuals. The typologies discussed have developed three general categories that may describe difficulties in human communication interaction—physical, psychological, and those related to message content. None of the authors, however, tested their conclusions.

More recent discussions of the problems or interferences with communication between individuals have focused on specific topics rather than attempted to develop large categories or typologies. Rogers[31] concluded that "the defensive exaggerations, the lies, the 'false fronts' . . . characterize almost every failure in communication."[32]

Roethlisberger[33] felt that the "difference of background, experience, and motivation were the chief blocks to communication."[34]

Other discussions of specific variables or concepts exist that, more often than not, were only labeled as barriers by the editors of books or journals seeking to fill a particular section on barriers to interpersonal communication[35] or the like. These singular, barrier-oriented papers covered such concepts as deception,[36] defensive behavior,[37] proxemics,[38] and physical attractiveness or physical stigmas,[39] among others.

EXPLICATION OF A THEORY

The above review generates several conclusions regarding interest in a given individual's ability to enter into, or carry on, verbal interactions with another. The interest of both lay and professional quarters has provided a variety of research on the subject. Unfortunately, one perplexing development accompanying this interest is that a good deal of confusion has developed over some of the more simple issues associated with the subject. The terms "barriers," "obstacles," and "hindrances" are among those terms used to account for communication breakdown or failures to communicate.

Little seems immediately obvious about these terms save that their use as labels is arrived at by convention rather than fixed by rule. The subtleties associated with these and related terms merit attention for the fact that these terms, which are a part of the vernacular for a wide portion of society, reflect both interest in and a need for information about those instances where, despite the imprecision of the notion, communication does break down. Smith's article, too, is interesting, for that article hits or misses the mark depending on one's point of view. Few current communication researchers would argue that communication is not a process, is not ongoing and dynamic, but linear. However, few would disagree that there are those times when something seems to happen—something seems to break down.

The desire of the public and of academe alike to describe, either metaphorically or literally, and understand this element of the communication process has provided valuable motivation to those preparing the typologies discussed. In fact, a second conclusion drawn from this review is that interest in the subject is wide ranging. The typologies reviewed chiefly reflect two disciplines, communication and psychology, but overall interest in the subject is evidenced by the many single articles reviewed representing additional areas (e.g., sociology) or fields of an area (e.g., clinical psychology or pathology) interested in accounting for, to use Ruesch's phraseology, "conditions which interfere with successful communication."

The terms "barriers," "obstacles," "hindrances," and "noise" are among the aphorisms used by these authors to account for or describe the distracting stimuli associated with the communication process. Yet descriptions alone are insufficient foundations when one seeks to document what are or are not barriers, or to produce a theory useful in accounting for or linking various particular barriers. Accomplishing these goals demands an empirically valid typology that specifies the domain of barriers and nonbarriers to interpersonal communication.

One particularly noteworthy conclusion to be derived after reviewing these materials is that while some researchers specifically strive to or even do offer a typology, none has actually measured or tested items defining the typology. A validated typology is particularly useful to researchers and clinicians, for in addition to gaining the ability to specify accurately what are and are not barriers, a typology aids theory development in that such typologies are based on broad and comprehensive studies of the general interrelationship among specific variables and categories of variables. Here, again, clarification and insight into the particular domain studied are achieved. More important, however, by gaining an understanding of the relationships, in this instance among conditions interfering with successful communication, one begins to conceptualize the operation of the conditions in everyday affairs and to move from mere classification to description.

This study has three objectives. First, it outlines a theory illustrating general patterns or uniformities particular to interpersonal conflict. This theory presents and examines a series of assumptions regarding the role of perceived barriers, obstacles, or the like in heightening dissonance between and among individuals. In doing so the theory establishes a point of departure for future investigations.

A second objective of the study is to develop a typology of barriers to interpersonal communication. Combined with the theory outlined, this typology stands to benefit those individuals concerned with the study of human interaction. The chief contribution of a typology rests with its ability to define the general domain of barriers and to specify the interrelationships among categories or groups of barriers. Thus, those professionals whose occupation is, by definition, to assist individuals in understanding themselves and their interactions with others, are likely to see such a typology as a useful tool for use when defining sources of communication-related problems encountered in actual practices.

The final objective of this chapter is to test elements of both the offered theory and typology in two instances: one specific to cross-cultural situations and the second across types of relationships. These studies allow for a test of both theory and typology—a means of exploring underlying relationships among different barriers experienced by individuals—and an opportunity to focus study on particular barriers across a variety of types of relationships.

The foundation of a theory describing the barriers of interpersonal communication is laid out in the remainder of this section. The focus of this portion of the chapter will (1) stipulate a general definition of the term "barrier"; (2) via a selected review of the literature, outline a theoretical description of the nature of barriers; and (3) conclude with an operational definition for use in the studies that follow.

Stipulative Definitions

A barrier to interpersonal communication is anything that prevents, restricts, or impedes the conveyance of meaning, by words or gestures, between two or more persons in a social setting. The key elements of this definition are the terms "barrier" and "interpersonal communication."

The *Oxford English Dictionary*,[40] English and English,[41] and Hayakawa[42] each provide pertinent perspectives on the definition of the term "barrier." These definitions are:

> Anything immaterial that stops advance, hostile or friendly, that defends from attack, prevents intercourse or union, or keeps separate and apart.[43]

> In psychology the term is used metaphorically for anything that restricts or impedes action. It may be a social obstacle, such as the scorn of associates or the threat of punishment. It may be a literal physical obstacle, such as a fence, or a physical obstacle such as rain or heat. Or, the barrier may be some internalized hindrance—a conflict, a moral scruple, a fear of failure. It is thus a very general term, though all these usages seem congruous with each other.[44]

> An obstacle is something that one must either remove or go around before being able to proceed. A barrier is an obstacle or obstruction that temporarily impedes progress, but is not necessarily impassable. A hurdle is a barrier that one must surmount if one is to continue. Hurdle usually suggests challenge and a good probability of success.[45]

From these definitions we are able to identify three essential qualities of a barrier: scope, intensity, and dimensionality.

Scope refers to the boundaries of the domain encompassing all barriers. Based on the above definitions, the scope of a barrier may range from the *Oxford English Dictionary's* "anything immaterial" to the Englishs' four categories: the literally physical, the physical, the social, and the internalized. Scope delineates sufficient, but not necessary, components of barriers. The essence of a barrier is determined by intensity.

Intensity, or the nature of X, is that quality with which X becomes, or becomes viewed as, a barrier, and without which X is viewed as a nonbarrier.

The Oxford definition is the most rigorous in specifying the intensity of a barrier: A barrier is anything that "stops," "prevents," or "keeps separate or apart." English and English are more moderate in their description of a barrier as something that "restricts or impedes." Finally, Hayakawa is the most flexible in qualifying a barrier as something that "temporarily impedes."

Given the possible range of barriers, each of these three distinctions is equally acceptable. Thus, when speaking of the intensity of barriers, intensity may be defined as the quality of X that temporarily impedes, restricts, stops, or prevents communication between at least two individuals.

In the interpersonal setting, that is, action between two or more persons, dimension defines the origin of barriers. In this sense, a barrier is said to be intra- or interpersonal in origin; that is, a barrier is a product of either an individual participant in the communication setting, or of the interaction itself of the participants in the communication setting. English and English, for example, cite the "scorn of associates or the threat of punishment" as a social or interpersonal barrier and the "fear of failure" as an illustration of an "internalized" or intrapersonal barrier. The interrelationship of these three characteristics might best be illustrated as a triangle.

The triangle represents the domain or scope of barriers to interpersonal communication to the extent that we might expect there to be fewer highly intense barriers in proportion to the entire domain. The highly intense barriers occupy the top of the triangle and, correspondingly, the moderately intense the middle, and the low intensity barriers the base. The entire triangle might be divided by the dimensionality of the barriers into intra- and interpersonal barriers.

Interpersonal communication is stipulated as the conveyance of meaning, by words or gestures, between two or more persons in a social setting. The limits of interpersonal communication are defined to include the following: congruent meaning, either literal or figurative; verbal or nonverbal acts of expression; persons in face-to-face encounters; and nonformal situations.

EMERGENT DEFINITIONS

The following section clarifies the definition of barriers to interpersonal communication by reviewing pertinent literature. Specifically, this section provides a general idea of factors contributing to interpersonal conflict.

The structure of the literature review is guided by the general visibility or apparent quality certain factors thought to contribute to conflict or dissonance possess. That is, certain barriers are harder to screen or mask when displayed in primary or secondary groups[46] than are private barriers. Aggression, anger, hostility, or obesity are examples of more publicly visible barriers than are dishonesty, depression, or negativism. Overall, this notion is based on the fact that the control of some barriers is beyond the power of the individual, whereas other factors may be conveniently masked while the individual is in the presence of others. The extent to which control may be exercised is a function of both the individual and the barrier. Additionally, control may be described in terms of degrees of control or response and, in this respect, such control can be linked to intensity as defined above. Finally, the locus of a barrier, whether in the primary or secondary group, does not detract from its impact as a barrier (save the fact that members of a primary group, because of their attachment or relationship to the individual, may be more understanding or tolerant of the individual).

Public Barriers

Rothenberg[47] observed a direct relationship between aggression and anger, hostility, hate, and violence. Additionally, he draws a tangential relationship between aggression and depression, hysteria, homosexuality, dependency, and its general role "in marital problems [where] we unearth distorted patterns of communication."[48] The general position of the literature regarding aggression as a possible barrier, however, depends largely upon which theory one chooses to accept as explaining the role of aggression in human affairs.

Freud,[49] Lorenz,[50] Ardrey,[51] Storr,[52] and Morris[53] argue that aggression is an instinct and therefore inborn. More generally, Sullivan,[54] Becker,[55] and Lidz[56] presumed that aggression was a derivative of anxiety and thus a factor more closely tied to culture. Berkowitz[57] and Dollard et al.[58] felt that aggression was a response to frustration, pain, and threat and therefore learned in the course of human development. Most recently, Bandura's[59] research on the imitative nature of individuals has done much to push this final assumption to the forefront in academic and social thought. The role of aggression and related variables, as studied through these theories, focuses on the individual per se, rather than on the role of the individual directly interaction in social relationships. Thus, in defining the role of aggression as a barrier vis-à-vis the individual, many researchers have been unable to provide documentation for their own particular theories outside the laboratory. For example, optimistic evidence suggesting that "pain cues" displayed by an attacked person inhibited further aggression[60] were only confounded with replication and further study.[61]

It is obvious that the possible barriers mentioned above exist in interpersonal relationships, but a pattern of operation of these barriers in the interpersonal setting is not so readily discernible. Typical of this situation are the studies that attempt to review the relationship between rate of speech and anxiety and anger. Kanfer[62] and Kasl,[63] for instance, find that rate of speech increases with anxiety and anger. Feldstein and Jaffee,[64] however, find the opposite to be true. Likewise, Fairbanks and Hoaglin[65] determine that subjects with a moderate rate of speech were perceived as more angry than fast or slow speakers, but Lalljee and Williams[66] conclude the opposite.

Argyle describes the general nature of aggression as follows:

> Aggression is not a drive that draws people together in social situations, but it is a drive that has a great effect on social behavior. When aroused it leads a person to harm people either physically, verbally, or in other ways. There are considerable variations between people and between cultures, in the amount of aggression that they display. Most of the social drives vary in strength between cultures, but this is particularly true of aggression—as is shown, for example, by the variation in murder rates in different areas.[67]

Furthermore, Buss points out that there are different forms of aggression: (1) physical, which includes the aggression in prejudice (e.g., race riots or lynchings); (2) verbal, as in threats or name-calling; or (3) indirect aggression, as in discrimination.[68] Finally, in addition to the fact that aggression may be perceived as a defensive tactic or as a form of hostility, aggression or aggressiveness may also be viewed as a necessary and socially acceptable means of achieving success or goals within this society.[69] Thus, while aggression, as an example, may be linked in theory with more negative concepts (e.g., hate, hostility, anger, or prejudice) it is not clear that previous research can identify aggression as a definite barrier to interpersonal communication. On the other hand, a case for physical characteristics of individuals operating as barriers to communication appears to be supported in the literature.

Byrne and Griffitt[70] point out that "attraction has been shown to be positively related to the physical attractiveness of targets in several investigations." They continue with this summary:

> In response to photographic stimuli, both male and female subjects indicated greater attraction toward physically attractive same and opposite-sex targets than toward unattractive ones. In later research more extreme differences in physical attractiveness and only opposite-sex targets were used; it was reported that attractiveness effects on the work partner scale and measures of the target's desirability as a dating and marriage partner are stronger for males than female subjects. Physical attractivenss seems to play an especially strong role in the dating situation. In studies of a prospective date whose photograph was available, actual partners in a computer dating experiment, and actual dates at a computer dance, physical attractiveness was found to be a strong and consistent determinant of interpersonal attraction.[71]

An important aspect of the Byrne and Griffitt review is that it outlines the role that physical attraction plays in drawing people together or in keeping them apart. Aside from the sources cited in this review, other investigations have focused on such issues as the role of attraction and attitude similarity or change[72] as well as subtleties of attraction including (1) hair length,[73] (2) body size,[74] (3) weight,[75] (4) posture or poise,[76] (5) clothing styles,[77] and (6) sloppiness.[78] In each case the results suggest that an aberration from the norm is perceived as negative influence upon social interaction.

Private Barriers

Unlike the more visible barriers to interpersonal communication, private barriers are distinct in that they may be either masked by the bearer or apparent only to those who make up the central core of the individual's interaction groups. Earlier in this study, anger and aggression were cited as examples of overt or public barriers to interpersonal communication. Another example is discrimination, which may be viewed as an overt expression or the manifestation of prejudice, a private barrier.

Prejudiced individuals tend to have narrow perceptions, lacking objectivity and flexibility in their opinions, and are defensive of, and reluctant to change, these opinions.[79] Similarly, the stereotypes used by prejudiced individuals operate as a barrier by limiting "their perceptions of the gradations of differences among people" and by "perpetuating self-fulfilling myths" about those stereotyped.

The impact of the stereotype on interpersonal communication is defined by the nature of stereotypes. Brigham[81] outlined six characteristics of the stereotype ranging from incorrect generalizations to the belief that the stereotype is, or can become, a product of habit passed on from generation to generation. Furthermore, the relationship between prejudice and the stereotype is cogently presented by Broom and Selznick:

> Because prejudice is arbitrary and categorical, it is eroded by close interpersonal contacts and the press of reality. [Prejudice] tends to be perpetuated by simplifying assumptions called stereotypes.[82]

The Active-Passive Nature of Barriers

As already mentioned, this discussion is dichotomized into the idea that a barrier may be visible to all witnessing its presence, or the barrier may be masked and known only to the possessor or those individuals making up the individual's primary group. This notion may be extended to describe the manner in which the barrier operates in the interpersonal setting. For example, a visible, public barrier may also be described as a passive barrier. These distinctions are more than academic extensions of the public and private classifications, for they serve to describe the nature of the barrier's operation in the interpersonal setting.

A public barrier actively affects communication because its cues — i.e., visibility—(1) indicate the presence of a barrier for the receiver, (2) prompt an immediate reaction on the part of the receiver, and (3) immediately affect the communication setting for both participants. On the other hand, a private barrier passively affects communication because any effect of the barrier is delayed and its presence is known only to the sender (possessor) of the barrier. In short, since the barrier is masked it offers no cues for the receiver, thereby allowing control of the communication situation (i.e., its continuance or termination) to rest solely with the possessor of the barrier.

To illustrate this point, one can consider the following examples. Anger, as a barrier, may exist in either a public or private mode. Correspondingly, it may also operate in either its active or passive states. For the sender, anger, operating as a public barrier in its active state, offers various physical and emotional cues of its presence, including loudness of voice or evident facial expressions, defensiveness, or general defiance. These cues, in turn, provoke immediate, reciprocal physical and emotional reactions on the part of the receiver. Finally, there is an immediate effect on the communication setting. Argument or similar face-to-face encounters, or complete withdrawal from the communication setting by the participants, are illustrations of possible effects of communication barriers.

Operating as a private, passive barrier, anger may not have an observable, immediate effect on dyadic communication. That is, rather than the barriers resulting in communication breakdown, conflict, or quasi-conflict, these barriers may at most cause confusion on the part of the person facing them. The difference in the end result of the two types of barriers rests with the different nature of each—the clearest distinction being that there are no cues identifying the presence of the private barrier.

One of the clearest examples of a passive, private barrier is rejection. In their study on the perception of feelings Taguiri, Brunner, and Blake[83] sought to measure an individual's ability to recognize accurately interpersonal acceptance and rejection. The results of this study indicate that subjects can perceive acceptance but not rejection of themselves by others. The authors conclude that rejection . . . is masked in our culture, and [our] subjects were no exception."[84] In a later study, Blumberg[85] arrives at a similiar conclusion in reference to positive and negative evaluations, finding that negative information tends to be withheld from the person being evaluated because of cultural norms.

A second example of a passive barrier is distrust. Distrust has been shown to be an important factor in specific or particular interpersonal situations such as counseling,[86] but, more important, in the general communication of information.[87] Distrust, like rejection, is masked; although individuals may interact with those they distrust, they do so in a guarded fashion, unable to believe or accept what is said or done.

A final illustration of the private, passive dimension of barriers is depression. Depression is one of the most ecumenical of all barriers, for few people ever escape experiencing feelings of depression in their lives.

Ruesch[88] describes depression as resulting from the "loss of a beloved person, collapse of an ideal, or failure to achieve some aspiration," and he isolates the communication behavior of a depressed person as characterized by "an attempt at reducing participation in group and interpersonal networks and confining the personal operations to repetitious performances."[89] Argyle has added that the depressed have

little energy and will brood and sit by themselves. They have a lower opinion of themselves than is warranted, and are obsessed with feelings of failure and guilt, and may contemplate suicide; they are completely lacking in self-confidence.[90]

Others have found the depressed to have less affection for family members and considerable resentment toward others and themselves.[91]

Regarding the active or passive nature of depression, depressed patients have been found to display less eye contact than nondepressed patients,[92] and Eckman and Rose[93] found that when shown photographs taken from depressed patients, subjects were able to discriminate between more depressed and less depressed stages of a patient's recovery. Depression, however, is not always readily evident. Ruesch cites the manic-depressive, or cycloid personality, as an example:

> Frequently one hears the comment that such-and-such a person seemed so well adjusted, that his movements and poise were so convincing that nobody expected him to suffer a breakdown. The difficulties that therapists experience in establishing rapport with depressed patients . . . are in part related to this loss of general expression. Therapists repeatedly have commented upon the somewhat phony and fraudulent impression these patients create.[94]

In this case manic-depressives' almost schizoid behavior operates to mask both their feelings and afflictions, thus placing it in the passive dimension of a barrier.

Operational Definitions

Scope, as defined earlier, serves the purpose of delineating sufficient, but not necessary, components of barriers, and in so doing defines the parameter of the barrier domain. Tafoya[95] identified the scope of the barriers domain through the use of a seven-point Likert-type scale in a self-report measure. In that study 228 possible barriers to interpersonal communication were listed along a scale ranging from very strong agreement to very strong disagreement that the item represented a barrier. Each point on the scale corresponded to a numerical value from 1 to 7. Thus, when Anger received a mean score of 2.0, one could generalize that the sample strongly agreed that anger is a barrier to interpersonal communication. Likewise, if an item received a mean score of 6.0, one concludes that there is strong agreement that that item is not perceived as a barrier to interpersonal communication.

Since for any given individual any particular item legitimately can be considered a barrier for that person, all items receiving a mean score of at least 3.0 (mild agreement that the item represented a barrier) were operationally defined as a barrier to interpersonal communication. The use of 3.0 in that instance served two purposes: first, it provided a means for distinguishing between perceived barriers and nonbarriers in the sample studied, and second, the 3.0 level effectively reduced the initially large item pool to a more manageable size, and, perhaps more important, one reliably reflecting the barrier's domain. In short, that early study served to define empirically items representing the domain of barriers to interpersonal communication by combining items thought, but not tested, to represent such a domain, and by having a group of subjects score the extent to which each item was perceived as representing the domain.

Tafoya's study serves as the basis for the two studies reported below. Items identified as barriers in that study served to define the measures used for the following studies. These studies are designed to accomplish two things. First, to identify, compare, and contrast typologies of perceived barriers (sources of interpersonal communication conflict) for interpersonal communication generally and cross-cultural communication specifically (Study I) and, second, to observe the effect context (i.e., cross cultural or not) may have on the rated intensity of a barrier (Study II).

MEASURING THE INTENSITY OF BARRIERS: A TYPOLOGY

In the preliminary study specific barriers were isolated, and those barriers were categorized through the use of various clustering techniques by types.[96] The typology developed identified two principal categories of barriers to interpersonal communication: *personal psychological barriers,* which prevent, restrict, or impede the transmission, by words and gestures, and the reception of accurate meaning between two or more persons in a social setting by directly affecting the possessor of the barrier. Another category is the *interpersonal behavioral style barriers* which prevent, restrict, or impede the transmission and reception of messages by directly affecting the individual exposed to the barrier. Examples of personal psychological barriers are timidity, fear of failure, worry, depression, and frustration, while stereotyping, dominance, and the desire to control another are typical of interpersonal behavioral style barriers.

Each of these two broad categories contained eleven subcategories, with each of these defined by several specific barriers. These subcategories, ranked in intensity and across main categories (personal psychological and interpersonal behavior style), are presented in Table 12.1.

TABLE 12.1   Typology of Barriers to Interpersonal Communication

Personal Psychological	GM	Interpersonal Behavioral Style
	2.20	Interpersonal aggression
	2.21	Defense mechanisms
Paranoia	2.50	Force
	2.54	Ego and ethnocentrisms
Isolation	2.70	Authoritarianism Negativisms
Mental disorders	2.80	Bitchiness
Personal insecurities	2.95	
Social insensibility	3.06	
	3.10	Misperception of nonverbal cues
Resentment	3.15	
Hopelessness	3.16	
	3.25	Social naivete
Neuroticism	3.30	
Physical discomfort		
	3.35	Immaturity
Secrets	3.40	
	3.50	Personal hygiene
Pain	3.65	

Measurement of the Intensity of Barriers

The Tafoya study concentrated on reducing the original data set containing 223 possible barriers to interpersonal communication to a data set containing perceived barriers to interpersonal communication; 83 items met the defined criteria, enabling them to be classified as barriers to interpersonal communication. These items served to define the measures used in Studies I and II to describe a typology and the intensity of barriers to interpersonal communication (Study I) and interpersonal cross-cultural communication (Study II). In order to assure that subjects were discriminating between barriers and nonbarriers in the studies, five additional items, representing nonbarriers, were added to the measures used. All totaled, 88 items were included in both measures.

Subjects

Participating in Study I were 309 students at a major midwestern university; 216 students at a major southeastern university participated in Study II. All subjects voluntarily participated in both studies.

Design of the Measures

As mentioned above, both measures contained the same 88 items and both measures allowed subjects to indicate, on a seven-point scale (ranging from very strong barrier to very weak barrier), the extent to which a particular item represented a barrier to interpersonal (Study I) and cross-cultural (Study II) communication. If a subject did not feel that a particular item did not represent a barrier, the subject indicated that this was the case for that item. All items were randomly placed in the measure.

Statistical Analyses

Standardized mean scores (Z scores) and principal component factor analysis were used to analyze the data gathered in the two studies. The standardized mean scores were used to differentiate intensity levels among the barriers (perceived contributors to interpersonal or cross-cultural conflict), and factor analysis was used to define relationships among barriers.

Results

Table 12.2 displays the means and Z scores for the items in the measures that define the upper and lower (most intense and least intense) ends of an intensity scale of barriers to interpersonal and intrapersonal communication. That is, those items falling beyond +1 standardized deviation (a strong barrier) and –1 (a weak barrier), excluding moderately strong or moderately weak barriers, are presented in Table 12.2.

A review of the data reveals at least four differences between the perceived intensity of factors seen as barriers to interpersonal and cross-cultural communication. First, in Study I, where barriers to interpersonal communication are examined, those barriers perceived as most intense tend to contain more personal psychological barriers (hate, dishonest, deception) and barriers of a more passive nature than those most intense barriers to interpersonal communication. The barriers to cross-cultural communication (Study II) tend to include more interpersonal behavioral style barriers and barriers more likely to affect actively communication (hostility or discrimination). Second, as one might expect, most intense barriers for the cross-cultural setting tend to reflect more situation-specific barriers (e.g., prejudice, discrimination, stereotyping, the inability to accept something different as equal, and the inability to adapt), while those addressing the interpersonal communication setting tend to reflect more general, non-situation-specific barriers.

**TABLE 12.2   Standardized Scores from Studies I and II,
Most Intense (+1) to Least Intense (−1)**

Study I		Study II	
Item	Z-Score	Item	Z-Score
Hate	2.17	Hate	1.94
Dishonesty	2.17	Prejudice	1.93
Deception	2.17	Hostility	1.65
Lying	1.76	Distrust	1.65
Distrust	1.76	Discrimination	1.56
Prejudice	1.55	Stereotyping	1.44
Lack of care for the		Dishonesty	1.32
feelings of others	1.35	Inability to accept	
Rejection	1.35	something different	
Hysteria	1.14	as equal	1.31
		Inability to adapt	1.24
Boredom	−1.12	Deception	1.22
Lack of eye contact	−1.12	Superiority feelings	1.12
Juvenile behavior	−1.12	Lack of flexibility	1.06
Despair	−1.12	Lying	1.05
Secrets	−1.12	Segregation	1.00
Bad breath	−1.32		
Body odor	−1.32	Bad breath	−1.00
First impressions	−1.32	Shyness	−1.05
Alcoholism	−1.32	Depression	−1.06
Lack of flexibility	−1.53	Timidity	−1.08
Feeble-mindedness	−1.53	Nagging	−1.10
Worry	−1.53	Secrets	−1.13
Pain	−1.94	Feeble-mindedness	−1.17
Fatigue	−1.94	Juvenile behavior	−1.18
Excessive rate of		Excessive rate of	
speech	−2.15	speech	−1.22
		Guilt	−1.24
		Despair	−1.59
		Worry	−1.71
		Boredom	−1.96
		Alcoholism	−2.05
		Pain	−2.36
		Fatigue	−2.64

There are more items (barriers) in the cross-cultural setting falling at least +1 standard deviation from the mean (13 versus 9) than in the general interpersonal setting, perhaps reflecting the complexity of communication interaction in this situation. Finally, a quick review of those barriers falling at the lower end of the distribution indicates that these low-intensity barriers tend to be the same for both samples in number and type. This suggests that a critical area for future research might center around the high-intensity items where variation between settings is most evident.

A review of the data in Table 12.2 indicates that, as expected, the extent to which an item might be perceived as having high, moderate, or low intensity (or effect on interpersonal interaction, whether that interaction is of a cross-cultural nature or not) can be graphically represented as triangular in shape. Certain variables, independent of context, appear to have more potential weight or impact on interaction than do others.

The most significant meaning of the data sets, however, rests with the interpretation of the results of the factor analyses conducted. Tafoya[97] indicated that factors contributing to conflict might be loosely classified into two categories: personal psychological and interpersonal behavioral style characteristics or traits associated with an actor. The distinction between these two categories is important, for this approach to interpersonal conflict may make for more manageable interpretations of why conflict might occur between individuals.

Classical approaches attempting to examine sources of conflict often neglect the perception of the participant as a source of information. These studies are useful in their own right, but the goal of this study is to move beyond describing types of conflicts, characteristics associated with a particular mode of conflict, or behaviors or acts associated with a mode of conflict. Rather, this study is designed to identify potential cognitive and behavioral conditions or states that seem to preclude a conflict.

Table 12.3 presents the factor-analytic solutions for the two studies. The criteria used for selecting factors and items defining factors were as follows: (1) a factor had to have a minimum of three items loading on it to be retained, (2) items needed primary loadings of .50 or better to be retained, and (3) an item had to have secondary loadings of or below .30 to be retained.

Reliability

These criteria were defined to provide factors that cleanly defined elements of a typology of perceived contributors to interpersonal and cross-cultural conflict. Table 12.3 also contains reported reliability (Cronbach's coefficient alpha) for the derived factors. An a priori level of .85 was established as acceptable for each study, and a level of .65 for each individual factor. This latter, lower level was felt to be sufficient given the inherently strong link of the coefficient alpha to n size. That is, high reliabilities can be an artifact of a data set if the n size is sufficiently

TABLE 12.3 Typology of Factors Across Studies I and II and Ranked by Factor Intensity

	Study I (Alpha = .95)			Study II (Alpha = .94)	
Factor Name	Alpha Reliability	Grand Mean	Factor Name	Alpha Reliability	Grand Mean
(Dishonesty)	.77	(2.06; .24)	(Prejudice)	.77	(2.06; .23)
ITEMS		LOADINGS	ITEMS		LOADINGS
Dishonesty		.78	Prejudice		.77
Lying		.78	Inability to accept		
Deception		.76	something different		
Hypocrisy		.55	as equal		.67
Selfishness		.54	Reluctance to change		.59
—Interpersonal Behavioral Style—			Lack of Flexibility		.58
			Discrimination		.58
(Defensiveness)	.77	(2.54; .14)	—Interpersonal Behavioral Style—		
Defensive Behavior		.60			
Paranoia		.59	(Dishonesty)	.76	(2.08; .14)
Negativism		.58	Dishonesty		.82
—Personal Psychological—			Lying		.73
			Deception		.68
(Control)	.79	(227; .09)	Distrust		.55
Manipulation		.80	—Interpersonal Behavioral Style—		
Desire to Control		.79			
Dominance		.68	(Hate)	.75	(2.27; .34)
Authoritarianism		.59	Hate		.74
—Interpersonal Behavioral Style—			Rejection		.63
			Segregation		.56
(Nagging)	.69	(2.7; .25)	—Personal Psychological—		
Nagging		.72			
Rudeness		.66	(Control)	.72	(2.46; .18)
Irritability		.61	Dominance		.74
—Personal Psychological—			Desire to Control		.68
			Authoritarianism		.58
(Timidity)	.76	(3.18; .13)	Superiority Feelings		.52
Timidity		.76	—Interpersonal Behavioral Style—		
Embarrassment		.74			
Shyness		.67	(Emotional	.85	(2.89; .12)
—Personal Psychological—			Instability)		
			Insanity		.79
(Depression)	.79	(3.29; .35)	Mental Illness		.68
Worry		.75	Hysteria		.58
Despair		.74	—Personal Psychological—		
Depression		.56			
—Personal Psychological—			(Jealousy)	.72	(3.35; .23)
			Low Self-esteem		.74
(Jealousy)	.71	(3.34; .22)	Envy		.66
Guilt		.71	Guilt		.57
Low Self-esteem		.69	—Personal Psychological—		
Envy		.58			
Isolation		.53	(Depression)	.73	(3.65; .27)
—Personal Psychological—			Despair		.75
			Frustration		.72
			Worry		.71
			—Personal Psychological—		

large.[98] The fact that average n size for each factor is never greater than five, but the average reliability across factors is greater than .73, suggests sufficient internal reliability for the factors representing the typology.

Overall reliability, too, exceeded a priori established levels for each study. The reliability for Study I (n = .25; i.e., only item factors out of the original 83-item data set) was .95, and for Study II (n = 25), .94.

Results of the Factor Analysis

Table 12.3 also carries information regarding a factor's variable names and primary loadings as well as the grand mean (as a heuristic measure of the factor's intensity), the factor's global name, and an indication whether the factor best reflects items typically classified as personal psychological or interpersonal behavioral style in nature. The global name was selected as one thought to best reflect the particular factor. Classification of a factor as mostly reflecting either personal psychological or behavioral style items was not done in so cavalier a fashion. In this case four trained raters were presented with a set of instructions containing specific definitions of the two categories and the 88 items from the original questionnaire. The raters were asked to indicate whether each item represented one or the other category, a combination of the two, or neither (as should be the case for such positively labeled items as cooperation, generosity, and the like). Only classification of the items in either of the first two categories was considered a correct response. In this case the average interrater reliability for items coded for Study I was .89, and .92 for Study II.

The results of the factor analyses for both studies uncovered a total of seven factors, after application of the criteria outlined above. The two studies shared four factors (dishonesty, control, depression, and jealousy) and there was a tendency for the highest and lowest intensity factors to be the same for the studies. The seven factors in Study I accounted for 48% of the variance, and the seven factors in Study II for 52% of the variance. Although both studies were based on the same basic instrument (i.e., changed only to reflect the desired cross-cultural nature of Study II), it is the presence of the factors not common to each that seems to contribute the most salient information about the domain of elements constituted as contributing to interpersonal or cross-cultural conflict.

A classical approach to defining the mix of different cultures visually is through the use of intersecting circles: for example, Venn diagrams. The idea behind this type of presentation is that while any two cultures, or individuals, may be inherently different, they do tend to share certain elements between them. The same appears here, but in this case, that is, given the nature of this chapter, what we see is that while certain states or behaviors or traits are context-bound (e.g., the prejudice and hate factors in Study II), other states or traits transcend cultural boundaries and are perceived as problematic regardless of context. Thus, some factors seem to reflect dimensions that (1) are more likely to contribute to conflict in one context than another, (2) are items reflecting behaviors or states that are not culture-specific in offensiveness, and (3) are items (factors) that may simply lose salience when thrust against a cultural backdrop (e.g., the timidity factor in Study I).

Some care must be taken not to concentrate too closely on specifics when examining these results, for to do so may lead to unfortunate misperceptions of what the overall domain of barriers or total collection of dimensions looks like holistically. For example, while the factors are presented in terms of their items' combined and averaged intensity ratings, one must not view this as any attempt to provide a linear explanation of the relationship among dimensions defining the domain of factors contributing to interpersonal or cross-cultural conflict. Seeking a simple linear solution in this instance is inappropriate, for, by definition, any of these items may contribute to conflict. Because of (1) the dynamic nature of both interpersonal same-cultural and cross-cultural interaction, and (2) the fact that none of these items or factors has been experimentally or otherwise causally linked to acts of conflict, one can only conclude that the subjects in these two studies perceived these items as potentially salient features underlying or reflecting possible conflict situations. It is interesting to note, however, that while personal psychological states tend to predominate overall, the interpersonal behavioral style factors tended to have the highest intensity ratings. The intensity ratings generally reflect a greater range and skewed distribution for the dimensions comprising Study II, thus possibly reflecting what may seem obvious: The cross-cultural context's dynamic nature not only reflects elements and products likely to be produced as culture's mix, but also that cross-cultural communication remains, in its simplest form, a facet of interpersonal communication.

CONCLUSION

These studies' results reflect the effusive nature of conflict. Both the theory and attempts to test that theory provide information useful in understanding the dynamic nature of conflict across interpersonal and cross-cultural settings. Yet perhaps the best way to describe the studies' results is by reviewing the studies's major themes vis-à-vis questions left unanswered by the studies. For example, while the theory presented was designed to isolate social characteristics of the nature of conflict-producing states or behaviors, only intensity was measured beyond the descriptive level. Thus, and assuming that for the moment we can do as Coleridge so aptly suggested one do in situations demanding critical but objective analysis—that we "suspend our disbelief" at least temporarily— we can pose several questions about elements of the theory outlined.

For example, what is the essence of the relationship among or between particular sets of public and private barriers? Admittedly the term "barrier" is used as a convention, but in light of the fact that identifiable states or behaviors exist that seem to be perceived as negatively affecting the communication process, it seems justifiable to wonder what the relationship is between more visible and those more covert barriers. "Prejudice" is a term used to describe a particular state when linked with the act or behavior of "discrimination." Now, apart from the temptation to argue the semantical nature of the words used here, it seems that we can present several questions yet unanswered regarding the relationship between these two barriers. For example: When does the private barrier prejudice take on its public manifestations? Is it only through the manifestation of a private barrier that communication is actively affected (and until that time only passively affected), or can private barriers actively and passively affect communication?

It is tempting to want to link, causally or otherwise, private and public barriers, particularly when they are part of the same factor of the typology presented. For instance, it is easy to suggest that prejudice causes discrimination. However, two points merit attention here. First, one cannot generalize that if, as this models suggests, there is a high-intensity private barrier behind a lower-intensity public barrier, then, in fact, there is only one barrier affecting the communication situation. Actually, all barriers affect the communication situation. Second, the extent to which a barrier affects a given situation is tied to two things: (1) the intensity of the barrier, and (2) the participants in the communication setting. For example, a barrier with low intensity (keeping in mind that intensity is a purely personal construct) may act only as a distraction to the communication process, while a barrier with high intensity will, most likely, be totally disruptive. Intensity is only one aspect of this conceptualization, for even a barrier with high intensity, when encountered in a communication setting, may not totally disrupt the communication process if the individuals encountering the barrier are willing and able to handle the situation. This point, however, is not within the scope of this study; it does merit further consideration and discussion.

A second point concerning the relationship between public and private barriers is that although an attempt has been made to illustrate that public barriers can be considered manifestations or extensions of private barriers, there are cases in which this does not hold true. For example, items that did not fall into factors reflect public and private barriers, yet without at least one necessary second item it is virtually impossible to construct legitimately a causal link among these items. Force is a public barrier of high intensity with no apparent private barriers accounting for its presence. However, it may be that force failed to fall into another factor because there were not other force-related items in the data set. (Although this is not entirely true for aggression, dominance and the desire to control are other seemingly related variables that are in the data set.) It could also be said that force was isolated because of measurement error. Aside from these two possibilities, the fact remains that this and other items stand alone in the factor analyses conducted, and they may stand alone simply because the are not related in the subjects' minds to other items representing possible contributors to conflict. Regardless of the argument accepted, the point remains that items classifiable as barriers but, given the criteria presented, not found in a developed factor, cannot be causally linked to other items in the study.

A second area in need of review are those cognitive and physiological aspects of human interaction that contribute to defining responses to both preconditions for conflict and actual conflict states. In some instances of higher intensity, private barriers are manifested in social and public situations. Intuitively the likelihood for these occurrences makes sense, for one would expect that highly intense, private barriers are actively working on the individual possessing the barrier, and that, over time, the individual must make some attempt to release the stress or dissonance associated with these barriers. Stress and dissonance, then, may be principal factors associated with the nature of barriers, with the stress produced by barriers affecting both the individual possessing and the individual exposed to the barrier. Where stress operates on the individual, instances of mental confusion or breakdown on one extreme, or a loss of self-esteem, depression, or mental disorder may result. Where stress operates on the individual exposed to the barrier, one may observe the effects of this condition holistically in what is commonly referred to as a breakdown in communication. What is interesting to note here is that while we adhere to a process approach to describing communication interaction—where communication never ceases or breaks down—to the layperson attempting to grapple with a stress-producing, dissonant situation, the inability to manage successfully (e.g., in a nonconflict manner) is likely to be aptly described metaphorically as a breakdown.

Classical descriptions of individuals washing their hands of or turning their backs on a situation beyond their control or ability in reality reflect methods for managing, albeit by not managing, the situation. Is it the barriers that produce the stress or response in a given situation? When we identify, list, and describe barriers to interpersonal or cross-cultural communication, are we in fact only presenting conditions or behavioral styles that, when encountered in the self or another, serve as a referent to gauge specific skills or competencies necessary to manage that which is encountered? The individual encountering a barrier and its resulting stress has at least three typical responses to the situation: withdrawal, assault, or forbearance. Typical communication-related situations resulting from these three responses might be outlined as the diagram in Table 12.4 suggests.

This simple illustration of possible alternatives suggests that in any given communication situation, when a barrier is encountered, the participants in the communication process may (1) withdraw from the situation, in which case communication ceases, or avoid the topic, in which case interaction may be continued in an altered though not unaffected manner. (2) They may respond with, for example, forms of physical or verbal assault, in which case the line of discussion is terminated; to deal with this new situation the individual(s) may attempt to displace any hostility by suppressing thoughts or feelings, in which case communication continues. However, the situation is altered because of the need and move to suppress. (3) There may be an attempt to forbear; that is, refrain from withdrawal or assault by, perhaps, recognizing that a problem exists, attempting to determine the basis or source of the problem, and moving toward some resolution of the problem. Thus, while each alternative is unique, all have one commonality: In each case the communication process is affected by the choice made.

SUGGESTIONS FOR FUTURE RESEARCH

Strictly speaking, the typologies developed above reflect only the perceptions of the sample participating in the two studies reported. Given this limitation, future investigations should consider using different samples in order to verify that the typologies isolated here

TABLE 12.4   Alternative Management Approaches to Conflict

Management Approach		Effect
Withdrawal:	(1) From the situation	(1) Communication ceases
	(2) From the stressful topic	(2) Process is altered; communication continues
Assault:	(1) Immediate hostility	(1) Communication ceases
	(2) Displaced hostility	(2) Process is altered; communication continues
Forebearance:	Barrier is recognized and dealt with	Process is altered; communication continues

reflect barriers to interpersonal communication generally and cross-cultural communication as a stratum of interpersonal communication.

More specifically, each of the several assumptions outlined in the chapter should be reviewed not only in terms of general samples, but also in terms of subsets of these samples. It is likely, for example, that perceptions of the barriers as sources of interpersonal or cross-cultural conflict may vary across sexes, age groups, or specific cultures. Thus, while the theory and typologies provide useful information to both academic and lay areas alike, the true utility of the information remains to be measured.

A second focus of subsequent studies should be the exploration of factors presented across different settings or contexts. For example, timidity and juvenile behavior were perceived as mild barriers to interpersonal and cross-cultural interaction. Keeping in mind that the focal setting for these studies was defined as social, one can only wonder how these two might be perceived in a business setting, where timidity may be viewed as a sign of weakness or lack of aggressiveness, and juvenile behavior as an indicator of immaturity or of being a poor leader. Thus, in some cases, particular settings may serve to define better what are or are not sources of interpersonal dissonance.

Lastly, assumptions suggesting that barriers vary in intensity may be classified in terms of their visibility, and affect interpersonal communication either actively or passively, should each be isolated and tested in controlled situations to verify whether these assumptions are indeed true.

Finally, each theoretical assumption outlined in the chapter should be examined in controlled situations. The assumption that barriers tend to vary in intensity is generally confirmed for the samples participating and should hold across other cultural samples. The actual identification of public and private barriers, however, and the manner in which these barriers affect interpersonal and cross-cultural communication within specific cultures remain to be verified. This chapter presents a foundation for future research, and the verification of the assumptions presented herein is critical to explaining precisely the role of communication in multicultural conflict situations.

NOTES

1. D. Berlo, *The Process of Communication* (New York: Holt, Rinehart & Winston, 1960).

2. Ibid, pp. 25-30.

3. D. Smith, "The Fallacy of the Communication Breakdown," *Quarterly Journal of Speech* 56 (1970): 343-46.

4. Ibid, pp. 343-44.

5. F. Heider, *The Psychology of Interpersonal Relations* (New York: John Wiley, 1958).

6. Smith, "Fallacy of Communication Breakdown," p. 346.

7. Alfred Korzybski, *Science and Sanity: An Introduction to Non-Aristotelian Systems and General Semantics* (Lakeville, CT: Institute of General Semantics, 1948).

8. Wendell Johnson, *People in Quandries: The Semantics of Personal Adjustment* (New York: Harper & Row, 1946).

9. Ibid., p. 470.

10. Ibid., pp. 487-89.

11. Samuel I. Hayakawa, *Symbol, Status, and Personality* (New York: Harcourt, Brace, 1963).

12. Ibid., p. 175.

13. Irving Lee, *Customs and Crises in Communication: Cases for the Study of Some Barriers and Breakdowns* (New York: Harper, 1954).

14. Ibid., p. 34.

15. Ibid.

16. Ibid., p. 36.

17. Irving Lee, *How to Talk with People* (New York: Harper & Brothers, 1952).

18. Ibid., pp. 44-46.

19. Daniel Katz, "Psychological Barriers to Communication," *Annals of the American Academy of Political and Social Science* 250 (1947).

20. Ibid., p. 17.

21. Ibid.

22. Ibid., p. 18.

23. Ibid.

24. J. Ruesch, *Disturbed Communication* (New York: W. W. Norton, 1957).

25. Ibid., p. 185.

26. Ibid., pp. 46-76.

27. William V. Haney, *Communication Patterns and Incidents* (Homewood, IL: 1960).

28. John Parry, *The Psychology of Human Communication* (London: University of London Press, 1967), pp. 84-126.

29. Ibid., p. 84.

30. Ibid., pp. 84-126.

31. Carl R. Rogers, "Communication: Its Blocking and Its Facilitation," in *Language, Meaning, and Maturity,* ed. S. Hayakawa (New York: Harper & Row, 1954), pp. 53-60.

32. Ibid., p. 59.

33. F. R. Roethlisberger, "Barriers to Communication Among Men," in *Language, Meaning, and Maturity,* ed. S. Hayakawa (New York: Harper & Row, 1954), pp. 61-68.

34. Ibid., p. 61.

35. B. R. Patton and K. Giffin, *Interpersonal Communication: Basic Text and Readings* (New York: Harper & Row, 1974).

36. E. Goffman, "On Face-Work: An Analysis of Ritual Elements in Social Interaction," *Psychiatry* 18 (1955): 213-31; S. Jourard, *The Transparent Self* (New York: Van Nostrand Reinhold, 1964); P. Watzlawick, J. H. Beavin, and D. D. Jackson, *Pragmatics of Human Communication* (New York: W. W. Norton, 1967).

37. J. Gibb, "Defensive Communication," *Journal of Communication* 11 (1961): 142-48; "Climate for Trust Formation," in *T-Group Theory and Laboratory Method,* ed. L. P. Bradford et al. (New York: John Wiley, 1964), pp. 279-309.

38. M. Argyle and J. Dean, "Eye-Contact, Distance and Affiliation," *Sociometry* 28 (1965): 283-304; R. Birdwhistell, *Introduction to Kinesics* (Louisville, KY: University of Louisville, 1954); E. T. Hall, *The Hidden Dimension* (New York: Doubleday, 1966); R. Sommer, *Personal Space* (Englewood Cliffs, NJ: Prentice-Hall, 1969); R. Barocas and P. Karaly, "Effects of Physical Appearance in Social Responsiveness," *Psychological Reports* 31 (1972): 495-500; E. Goffman, *Behavior in Public Places* (New York: Free Press, 1963); R. Kleck, "Physical Stigma and Task Orientation," *Human Relations* 22 (1969): 51-60.

39. D. Regan, E. Strauss, and R. Razio, "Liking and the Attribution Process," *Journal of Experimental Psychology* 10 (1974): 385-97.

40. *Oxford English Dictionary* (Oxford: Clarendon Press, 1933), "barrier."

41. Horace B. English and Ava C. English, *A Comprehensive Dictionary of Psychology and Psychoanalytic Terms* (New York: Longmans, Green, 1958).

42. S. I. Hayakawa, *Funk & Wagnalls Modern Guide to Synonyms and Related Words* (New York: Funk and Wagnalls, 1968).

43. *Oxford English Dictionary,* "barrier."

44. English and English, *Comprehensive Dictionary,* p. 60.

45. Hayakawa, *Modern Guide to Synonyms,* p. 407.

46. G. C. Homans, *The Human Group* (New York: Harcourt, Brace, Jovanovich, 1950), 454-60.

47. A. Rothenberg, "On Anger," *American Journal of Psychiatry* 128 (1971): 454-60.

48. Ibid., p. 86.

49. S. Freud, *Beyond the Pleasure Principle* (1920), in *Complete Psychological Works,* vol. 18. ed. and trans. F. Strachey (London: Hogarth Press, 1961), pp. 59-145; idem, *Civilization and Its Discontents* (1930), Ibid., vol. 21, pp. 3-64.

50. K. Lorenz, *On Aggression* (New York: Harcourt, Brace & World, 1966).

51. R. Ardrey, *The Territorial Imperative* (New York: Atheneum, 1966).

52. A. Storr, *Human Aggression* (New York: Atheneum, 1968).

53. D. Morris, *The Naked Ape* (New York: McGraw-Hill, 1968).

54. H. S. Sullivan, *Clinical Studies in Psychiatry* (New York: W. W. Norton, 1956).

55. E. Becker, "Anthropological Notes on the Concept of Aggression," *Psychiatry* 25 (1962): 328-38.

56. T. Lidz, *The Person* (New York: Basic Books, 1968).

57. L. Berkowitz, *Aggression: A Social Psychological Analysis* (New York: McGraw-Hill, 1962).

58. J. Dollard, L. Doob, and N. Miller, *Frustration and Aggression* (New Haven, CT: Yale University Press, 1967).

59. Albert Bandura, "Influence of Models' Reinforcement Contingencies on the Acquisition of Imitative Responses," *Journal of Personality and Social Psychology* 1 (1965): 589-95; idem, *Principles of Behavior Modification* (New York: Holt, Rinehart & Winston, 1969).

60. S. M. Berger, "Conditioning through Vicarious Instigation," *Psychological Review* 69 (1962): 450-66; Robert A. Baron, "Aggression as a Function of Magnitude of Victim's Pain Cues, Level of Prior Anger Arousal, and Aggressor-Victim Similarity," *Journal of Personality and Social Psychology* 18 (1971); 48-54; idem, "Magnitude of Victim's Pain Cues and Level of Prior Anger Arousal as Determinants of Adult Aggressive Behavior," *Journal of Personality and Social Psychology* 17 (1971): 236-43; J. R. Green, "Climate for Trust Formation," in *T-Group Theory and Laboratory Method*, ed. L. R. Bradford, J. R. Gibb, K. D. Benne (New York: John Wiley, 1964).

61. S. Feshback, "The Function of Aggression and the Regulation of Aggressive Drive," *Psychological Review* 71 (1964): 257-72; R. R. Sears, "Personality Development in the Family," in *The Child*, ed. J. M. Seidman (New York: Holt, Rinehart & Winston, 1958); A. Bandura, "Social Learning Theory of Aggression," in *Control of Aggression: Implications From Basic Research*, ed. J. F. Knutsen (Chicago: Aldine-Atherton, 1971); R. A. Baron, "Aggression as a Function of Victim's Pain Cues, Level of Prior Anger Arousal, and Exposure to an Aggressive Model," *Journal of Personality and Social Psychology* 29 (1974): 117-24.

62. F. H. Kanfer, "Verbal Rate, Content, and Adjustment Ratings in Experimentally Structured Interviews," *Journal of Abnormal Social Psychology* 58 (1958): 305-11; F. H. Kanfer, "Verbal Rate, Eyeblink and Content in Structured Psychiatric Interviews," *Journal of Abnormal Social Psychology* 61 (1959): 341-48.

63. S. V. Kasl and G. F. Mahl, "The Relationship of Disturbances and Hesitations in Spontaneous Speech to Anxiety," *Journal of Personality and Social Psychology* 1 (1965): 425-533.

64. S. Feldstein and J. Jaffee, "The Relationship of Speech Disruption to the Experience of Anger," *Journal of Consulting Psychology* 26 (1963): 505-13.

65. G. Fairbanks and L. W. Hoaglin, "An Experimental Study of the Durational Characteristics of the Voice During Expression of Emotion," *Speech Monographs* 8 (1941): 85-90.

66. M. G. Lalljee and M. Williams, "Speech Rate and Speech Disturbance in the Perception of Anxiety," *Language and Speech* 17 (1974): 80-86.

67. Michael Argyle, *The Psychology of Interpersonal Behavior* (London: Cox & Wyman, 1972).

68. A. H. Buss, *The Psychology of Aggression* (New York: Harper & Row, 1959), 165-89, 245.

69. K. Menninger, *Man Against Himself* (New York: Harcourt Brace & World, 1938); P. Thompson and P. Mullahy, *Psychoanalysis: Evolution and Development* (New York: Heritage House, 1950).

70. Donn Byrne and William Griffitt, "Interpersonal Attraction," *Annual Review of Psychology* 11 (1973): 317-36.

71. Ibid., p. 321.

72. Icek Ajzen, "Effects of Information on Interpersonal Attraction: Similarity versus Affective Value," *Journal of Personality and Social Psychology* 29 (1974): 374-80; L. R. Good and K. C. Good, "On Perceiving Probability of Marital Success," *Psychological Reports* 31 (1972): 300-2; J. H. Harvey and D. R. Kelley, "Effects of Attitude Similarity and Success-Failure upon Attitude Toward Other Persons," *Journal of Social Psychology* 90 (1973): 105-114; L. Knecht, D. Lippman, and W. Swap, "Similarity, Attraction, and Self-Disclosure," *Proceedings of the Eighty-First Annual Convention of the American Psychological Association, Montreal* 8 (1973): 205-6; B. D. Layton and C. A. Insko, "Anticipated Interaction and the Similarity-Attraction Effect," *Sociometry* 37 (1974): 149-62; C. A. Insko et al., "Implied Evaluation and the Similarity-Attraction Effect," *Journal of Personality and Social Psychology* 25 (1973): 297-308; G. F. Mascaro and W. Graves, "Contrast Effects of Background Factors on the Similarity-Attraction Relationship," *Journal of Personality and Social Psychology* 25 (1973): 346-50; M. K. Moss and F. Andrasik, "Belief Similarity and Interracial Attraction," *Journal of Personality* 41 (1973): 192-205; W. C. Scott, "The Linear Relationship Between Interpersonal Attraction and Similarity: An Analysis of the 'Unique Stranger' Technique," *Journal of Social Psychology* 91 (1973): 117-25; P. H. Wright and A. C. Crawford, "Agreement and Friendship: A Close Look and Some Second Thoughts," *Representative Research in Social Psychology,* 2 (1971): 52-69; P. H. Wright and K. D. Wright, "Attitude Similarity and Their 'Anticipated Rewards' as Predictors of Attraction to a Hypothetical Stranger," *Representative Research in Social Psychology* 3 (1972): 131-40.

73. Alan L. Chaikin, Valerian J. Derlega, John Yoder, and David Phillips, "The Effects of Appearance on Compliance," *Journal of Social Psychology* 92 (1974): 26-30; K. C. Mace, "The 'Over-Bluff' Shoplifter: Who Gets Caught?" *Journal of Forensic Psychology* (1972): 26-30; R. J. Pellegrini, "Impressions of the Male Personality as a Function of Beardedness," *Psychology* 10 (1973): 29-33; P. Rom, "Hair Style and Life Style," *Individual Psychology* 10 (1973): 22-25; T. L. Rosenthal and G. M. White, "On the Importance of Hair in Students' Clinical Inferences," *Journal of Clinical Psychology* 28 (1972): 43-47.

74. E. Kretschmet, *Physique and Character* (London: Kegan Paul, 1925); W. Sheldon and S. Stephens, *The Varieties of Temperament* (New York: Harper, 1942); W. Wells and B. Siegel, "Stereotyped Somatotypes," *Psychological Reports* 8 (1961): 77-78.

75. J. J. Hartnett, K. G. Bailey, and C. S. Hartley, "Body Height, Position, and Sex as Determinants of Personal Space," *Journal of Psychology* 87 (1974): 129-36; E. E. Rump and P. S. Delin, "Differential Accuracy in the Status-Height Phenomenon and an Experimenter Effect," *Journal of Personality and Social Psychology* 28 (1973): 343-47.

76. E. Corbin, "Muscle Action as Nonverbal and Preverbal Communication," *Psychoanalytic Quarterly* 31 (1962): 351-63; W. James, "A Study of the Expression of Bodily Posture," *Journal of General Psychology* 7 (1932): 405-36; A. Raskin, "Observable Signs of Anxiety or Distress During Psychotherapy," *Journal of Consulting Psychology* 26 (1962): 389-96.

77. L. Aiken, "The Relationships of Dress to Selected Measures of Personality in Undergraduate Women," *Journal of Social Psychology* 59 (1963): 119-28; N. Compton, "Personal Attributes of Color and Design Preferences in Clothing Fabrics," *Journal of Personality* 54 (1962): 191-95; J. Flugel, *The Psychology of Clothes* (London: Hogarth Press, 1930); R. Hoult, "Experimental Measurement of Clothing as a Factor in Some Social Ratings of Selected American Men," *American Sociological Review* 19 (1954): 324-

78. L. Bickman, "Social Roles and Uniforms: Clothes Make the Person," *Psychology Today* 7 (1974): 49-51; Joseph Cooper, John M. Darley, and James E. Henderson, "On the

Effectiveness of Deviant and Conventional Appearing Communicators: A Field Experiment," *Journal of Personality and Social Psychology* 29 (1974): 752-57; P. Crossweller, M. A. Godron, and W. H. Tedford, "An Experimental Investigation of Hitchhiking," *Journal of Psychology* 82 (1972): 43-47; C. B. Keasey and C. Tomlinson-Keasey, "Petition Signing in a Naturalistic Setting," *Journal of Social Psychology* 89 (1973): 313-14; M. B. Littrell and J. B. Eicher, "Clothing Opinions and the Social Acceptance Process Among Adolescents," *Adolescence* 8 (1973): 197-212; B. Smucker and A. M. Creckmore, "Adolescents' Clothing, Conformity, Awareness, and Peer Acceptance," *Home Economics Research Journal* 1 (1972): 92-97.

79. A. W. Coombs and D. Snygg, *Individual Behavior* (New York: Harper & Row, 1959), pp. 165-89.

80. Patton and Giffin, *Interpersonal Communication*.

81. John C. Brigham, "Ethnic Stereotypes," *Psychological Bulletin* 76 (1971): 15-38.

82. Leonard Broom and Philip Selznick, *Sociology* (New York: Harper & Row, 1973), p. 467.

83. R. Taguiri, J. S. Brunner, and R. R. Blake, "On the Relation Between Feelings and Perception of Feelings Among Members of Small Groups," in *Readings in Social Psychology,* ed. E. E. Maccoby, T. M. Newcomb, and E. L. Hartley (New York: Holt, Rinehart & Winston, 1958), pp. 110-16.

84. Ibid., p. 116.

85. Herbert H. Blumberg, "Communication of Interpersonal Evaluations," *Journal of Personality and Social Psychology* 23 (1972): 157-62.

86. M. Deutsch, *Conditions Affecting Cooperation* (Washington, DC: Final Technical Report of ONR, 1957); "Cooperation and Trust: Some Theoretical Notes," *Nebraska Symposium on Motivation* (Lincoln: University of Nebraska Press, 1962); Jack Gibb, "Defensive Communication"; F. Friedlander, "The Primacy of Trust as a Facilitator of Further Group Accomplishment," *Journal of Applied Behavioral Science* 6 (1970): 387-400; S. R. Strong, "Counseling: An Interpersonal Influence Process," *Journal of Counseling Psychology* 15 (1968): 215-24; S. R. Strong and L. D. Schmidt, "Trustworthiness and Influence in Counseling," *Journal of Counseling Psychology* 17 (1970): 197-204.

87. P. Blau and W. R. Scott, *Formal Organizations* (San Francisco: Chandler, 1962); K. Griffin, "The Contribution of Studies of Source Credibility to a Theory of Interpersonal Trust in the Communication Process," *Psychological Bulletin* 68 (1967): 104-20; E. E. Jones, K. Gergen, and R. G. Jones, "Tactics of Ingratiation Among Leaders and Subordinates in a Status Hierarchy," *Psychological Monographs* 77 521 (1973); G. Mellinger, "Interpersonal Trust as a Factor in Communication," *Journal of Abnormal and Social Psychology* 52 (1956): 304-09; W. Reid, "Upward Communication in Industrial Hierarchies," *Human Relations* 15 (1962): 3-16; D. E. Sand, "Trust and Managerial Problem Solving," *Administrative Science Quarterly* 17 (1972): 229-40.

88. Ruesch, *Disturbed Communication*.

89. Ibid., p. 138.

90. Ibid., p. 176.

91. Ruth Bullock, "The Weeping Wife—Marital Relationships of Depressed Women," *Journal of Marriage and the Family* 34 (1972): 488-95; M. M. Weissman, "The Depressed Woman: Recent Research," *Social Work* 17 (1972): 19-25.

92. M. K. Hinchliffe, M. Lancashire, and F. J. Roberts, "A Study of Eye-Contact Changes in Depressed and Recovered Psychiatric Patients," *British Journal of Psychiatry* 549 (1971): 213-15; P. Waxer, "Nonverbal Cues for Depression," *Journal of Abnormal Psychology* 83 (1974): 319-22.

93. P. Ekman, *Progress Report to the National Institute of Mental Health* (Bethesda, MD: National Institute of Mental Health, 1965).

94. Ruesch, *Disturbed Communication*, p. 139.

95. D. Tafoya, "Barriers to Interpersonal Communication: A Theory and Typology," (Ph.D. diss., University of Michigan, 1976).

96. Ibid., p. 76.

97. Ibid.

98. J. Nunnally, *Psychometric Theory* (New York: McGraw-Hill, 1967).

IV

**CONTRIBUTIONS FROM
OTHER DISCIPLINES**

13

Codes and Contexts
An Argument for Their Description

RALPH E. COOLEY • *University of Oklahoma*

My purpose in this chapter is to present a position that represents my current views of intercultural communication for your consideration. I have proceeded from two assumptions that are not generally held in intercultural communication, nor in the general field of communication of which it is a part, and therefore I want to make them explicit and to challenge you to examine their appropriateness and to argue for their replacement or reformulation.

My first assumption is that the study of codes should be one of the central concerns to the study of communication. Coming to the field from the outside as I have, I cannot testify to our past history, but it is certainly true today that many, if not most of us do not operate from this assumption. In most of today's research the study and understanding of the code being used to communicate is not only not central to the question; in many cases it is not even considered relevant. I maintain that the study of codes is at least as relevant as the many other issues that are being considered and that such studies do not have such a central place in our literature today. Not only are there very few code studies extant in the literature,[1] but an examination of those studies using noncode variables shows that these often suffer from a lack of under-standing of the code and so come up short of real insight into communi-cation processes.

As one example of work that suffers because it contains no central interest in the code, Huber Ellingsworth proposed a theory of adaptive intercultural communication[2] in which I understand code to be crucial to all of his resulting propositions. Even his minimal condition for intercultural communication to occur depends on an understanding of what code is and how to analyze it. Yet a concern for code is not apparent in Ellingsworth's presentation. He spends

EDITOR'S NOTE: *Ralph Cooley passed away while this volume was going to press. He will be missed by all of us.*

just over five lines discussing it as part of the general category "communication style," which is part of the setting. This proposal seems to me to be quite typical of the thinking we are producing today, in which code is either not considered to be very relevant or is assumed to be outside of the realm of the theory being propounded.[3]

My second assumption is that a body of descriptive research centering on codes is sorely needed in the study of communication today. We lack a general descriptive base from which to formulate theory and hypotheses, to make reasoned decisions concerning relevant choices of variables, and to supply a context within which our current theories can be examined to see if they are valid and relevant. Such a base is necessary even for those studies that do not focus on the code itself; many standing studies using variables other than code variables depend on an understanding of the code for their validity. Currently we have only our intuitions as code users and scholars, and bits and pieces of our colleagues' research, to supply us with this base. It seems to me that in our haste to become scientists we have overlooked the fact that the harder sciences, which we have used as models, often spent generations developing descriptive, taxonomic base from which they could progress. We have not developed such a base in the field of cummunication. Its development is crucial to the understanding of intercultural encounters where there is more than one code in use. Further, we who are interested in contributing to this descriptive base need to be concerned with the development of a unified set of methodologies, so that our products will be comparable.

It is appropriate here to attempt to define what I mean by code. I have abandoned the word "system" in the title of this chapter because it is redundant: The term code entails systematicity. A *code* is a culturally defined, rule-governed system of shared arbitrary symbols that is used to transmit meaning. This is a very broad definition, including within its scope both oral and written language: those paralanguage phenomena (such as pitch, stress, and loudness) systematically related to oral language; certain nonverbal phenomena characterized by their systematicity (gesture, facial expression, and parts of gaze and posture); and, finally, the composition of discourse: silence, interruptions, turn-taking, the organization of talk, choice of dialect or language, bilingual/bidialectal behaviors, and the like.

While broad in scope, this definition is not a loose one. It restricts the use of the label to those systematically varying symbols that are not simply artifacts of being human (pupil dilation, fundamental freuqency variations due to age and sex, tears, and the like), or clothing, housing patterns, and other phenomena sometimes included in discussions of nonverbal behaviors. These phenomena do communicate meaning, but there is no evidence of system structure or systematic cultural definition.

Codes exhibit certain properties. The relation between meaning and symbol or unit of behavior is arbitrary. Their structure, tokens, and use are rigidly controlled by the using society, although this control does not keep change from occurring. They commonly possess a complex, hierarchically arranged internal structure. This hierarchical structure is most apparent in verbal and written codes, but has been shown to hold in paralanguage behaviors[4] and in gesture and posture.[5] Finally, the various types of phenomena (verbal, nonverbal, paralanguage, and discourse) exhibit interrelationships that indicate the presence of a parallel structure.

Code is the vehicle for the transmission of meaning and is therefore placed at the center of communication research. Because it is so tightly related to culture, the code is the arena where the individual and cultural values, priorities, and understandings (or lack of them) are displayed in the communication event. As a result, it is available to us to use as a key to understanding culture. The code is also the tool by which the participants negotiate and define new understandings, new joint priorities, and new values, and so it is available as a key to understanding the intercultural communication process.

The difficulty with investigating codes is that their structures are inherently very complex, arranged both vertically within phenomena types and horizontally across them. Verbal behavior is vertically, or hierarchically, organized: Conversations take place in turn by turn, but turns are sometimes composed of sentences, which are composed of clauses, which are composed of phrases and words, which are composed of sounds.[6] Verbal behavior is horizontally related to nonverbal behaviors: Gestures are known to be related to clausal structures—in order to show contrast and emphasis, for example—and also to syllable structure through rhythm. On the other hand, gesture is also analyzable into vertical levels: Large movements of the arms are made up of ordered layers of movement of the shoulder, the upper arm, the forearm, and the hand. One of the best demonstrations of this multiple horizontal and vertical structure is Adam Kendon's study of greeting behavior, which examines body orientation, gaze behavior, and gesture.[7] Kendon demonstrates the structural relationships between these nonverbal behaviors at several levels. The entire study is couched in the context of the social and situational constraints on both types of behavior.

A code transmits meaning. Without making any attempt to define what meaning is, I want to attend to the differences in kinds of meaning and examine some of the ways these meanings are transmitted by a code. It is useful to differentiate between semantic meaning, which I will limit to dictionary meaning, and functional meaning, the reflection of the speaker's communicative intent. Searle labels this differentiation utterance meaning versus speaker meaning.[8] Speaker meaning is often discussed under the heading of pragmatics. Semantic and functional meanings are reflections of the values and world view of the society. Their occurrence can be shown to be subject to some of the same rules that govern the structure of the entire discourse. However, the kinds of social meaning they express are limited in ways other social meanings are not. They mainly affect the short stretches of the code by which they are realized. They have varying degrees of cumulative effect on the social impact of the discourse, but no single occurrence of a lexical item or speech act will carry social meaning across the entire conversation.

There is another kind of social meaning that encompasses code phenomena of a different type. These meanings straightforwardly represent how a culture values itself and others, in what ways it is appropriate for its members to interact in certain situations, and how its world of communication is organized. These social meanings are expressed in the code at all levels, both vertical and horizontal: The choice of style,[9] dialect,[10] or language;[11] in those cases where a group's repertoire is large enough to allow such a choice; politeness phenomena; the understanding of how assertions are to be interpreted;[12] how one's talk is organized;[13] the choice of talk or silence, eye contact, posture, and gesture.[14] The ways of talking that a society/culture evidences give the observer an opportunity to understand who its members perceive themselves to be and how they have decided to get along together and with others.

An example from a recent protest and boycott in the St. Louis high schools will demonstrate the complexity of this sort of meaning and its potential for misinterpretation across cultures. A White woman student is reported to have said: "I was bothered by a bunch of black guys who called me a honky and asked me how I danced. It's not the kind of thing a white guy would say."[15] It was not simply the use of the term "honky" or the question about her dancing, however it was phrased, that the woman found threatening, but the occurrence of these and other stylistic and discourse phenomena (including the fact that she was asked the question in the first place) that relate to male-female interactions in Black culture. These phenomena are governed by rule sets reflecting the appropriate use of language to accomplish certain ends in Black culture, but not in White culture.

Codes, then, can be seen to exhibit complex internal relationships and equally complex relationships to the using members' culture. We need, first of all, to have descriptive studies that will display all of the various levels of code behavior and their interrelationships. Then we need to examine those behaviors to determine which ones are meaningful in what contexts. Not all of them are likely to be equally meaningful, and some of them may not be meaningful at all. We need also to study what kinds of meaning each transmits. It is safe to assume that there will be variations in both meanings and behaviors from context to context, and so we must examine a sufficient number of contexts to understand what these variations are. The range of contexts we examine must include both single-culture contexts for baseline data, and intercultural contexts.

NATIVE AMERICAN CULTURE

A very large number of cultures are represented in the population of the United States. I would like to discuss one set of these cultures, that of Native Americans, in order to illustrate the need for the sort of research I am suggesting. I will limit my discussion to Native Americans in Oklahoma. Their circumstance is typical of many of the North American tribes, even though they are unique in at least two ways: They are not indigenous to the area and they are not reservation Indians. With the exception of linguists and anthropologists, very few scholars have bothered to study Oklahoma Indians until the last few years and very little is known, other than anecdotally, about their modern intercultural situation, which ranges from full assimilation for some to minimal assimilation for many. These latter are mainly very poor rural Indians in the eastern part of the state who have little contact with Whites, speak little or no English, and maintain many of their traditions. Strong negative stereotyping is often the case, regardless of the degree of assimilation.

Two groups of scholars at the University of Oklahoma have been examining these stereotypes because of their relevance to the educational setting. Lujan et al. have investigated the stereotype of the Indian student as reticent and nonparticipative in the classroom.[16] They recognize that such behavior does exist in the classroom but that it is not typical in other situations. They suggest that reticence is a coping strategy and offer insights into its sources. Another group has investigated the stereotype of the Indian speaker as rambling and unorganized.[17] Their analysis demonstrates that such speeches are organized according to a different set of principles than Whites have been trained to recognize. Siler and Labadie-Wondergem pursue this thesis and examine the relationship between these organizational patterns and Native American culture, and demonstrate that these patterns are reflexes of a pervasive set of values in Native American culture.[18]

As valuable as these code-oriented studies may be, they are still subject to the same sort of criticisms with which I began this chapter. They begin with the intercultural setting (the classroom) and are limited to a small set of contexts. Further, each examines only one aspect of code behavior, without reference to either vertically or horizontally related behaviors. I am not suggesting that these studies should not have been done, but if we continue to do only this type of study we are left with descriptions of single-code behaviors in limited social contexts with no way of knowing how they relate to the multitude of other code behaviors these speakers evidence. We cannot, then, attach meaning to the behaviors with any confidence since we have no way of knowing whether meaning adheres to them alone, to a combination of behaviors of which they are a part, or to some other behavior with which they co-occur. Even if we could confidently attach such meanings, we have no way of placing those meanings in a cultural context because no studies exist of either behavior in other situations in either culture. As a result we are left with only our ethnocentric scholarly intuitions as a basis for our generalizations.[19]

In order to understand adequately the communication process in the intercultural classroom, we need a data base including, at a minimum, studies of the entire range of code behaviors listed earlier in the following settings in both the relevant Native American culture and the local White overculture.[20] First, the home—characterizing both the behavior of children and adolescents together and their interactions with adult caregivers, including contexts of instruction, correction, and punishment. Anecdotal data suggest that adult strategies in these contexts vary widely in these two cultures. Second, a sufficient number of settings housing adult-to-adult behavior give us some understanding of the appropriate ways that people interact with members of their own sex and with members of the opposite sex within each culture. The settings should include both social and professional/job contexts. These studies will give us an understanding of the communication behaviors and strategies each culture considers appropriate to train its younger generation to use as adults.

Finally, the school setting needs to be described carefully. Here the interactive communication behaviors of members of each culture are characterized as contributions to the intercultural process. Now we can see these behaviors in the context of their actors' cultures, and culturally appropriate meanings can be attached to them. In addition, the reactions of each participant to the other's behaviors can be used to help us interpret what meanings they have attached to those behaviors. Such an ordered approach comes far closer to offering a complete understanding of the intercultural process in classrooms containing Native American students and White teachers than what we are doing at present. It supplies us with a description of a wide range of code behaviors so that we can understand them in relation to each other; it describes those behaviors in the context in which they have occurred so that contextual meaning can be attached; and it grounds that description in the larger cultural context which, after all, determines the participants' interpretations of their own and others' behaviors. Out of that larger description we can begin to understand and characterize the intercultural communication taking place in this setting.

A SUGGESTED APPROACH

What methodologies are available to utilize in such investigations? What methodologies will produce usable descriptions of the complex code of behaviors and yet will remain faithful to the context so that meanings can be attached to those behaviors? It seems to me that there are some that are available, either individually or in combination, to tackle this problem. They are not ends in themselves, but simply tools to use to gain insights other tools do not offer. I am suggesting that we use them to analyze large amounts of very comlex data so that those data can become usable. We can then address questions of meaning and strategy in ways that may be more fruitful than those we are now using. I will briefly discuss three such methodologies—sociolinguistics, ethnomethodology, and the ethnography of speaking—touching on their rationale, scope, and results.

Sociolinguistics takes as its subject matter the study of language in its social context. It has been with us, in an official form, for nearly two decades. Joshua Fishman described the goals of sociolinguistics as

(1) The description of the linguistic and functional characteristics of the language varieties involved in the verbal repertoire of a speech community.
(2) The discovery of the societal rules or norms that explain and constrain language behavior and the behavior toward language in speech communities.
(3) The determination of the symbolic value of language varieties for their speakers.[21]

I understand these goals to be even more valid now than they were in 1970, even though the methodologies and phenomena of interest have changed somewhat. Early sociolinguists were mostly interested in phonological and grammatical phenomena, but currently there is a great deal of interest in discourse-level phenomena such as the organization of narrative[22] and the interpretation of contributions to conversations.[23]

Sociolinguists regularly use linguistic analytic methods to examine what we are calling code behaviors: to isolate them and to illustrate their interrelationships. This is one of their strengths—their use of a rigorous set of methods to examine language. Sociolinguists, however, differ from other types of linguists in the data base they find appropriate. They concentrate on *language in use*, not on their intuitions about language, as their primary data. Finally, sociolinguists use sociological methods to demonstrate the relationships between the language behaviors of interest and the social norms of the community. Among other things, they have supplied us with a great deal of valuable data on the structure and use of language in Black and Puerto-Rican communities in this country, on the structure and function of pidgins and creoles, which develop as code systems between two communities without a common language, and on the progress of language change.

Ethnomethodology is the study of how people construct their everyday, ordinary activities and use those constructions to make their behaviors accountable and reportable.[24] Since talk is the main means people have for such construction and accounting, talk becomes a primary source of data for ethnomethodologists, even those who are not essentially interested in examining only talk (as Garfinkel himself is not, for example). Ethnomethodologists do not utilize a rigorous set of methods for dealing with the structures and units contained within talk, and therefore we can find holes in their work.[25] Notwithstanding this weakness, their rigorous handling of large amounts of data in order to determine patterns, interpret them, and generalize from those interpretations offers a great deal of value to communication scholars interested in code behaviors. An increasing body of very interesting work on the structure and function of verbal interaction, especially conversation, is emerging from the field of ethnomethodology. It is safe to say that anyone in communication who is working on conversational interaction acknowledges some debt to ethnomethodology.

One of the strengths of sociolinguistics and ethnomethodology is their reliance on context. Mishler points out that

human action and experience are context dependent and can only be understood within their contexts. We rely on context to understand the behavior and speech of others and to ensure that our own behavior is understood, implicitly grounding our interpretations of motives and intentions in context.[26]

If we wish to determine the context-bound norms or rules toward code use and function, as sociolinguistics (and communication) does, or if we wish to interpret and account for context-bound, everyday conversational behavior, as ethnomethodology (and communication) does, then we must place context squarely in the middle of our investigation, as they do. Only by doing so can we arrive at some understanding of the meanings that attach to the behaviors in which we are interested.

If meaning is context bound, how can we arrive at contextual descriptions that have anything to say to each other? One way, it seems to me, is to follow some set of principles for organizing contexts according to the place that they have in a given society's organization of its everyday world. Dell Hymes offers us such a way in his call for the development of a field called the Ethnography of Speaking. Hymes sees the goal of this field to be a description of speech that understands speech to be systematic cultural behavior, necessarily concerned with the organization of diversity.[27] Here and elsewhere he outlines a taxonomic framework for studying the organization of communication. For Hymes,

> The starting point is the ethnographic analysis of the communicative conduct of a community. One must determine what can count as a communicative event, and as a component of one and admit no behavior as communicative that is not framed by some setting and implicit question. The communicative event thus is central.[28]

Hymes acknowledges his debt to communication theory and to Roman Jakobson as he lists the components of an ethnographic description of communication: participants, channels, codes, settings, message forms and genres, attitudes and contents, and the events themselves.[29] These components are separate, not intended to be collapsed together, as we so often tend to do.

Even if one is not doing ethnographies, the explicit inclusion of these components into one's descriptions will do two things. First, it will inevitably result in a body of data that can be organized according to communicative contexts within and across cultures. We can then begin to understand the range of events that serve to express and perpetuate values within a culture and begin to compare similar events across cultures. Second, it serves as a general framework for investigation within which we can follow those methodologies appropriate to the specific issue in which we are interested. If our goal is the understanding of code or the relationship between code and some other components of the event, then sociolinguistic or ethnomethodological methods seem especially appropriate.

We do not necessarily need to become ethnographers, sociolinguists, or ethnomethodologists in order to accomplish these goals. We do need to become skillful enough to incorporate those methods into our work. More important, we need to encourage our students to become skillful practitioners and to invite ethnographers, sociolinguists, and ethnomethodologists into the body of scholars that we gather around us in search of an understanding of the intercultural communication process.

NOTES

1. Even using very relaxed definitions of language, a review by H. W. Cunmings of the feature article in *QJS, HCR, Communication Education,* and *Communication Monographs* from 1969 to 1979 uncovered only 60 articles on language.

2. Huber W. Ellingsworth, "Adaptive Intercultural Communication," this volume.

3. See John J. Gumperz, "Sociocultural Knowledge in Conversational Inference," in *Georgetown University Roundtable on Languages and Linguistics 1977,* ed. M. Saville-Troike (Washington, DC: Georgetown University Press, 1977), for a discussion of code phenomenon demonstrating that code is much more complex than Ellingsworth's adaptation can handle.

4. Kenneth L. Pike, *Tone Languages* (Ann Arbor: University of Michigan Press, 1977).

5. W. S. Condon and W. D. Ogston, "Sound Film Analysis of Normal and Pathological Behavior Patterns," *Journal of Nervous and Mental Disease* 143 (1966): 338-46; Adam Kendon, "A Description of Some Human Greetings," in *Studies in the Behavior of Social Interaction,* ed. A. Kendon (Bloomington: University of Indiana Press, 1977).

6. I am intentionally using the term rather loosely in order to avoid a very lengthy discussion of the definition and usefulness of the concept of sentence.

7. Kendon, "Description of Some Human Greetings."

8. John Searle, "Indirect Speech Acts," in *Syntax and Semantics,* vol. 3, ed. P. Cole and J. Morgan (New York: Academic Press, 1973).

9. John L. Fisher, "Social Influence in the Choice of a Linguistic Variant," in *Language in Culture and Society,* ed. Dell Hymes (New York: Harper & Row, 1964).

10. William L. Leap, "The Study of American Indian English," in *Studies in Southwestern Indian English,* ed. W. L. Leap (San Antonio, TX: Trinity University, 1977).

11. John J. Gumperz, "Communication in Multilingual Societies," in *Language in Social Groups: Essays by John J. Gumperz,* ed. Anwar S. Dil (Stanford, CA: Stanford University Press, 1971).

12. Thomas Kochman and Alan Harris, "Methodology to Examine the Race and Culture Correlation" (Paper delivered at the 1980 International Communication Association convention, Acapulco, Mexico, May 1980).

13. Ralph E. Cooley, "Spokes in a Wheel: A Linguistic and Rhetorical Analysis of Native American Public Discourse," in *Proceedings of the Fifth Annual Meeting of the Berkeley Linguistic Society* (Berkeley: Berkeley Linguistic Society, 1979).

14. W. von Raffler-Engel, "Some Rules of Socio-Kinesics," in *Proceedings of the Fourth International Congress of Applied Linguistics*, vol. 2, ed. G. Nickel (Stuttgart: HochschulVerlag Stuttgart, 1976).

15. *Oklahoma Journal*, September 13, 1980.

16. Phillip Lujan, W. R. Kennan, L. B. Hill, and L. Long, "Communication Reticence and Native Americans in the Classroom" (Paper delivered at the Speech Communication Association convention, San Antonio, November 1979).

17. Ralph E. Cooley and Roger Babich, "The Structure of Native American Public Speeches" (Paper delivered at the Second Annual Southeastern Native American Bilingual Education Conference, Jackson, MS, March 1979); Cooley, "Spokes in a Wheel."

18. Ina Siler and Diana Labadie-Wondergem, "Cultural Factors in the Organization of Native American Speeches" (Paper delivered at the Eighth Annual Southwest Area Language and Linguistics Workshop, Arizona State University, April 1979).

19. At the 1980 ICA convention there was considerable discussion about the ethics of doing intercultural resarch without a representative from both cultures on the research team. Viewed from the perspective of this chapter, adding a representative from each culture is only part of the solution, since it can only add another set of ethnocentric intuitions to the research team. The problem will not be solved until our investigations are gounded in theory constructed on a broad data base.

20. The assumption here is that the White school teacher is a representative of that overculture and that his or her behavior reflects not only values of the overculture, but also that overculture's interpretations of students' behavior and its expectations about how the students should modify their behaviors to conform to the overculture's norms.

21. Joshua A. Fishman, *Sociolinguistics: A Brief Introduction* (Rowley, MA: Newbury House, 1969), p. 3.
Conversation (New York: Academic Press, 1977).

22. William Labov and Joshua Waletzky, "Narrative Analysis," in *Essays on the Verbal and Visual Arts* (Seattle: University of Washington Press, 1967).

23. William Labov and David Fanshel, *Therapeutic Discourse: Psychotherapy as Conversation* (New York: Academic Press, 1977)

24. Harold Garfinkel, *Studies in Ethnomethodology* (Englewood Cliffs, NJ: Prentice-Hall, 1967), pp. 1-3.

25. For example, one of the weakest parts of Harvey Sacks et al.'s rules for turn-taking is the lack of any rigorous definition of the internal structure of the turns themselves. A clear understanding of how rules apply depends on such a definition, and a resercher who intends to use those rules as a framework for investigating conversational dominance, for instance, must first arrive at a definition for her- or himself—with the resulting risk of deviating from the rules themselves. See H. Sacks et al., "A Simplest Systematics for the Organization of Turn-Taking for Conversation," in *Studies in the Organization of Conversational Interaction*, ed. J. Schenkein (New York: Academic Press, 1978).

26. Elliot G. Mishler, "Meaning in Context," *Harvard Educational Review* 49 (1979): 2.

27. Dell Hymes, "Sociolinguistics and the Ethnography of Speaking," in *Social Anthropology and Language*, ed. E. Ardener (London: Tavistock, 1971), p. 51.

28. Dell Hymes, *Foundations of Sociolinguistics* (Philadelphia: University of Pennsylvania, 1974), p. 9.

29. Ibid., p. 10.

14

Language Theory and Linguistic Principles

NOBLEZA ASUNCION-LANDE ● *University of Kansas*

Linguists have long been aware of the significance of language in human interaction. This is seen in the writings of language scholars from the ancient past to the present time. Their statements about linguistic phenomena can provide insights into the role of language in intercultural communication, and can provide a linguistic framework on which to organize a theory of intercultural communication.

Linguistics as defined in this chapter refers to the scientific study of language. The important foci of lingustic study are a precise description of a particular language and its role in human life and society, and a logical description of a general grammar of language that can provide an understanding of communicative ability.

The purpose of this chapter is to relate developments in linguistics to the development of theory in intercultural communication. Certain Asian theoretical concepts from the past have exercised an influence on current thinking concerning the features of human language, and its connection with other systems of communication. Some of the more significant ones will be mentioned. Major concepts of modern linguistics and their implications for intercultural communication theory will be discussed.

Certain theoretical assumptions about language from the ancient and remote past have exercised an influence on current thinking concerning the features of human language and its connection with other systems of communication. I shall mention some of the more significant ones.

Chinese linguistic studies from the second century A.D. onwards viewed the phenomenon of linguistic change as an important part of the phonetic study of the language. The causes of linguistic change were discussed and scholars referred to the factors of linguistic contacts and mixtures. In this context multilingualism was a recognized fact of life. The linguistic scholars devoted their efforts to lexicography and phonology. This led to a systematization of rules and the standardization of the pronunciation of characters.

Chinese grammatical theory distinguished between "full" and "empty" words.[1] A full word signified the object that constituted the matter of discourse; an empty word did not signify anything of itself but merely contributed to the total meaning of a sentence by imposing upon it a certain form or organization. Chinese linguistic scientists attempted to discover the full semantic properties of a word. They concluded that it was difficult to capture the meaning, much less the spirit, of an old word or phrase. The meaning of a written word must be "talked into being."[2] Furthermore, meaning could not exist independently of context. It was necessary to recreate the context of when it was written, that is, the personalities, the problems and conditions of the time, the intentions of the speakers.

Indian linguistic studies, which go back further than European linguistic scholarship, had their origin in the need to preserve intact the text and pronunciation of the Vedic hymns. The precise and accurate recitation of these hymns was deemed essential to their efficacy in Hindu ritual.

India's best-known piece of linguistic study is Panini's Sanskrit grammar. It is believed to date between 600 and 300 B.C. The grammar consists of approximately 4000 rules and lists of basic roots to which reference is made in the rules. The rules are ordered in sequence in such a way that the scope of a particular rule is defined or restricted by the preceding rules.

In India general linguistic theory was debated by scholars. Language was considered against the background both of literary studies and of philosophical inquiry. Various questions involved in understanding the nature of word and sentence meanings were discussed from different points of view. Indian linguists considered the extent to which onomatopoeia could be taken as a model for a description of the relationship between word and thing. Meanings were seen to be learned both from observation of the contexts of situation in which words were actually used in sentences and from direct statements by elders and teachers concerning particular words and their uses. Much attention was also paid to the relations between what was considered the primary meaning of a word, which was said to be understood first, and the various meanings arising from its metaphorical use both in everyday communication and for particular literary effects.

A question that has not really been resolved, even up to the present time, is that of the semantic relation between a sentence and its component words. One set of Indian thinkers were of the view that the sentence is built up of words, each contributing its meaning to the total meaning of the sentence. But an opposite view regarded the sentence as a single undivided utterance conveying its meaning in a flash, just as a picture is first perceived as a unity notwithstanding subsequent analysis of its components.

Arab linguistic studies sprang up from the Koran. As the sacred book of the Islamic faith, the Koran was the bond of unity over the entire Arab world. An Islamic stricture, which is true even today, is that the Koran must not be translated. Non-Arab converts to Islam must learn Arabic to read and understand it. The needs of these converts and the bureaucracy to learn the language of Islam gave rise to linguistic expositions and debate. One set of thinkers laid stress on the strict regularity and the systematic nature of language as a means of communication about the world. Linguistic scholarship focused on orderly and precise descriptions of the language, the organs of utterance, and the different configurations of the vocal tract. This laid the foundations for grammatical description and teaching of Arabic from then on. An opposite view gave more importance to the diversity of language as it was actually found, including dialectical variations and textual occurrences as they were accepted. This influenced the thinking on the study of the vernaculars as worthy of intense scholarly effort and to the notion popular to this day that there is no human language that is in a primitive or in an advanced state of development.

This bird's eye view of Ancient Eastern linguistic theories suggests why these theories still exercise influence today. The challenge for intercultural communication theorists is to discover specific features of Eastern theory that can contribute to a general theory capable of explaining or predicting communication phenomena and that can be accepted by both Eastern and Western scholars.

Modern linguistic theory in fact has been eclectic in absorbing some elements of Eastern linguistic thinking. In their quest for universal features of human languages, modern linguistic scientists have come up with certain conceptual formulations.

There is a general belief that all human language have a deep and a surface structure. The *deep structure* of a sentence refers to its semantic interpretation, while the *surface structure* refers to the organization of a sentence into categories and phrases directly associated with the physical signal. The implication of this concept for communication theory lies in the belief that the deep structure of a sentence suggests the intimate connection between languge and culture. It also leads to the conception of an underlying universal grammar for all known languages.

Context of situation refers to the "meaning potential" of language. When one speaks, one makes a choice as to whether to make a statement, ask a question, generalize or particularize, repeat or add something new, and the like. The system of available options is the grammar of the language, and the communicator makes selections within this system not in a vacuum but in the context of speech situations.

The *etic* and *emic* approaches for the description of behavior extend the use of basic structural units beyond languge and apply them to human behavior in general. As such, they provide a basis upon which a predictive science of behavior can be made. The etic approach to behavior prepares an observer to recognize quickly the different kinds of events and to help him or her see slight differences between similar events. The value of an emic study is that it leads to an understanding of the way in which a language or culture is constructed, not as a series of miscellaneous parts but as a working whole; it helps one to appreciate and understand the culture and the individuals as the latter play out their roles in their ordered contexts; it also enables one to define similarities and differences of behaviors in cultural contexts.

The principle of language change enables linguists to determine the process of linguistic change over time. Whether or not a country has an official language set that is maintained by an academy or in the form of prescriptive grammars or dictionaries, the actual language of its speakers keeps changing, not only from generation to generation, but also during the lifetime of a single person. Since language is a set of habits maintained chiefly through the interaction between members of a speech community, it will change if the frequency of intercommunication is diminished. There are many factors in linguistic change but what is important to the intercultural communicator are the changes that result from influences between speaker groups. Different groups of speakers, be they age groups, social classes, dialect groups, or speakers of different national languages, have of course always had some degree of intercommunication and thus have influenced one another's speech. The most important is the influence of parents on children. This is the way a language is transmitted and maintained. Education also plays an important part in the influence of one group on another. This is done when people become aware of the styles of speaking in the different periods of history. Another example is when a speaker overcorrects to imitate a supposedly higher form of speech. Another form of influence is that of borrowing between dialects and languages. This is a quite common phenomenon especially as intercommunication is increased between peoples from different cultures and countries.

The potential of language theory for building a theory in intercultural communication is quite significant. It may provide clues for developing the linkage between language and communication and communication and culture. It may point to some specific directions for studying the nature of communication in cross-cultural contexts. It can prove helpful in dealing with the "process" phenomenon of intercultural communication. Process in linguistics relates to the interconnectedness of actions, events, states and relations, and the persons, objects, and abstractions associated with them. For these reasons, it is important that linguistic principles and language theory should form part of the framework for a theory of intercultural communication.

NOTES

1. R. H. Robins, *A Short History of Linguistics* (London: Longmans Green, 1967), p. 105.

2. R. T. Oliver, *Culture and Communication* (Springfield, IL: Charles C. Thomas, 1962), p. 142.

15

Culture and the Attribution Process
Barriers to Effective Communication

PETER EHRENHAUS ● *Rutgers University*

> Two strangers walking down a city street approach each other. They draw near. One says, "Hello." They pass. The other ponders, "I wonder what that was all about?"

Communications sustains all human relationships. It is necessary but insufficient for organizing social life. That organization—the definition, shape, and development of relationships—is further contingent upon the significance interactants attribute to the messages through which their relationships are constituted. My concern in this chapter is to examine both the mediation of culture upon the attribution process and the consequences of intercultural communication.

The argument I develop in this chapter is based in attribution theory. That theory, and the research it has generated, is concerned with understanding the manner in which persons organize and assign meaning to the events and actions they experience and observe. The theory has important implications for intercultural communication.[1] The purpose of this chapter is to explore some of those implications.

The chapter is developed in two sections. First, I provide a brief overview of the attribution process. I emphasize the role of direct communication in that process, and I develop conceptual definitions of effectiveness and interpersonal coherence consistent with that process. Second, I discuss the role of culture in the attribution process, relating it specifically to the cognitive mechanisms by which experience is organized. I discuss differences in cultures' interpretive structures, using Hall's distinction between high- and low-context cultures.[2] The chapter concludes with comments upon the implications of those differences for effective, coherent intercultural communication.

ATTRIBUTION, COHERENCE, AND EFFECTIVENESS

Attribution theory stems from the work of Fritz Heider.[3] It concerns itself with the manner in which persons organize the stream of information they receive from their environment into meaningful events and actions—how persons make sense of the world around them. In regard to social behavior, attribution concerns the process by which a person organizes the continuous stream of information provided by another's behavior into meaningful units that provide the basis for social inference and social action.

Heider views the attribution process as a continuous causal stream,[4] and not as a series of discrete, sequential stages of information processing. It is neither exclusively nor primarily concerned with inference-making. It does concern the interactive process by which the individual bridges the world outside with his or her perceptual experience and comprehension of that world.

An analysis of the attribution process begins with the objects toward which the individual's attention is directed. Let us assume this object is another individual. According to Heider, the world beyond the individual is inaccessible to direct experience. We cannot, for example, directly apprehend another's thoughts, intentions, or understandings. We can only gain information about another through the mediation of the physical world. We can observe, we can be informed, or we can directly engage another in communication. In the case of direct communication, we have contact with the messages constituting the interaction.

However, we do not merely have contact with messages; messages are perceptually organized into meaningful units of information.[5] These units of organized experience enable attributions of meaning to the messages, and to the other as inferred through the messages.

This framework may seem cumbersome, and inconsistent with the fluidness of social interaction as we experience it. In fact, the process of attribution would be impeded if each human experience and interaction were encountered anew, strange and dissimilar to all others. However, attributors approach interactions with expectations, which enable us to organize and assign significance to experience and interaction. Working with these expectations, the process of attribution occurs in automatic fashion.[6] We most frequently perceive and comprehend simultaneously. Occasions do arise when our expectations are clearly not met, when they cannot fit the experience, or when our uncertainty for the interaction precludes clear expectations; in these circumstances, attribution proceeds as controlled information processing. Understanding, should it arise, occurs subsequent to perception. We must impose meaningful units upon the continuous stream of information, and draw plausible inferences from those perceived units.

For the stream of communication to be coherent, an attributor must be able to organize the structure and sequence of the messages into personally and socially meaningful units.[7] Consider the vignette that opened the chapter. The main character was unable to attribute meaning, the practical implication of the everyday utterance of "hello," as it occurred in the context of walking down a city street. You, the reader, may have found it humorous, because such a simple structured expectation for interaction in that context was not shared by the character. You might have wondered what caused the character's uncertainty, why such a common expectation for interaction on a public thoroughfare was not shared. As you wondered, you may have tested various explanations for their plausibility—the character was of some remote culture, or was insane, or was a psychoanalyst, or was a frightened resident of a terrorized urban environment. You may have chosen the last explanation as most plausible, since the vignette informs you that the encounter occurred on a city street, and you found that situational information salient to your inference-making.[8] That is, you identified the information about the location of the interaction significant for developing a relevant and reasonable explanation of the various features of the encounter. Regardless of your conclusion, your attributional search was virtually instantaneous. Your appreciation was immediate upon perception. The fluidness of your experience was unimpeded.

When two persons converse, both engage in the process of attribution. Both attribute meaning to the messages that constitute the interaction and to the other as inferred through the messages.[9] Communicators are interdependent, linked through the stream of messages they jointly generate and to which they both have access. A conversation is both cause and consequence of two conversants' attribution processes as they strive to create coherence. Each attributor must structure the continuous flow of information from the other's messages into meaningful units that collectively cohere, particularly in light of his or her own contributions. However, the ability of two attributors to construe their communicative interaction coherently does not ensure that the two versions of coherence are congruent. From the perspective of attribution theory, interpersonal incoherence can accompany personal coherence. I propose the following conceptions to clarify the implications of the attribution process for communicative interaction.

(1) Interpersonal coherence is the sine qua non of each and every communicative exchange. While attributors may presume coherence, it is a goal to be strived for continually.

(2) Interpersonal coherence results when both attributors structure the continuous stream of communication similarly, and cue structures of expectation congruently.

(3) Interpersonal coherence may be achieved and lost repeatedly through-out an interaction, although the linguistic contributions of the com-municators may be smoothly coordinated.

(4) Effectiveness in communicative interaction is defined by the relative proportion of interpersonal coherence that is achieved. The higher the ratio of attributional congruence, the greater the effectiveness of the interaction.

CULTURAL INFLUENCES ON
THE ATTRIBUTION PROCESS

The structuring principles that guide attributors to organize actions into meaningful units and to make action coherent are known by different label—frames, scripts, schemata. All of these terms refer to structures of expectations.[10] These conceptual structures are inductively derived and probalistic, and they are based upon our experiences of the world within some culture or series of cultures. We use them to organize our knowledge about the world and to make predictions about newly encountered events, information and interaction.[11]

The link between these structures of expectations and culture is fundamental. Freedle offers two conceptions of culture in terms of these structures. In one, culture is "a set of schemata for concretizing habitual ways to perform activities including those involving language."[12] Culture is a series of structured expectations for making action and language use routine. These expectations guide and enable fluid social interaction. Similarly, Hall refers to situational frames, "made up of situational dialects, material appurtenances, situational personalities, and behavior patterns that occur in recognized settings and are appropriate to specific situations."[13] Reading situations properly—determining the proper structuring principle for participating in and interpreting interaction—is a matter of making the correct attributions.

In Freedle's other view, culture is "a set of interactive schemata for habitual ways in which interacting individuals can dynamically discover what each person intends to convey *given the immediate context and shared presuppositions of the culture.*[14] Culture is the collection of expectations by which we construct, test, and modify our interpretations of the discourse and of the other's purposes as inferred through the discourse. Here, culture is not a fixed set of expectations imposed upon interaction. Rather, as Frake suggests, "culture provides principles for framing experience as eventful in particular ways."

Culture does not impose a cognitive map upon persons, but provides them with a set of principles for map-making and navigation. The mapping process results in a "whole chart case of rough, improvised, continually revised sketch maps. Different cultures are like different schools of navigation designed to cope with different terrains and seas."[15]

Both of Freedle's views of culture provide workable bases for learning about the relationship of culture to the attribution process. The former view directs our attention to stable cognitive structures. How are those structures cued? What features of a stereotyped interaction become attributionally salient within a particular structure of expectation? The latter view directs our attention toward cognitive processing. In what way does attribution direct the dynamic discovery process of which Freedle speaks? How do these map-making principles of which Frake speaks lead persons to develop particular attributional predispositions? In the remainder of this chapter, I will offer a series of propositions concerning the mediation of culture upon attribution. I will conclude with comment upon the implications of culturally based attributional differences for effective intercultural communication.

> *Hypothesis 1:* High-context culture (HCC) members are attributionally sensitive and predisposed toward situational features and situationally based explanations. Low-context culture (LCC) members are attributionally sensitive and predisposed toward dispositional characteristics and dispositionally based explanations.

Hall observes that cultures differ considerably in both the manner and extent to which their expectations for action and language use are informed by their reliance on the immediate context and on the implicit, shared presuppositions of the culture.[16] His distinction is that of high-context and low-context cultures. In HCCs, considerable information to focus expectations and guide the attribution of meaning is embedded in the physical context or is internalized in the person (i.e., the person has internalized the culture's presuppositions). For such a system to be effective, its users must become highly sensitive to situational features for guiding their own behavior and for making predictions about other persons' behavior. In HCCs, communicative behavior is proportionally more a product of situational forces than of the internal characteristics of the interactants. Relatively less information needs to be explicitly encoded. The situationally sensitive attributor is predisposed to the availability of information in the immediate context.

In LCCs, relatively little information to focus expectations and guide the attribution process is available in the physical context or is presumed to be shared by the interactants. Limited contextual information requires messages to be high in information value. Communication is presumed to reflect more the character of the interactants than the character of the situation, since constraints upon their behavior are fewer than in HCCs.

Individuals develop attributional sensitivities and predispositions to enable fluid attribution and interaction within their own cultures. Different features of the interaction are seen by culturally disparate attributors as salient, and these differing salient features cue each attributor to rely upon his or her familiar structures of expectations.

Tannen provides evidence of the mediation of culture upon structures of expectations.[17] She examines evidence of expectations in language production. The study concerns the relationship of expectations to the production of narrative; the findings can apply to intercultural interaction as well. Subjects viewed a brief silent film and provided narratives of the action. The film showed a series of actions: a man picking pears from a tree and placing them in baskets, a boy on a bicycle stealing a basket, the young thief having a bicycle accident in the presence of a girl, his rescue by other boys, their reward of pears, and their being observed eating pears by the man who picked them. The film was shown to Greeks and Americans. Tannen found that the two cultural groups had diverse and sometimes contradictory expectations guiding their narratives. Some of these differences were revealed in their moral judgments, their specific inclusion or deletion of information presented in the film, and in their manufacturing novel elements to fit their narratives. The narratives fit subjects' expectations for what events could occur, how and why they occurred, and what motives guided the characters.

Zadny and Gerard experimentally demonstrate the power of expectations in the attribution process.[18] When attributors expect certain actions to be guided by particular intentions, they attend to and recall action bearing on those intentions. Attributors identify intent-relevant features of action as salient. This tendency to identify features of action as salient enables attributors to parse the continuous flow of information into meaningful units consistent with their structures of expectations. Further, the ability to construct a coherent explanation justifies the appropriateness of those expectations that guided the attribution process.

> **Hypothesis 2:** In initial intercultural interactions, HCC and LCC communicators will seek out information deemed salient by each. This search, based upon the presuppositions of their respective cultures, will be the source of misattributions about each other.

A variety of studies indicate important differences between HCCs and LCCs regarding what information is salient for learning about others, what style of exchanging information is desirable, and what topics are acceptable and when they should be broached. Gudykunst finds that in HCCs, the type of information that is salient for learning about another and being able to predict that person's behavior and character pertains to social background.[19] Compared to LCCs, more questions asked of another pertain to social background, and this information is the basis for a broad range of assumptions. In their comparative study of Chinese and Americans, Alexander, Cronen, Kong, Tsou, and Banks find that the Chinese subjects believe they can infer an individual's intellectual and academic potential by knowing demographic data about a person.[20] By contrast, Gudykunst and Alexender et al. find that LCC members seek out large quantities of information about another, which emphasizes the personal rather than the social.

These differences in perceived salience reflect the attributional sensitivities required to master each type of culture. As Freedle suggests, we can consider culture as a set of schemata for discovering the other's intentions given the context and shared presuppositions of the culture. In an HCC, social background is a contextual fact acting as a constraint upon one's behavior. Further, the implications of knowing the culture's presuppositions are self-reflexive: One is aware of one's background, one shares it with another, both are aware that such contextual information should constrain behavior, and one implicitly allows it to constrain behavior. In this manner, sociographic information becomes a valuable tool for attributing intentions, characteristics, and abilities to others, and for making them predictable. The predictive validity of sociographic information relies upon the heuristic of representativeness.[21] HCC attributors classify and make predictions about another on the basis of that person's group membership. Because of the utility of this inferential shortcut, HCC attributors become more predisposed toward the heuristic than do LCC attributors.

In contrast, situational constraints are few in LCCs (i.e., the members of such cultures allow them to be few). Consequently, the predictability of an individual becomes contingent upon acquiring information specific to that individual. Social background information becomes relatively trivial; LCC attributors must learn about the other qua individual, rather than about the other qua group member.

Conversational styles, in a general sense, also differ between HCCs and LCCs. Gudykunst finds that initial interactions by members of HCCs tend to be relatively cautious, while LCC persons tend to be relatively open and verbose. Verbosity would tend to be consistent with the need to acquire large amounts of personal data. Further, as Elliot, Jensen, and McDonough indicate, the significance attributed to these different styles also differs.[23] Within the LCC of the United States, higher levels of verbosity are positively related to perceived attractiveness. In the HCC of Korea, less verbosity is perceived as more attractive. Americans attribute lower levels of verbosity to reticence, a dispositional characteristic.

Finally, Alexander et.al. indicate that Chinese and U.S. sequence topics differ in conversation.[24] Topic placement concerns a sequence of related events in a coherent manner, quite similar to the various concept of scripts, frames, and schemata. Such structures of expectations provide the basis for making judgments about the event sequence. And, as Hall states, "As in all HCC systems, the forms that are used are important. To misuse them is a communication in itself."[25] The range of appropriate topics also differs between these two cultures. More topics are prohibited in the Chinese culture. More are obligated in the U.S. culture; this obligation is consistent with the need to acquire a great range of personal data to reduce uncertainty about the other.

Hypothesis 3: Intercultural communicators are particularly likely to commit the "ultimate attribution error."

Attribution research has produced a series of findings suggesting that observers systematically underestimate the contextual and social constraints upon actors and overestimate the personal dispositions of actors as explanations of their behaviors. [26] Pettigrew believes this bias is exaggerated by cultural differences between the actor and the observer, and that the bias extrapolates from the actor as an individual to the actor as a member of an outgroup.[27] When observers are asked to explain the behavior of outgroup members, acts perceived as negative are overattributed to the personal characteristics of the individuals; special explanations account for positive acts by outgroup members.

Pettigrew argues that this ultimate attribution error is at its most extreme in individuals who are prejudiced. However, all persons are subject to patterned differences in the manner in which they interpret the behavior of members of their own group and of other groups. Consequently, the ultimate attribution error is ubiquitous. Only its intensity is variable.

There is considerable support for Pettigrew's position. Wang and McKillip find that Chinese international students in the United States and U.S. nationals attribute higher levels of culpability to outgroup members in making judgments about fines for automobile accidents.[28] Duncan finds that whites are more inclined to attribute negative acts to personal dispositions when the actor is black, and to attribute the cause of those same acts to situational factors when the actor is white.[29] Taylor and Jaggi find further evidence for the ultimate attribution error in a South Indian context.[30] Hindus say the favorable actions of members of their own group are due to personal dispositions and unfavorable actions are due to situational factors; the pattern was reversed when Hindus judged the same actions performed by Muslims.

As Kanouse and Hanson observe, attributors have a reliable tendency to overemphasize negative information about others.[31] Negative behavior is more informative, carrying greater weight; it stands in contrast to standards of behavior and expectations emphasizing the positive. Such distinctiveness makes negative information salient for the attribution process. An actor's deviations from the norm are more revealing than is conformity with the norm.

Where culture is a mediating factor, the Kanouse and Hanson finding is more applicable to attributions about outgroup members, regardless of whether the attributors are members of HCCs or LCCs. We can only speculate about the reasons such charity is shown in group members. In HCCs, obligated, prohibited, and permissible behavior choices are informed extensively by contextual cues and by the shared presuppositions of the culture that the interactants share. It becomes increasingly unlikely, therefore, than an ingroup member would intentionally behave in an undesirable fashion, particularly since persons of HCCs "sync on a conscious level."[32] Some unknown factor in the situation of the deviant actor must be behind the behavior. In LCCs, a broad range of permissible behavioral options is available. It is therefore unlikely that a negative behavior would be selected with such a large array of acceptable behaviors. Some unknown situational factor must be operating.

The likelihood of perceiving some action as negative is as significant as the effect of the ultimate attribution error. It lies at the heart of the question of effectiveness in intercultural communication.

CONCLUSION

When two persons of different cultures meet, converse, attempt to learn about each other, or simply try to accomplish some social task, they do so with the expertise acquired within their own cultures. That expertise includes the expectations for organizing and interpreting social action and the particular attributional sensitivities and predispositions that have made those expectations successful in past encounters.

This chapter has examined some differences in those attributional sensitivities and predispositions. Some attributors appear to be more sensitive and inclined to search for salience cues in the context of the encounter; others search for salience cues directly in the apparently unconstrained behavior of the participants. Some seek general background information about others, presuming it to be valid for inference-making; others presume interpersonal knowledge and predictability comes only from delving into a gamut of personal data. And all are more likely to make unduly harsh disposition attributions to others who differ from themselves when their behavior appears undesirable or awkward; the judgment about the desirability or appropriateness of any behavior relies upon our expectations for how some situated social activity should develop.

While the map-making principles are those of each attributor's culture, the terrain and seas of intercultural contact can be unfamiliar in obvious and subtle ways. Those principles may work well enough to give each attributor a sense of personal coherence, but the interaction may be relatively ineffective. Making sense simply does not mean making sense accurately.

NOTES

1.   Peter Ehrenhaus, "Attribution Theory: Implications for Intercultural Communication," in *Communication Yearbook 6,* ed. Michael Burgoon (Beverly Hills, CA: Sage, 1982).

2.   Edward T. Hall, *Beyond Culture* (Garden City, NY: Anchor, 1977).

3.   Fritz Heider, *The Psychology of Interpersonal Relations* (New York: John Wiley, 1958).

4.   Fritz Heider, "A Conversation with Fritz Heider," in *New Directions in Attribution Research,* Vol. 1, ed. J. H. Harvey, W. J. Ickes, and R. F. Kidd (Hillsdale, NJ: Lawrence Erlbaum, 1976).

5.   Darryl Newtson, "Attribution and the Unit of Perception in Ongoing Behavior," *Journal of Personality and Social Psychology* 28 (1973): 28-38.

6.   W. Schneider and R. Shiffrin, "Controlled and Automatic Human Information Processing: I. Detection, Search, and Attention," *Psychological Review* 84 (1977): 1-66; and R. Shiffrin and W. Schneider, "Controlled and Automatic Information Processing: II. Perceptual Learning, Automatic Attending, and a General Theory," *Psychological Review* 84 (1977): 127-90.

7.   Newtson, "Attribution and the Unit of Perception"; and D. Newtson, "Perception of Ongoing Behavior," in *New Directions in Attribution Research,* vol. 1, ed J. H. Harvey, W. J. Ickes, and R. F. Kidd (Hillsdale, NJ: Lawrence Erlbaum, 1976).

8.   S. Taylor and S. Fiske, "Salience, Attention, and Attribution: Top of the Head Phenomena," in *Advances in Experimental Social Psychology,* vol. 11, ed. L. Berkowitz (New York: Academic Press, 1978), pp. 249-88.

9.   Helen Newman, "Interpretation and Explanation: Influences on Communicative Exchanges within Intimate Relationships, *Communication Quarterly* 29 (1981): 123-31. Newman writes of "implicit attribution-making," which are "embedded in the very perception and interpretation of communicative messages at the time such messages are experienced" (p. 124).

10.   R. N. Ross, "Ellipsis and the Structure of Expectation," *San Jose Occasional Papers in Linguistics* 1 (1975): 183-91. Cited in Deborah Tannen, "What's in a Frame? Surface Evidence for Underlying Expectations," in *New Directions in Discourse Processing,* vol. 2, ed. Roy O. Freedle (Norwood, NJ: Ablex, 1979), p. 137-81.

11.   Ibid., pp. 138-39.

12.   Roy Freedle, "Introduction to Volume 2," in *New Directions in Discourse Processing,* vol. 2, ed. Roy O. Freedle (Norwood, NJ: Ablex, 1979), p. xii.

13.   Hall, *Beyond Culture,* p. 129.

14.   Freedle, "Introduction," p. xiii. Emphasis added.

15.   Charles O. Frake, "Plying Frames Can Be Dangerous: Some Reflections on Methodology in Cognitive Anthropology," *Quarterly Newsletter of the Institute for Comparative Human Development* 1 (June 1977): 6-7.

16.   Hall, *Beyond Culture,* chapters 6-7.

17.   Tannen, "What's in a Frame?"

18.   J. Zadny and H. Gerard, "Attributed Intentions and Informational Selectivity," *Journal of Experimental Social Psychology* 10 (1974): 34-52.

19.   William Gudykunst, "Uncertainty Reduction and Predictability of Behavior in Low and High Context Cultures: An Exploratory Study," *Communication Quarterly,* in press.

20.   Alison Alexander, Vernon Cronen, Kyung-Wha Kong, Benny Tsou, and Jane Banks, "Patterns of Topic Sequencing and Information Gain: A Comparative Study of Relationship Development in Chinese and American Culture" (Paper delivered at the Conference of the Speech Communication Assocation, New York, 1980).

21.   A Tversky and D. Kahneman, "Judgment under Uncertainty: Heuristics and Biases," *Science* 185 (1974): 1124-31.

22.   Gudykunst, "Uncertainty Reduction and Predicability."

23.   Scott Ellio, Arthur Jensen, and Matthew McDonough, "Perception of Reticence: A Cross-Cultural Investigation" (Paper delivered at the Conference of the International Communication Association, Minneapolis, 1981).

24.   Alexander et al., "Patterns of Topic Sequencing."

25.   Hall, *Beyond Culture,* p. 113.

26.   E. E. Jones and R. E. Nisbett, "Actor and the Observer: Divergent Perceptions of the Causes of Behavior," in *Attribution: Perceiving the Causes of Behavior,* ed. E. E. Jones, D. E. Kanouse, H. H. Kelley, R. E. Nisbett, S. Valins, and B. Weiner (Morristown, NJ: General Learning Press, 1972), pp. 79-94; and L. Ross, "The Intuitive Psychologist and His Shortcomings: Distortions in the Attribution Process," in *Advances in Experi-*

mental Social Psychology, vol. 10, ed. L. Berkowitz (New York: Academic Press, 1977), pp. 174-221.

27.   Thomas F. Pettigrew, "The Ultimate Attribution Error: Extending Allport's Cognitive Analysis of Prejudice," *Personality and Social Psychology Bulletin* 5 (1979): 461-76.

28.   G. Wang and J. McKillip, "Ethnic Identification and Judgments of an Accident," *Personality and Social Psychology Bulletin* 4 (1978): 269-99.

29.   B. L. Duncan, "Differential Social Penetration and Attribution of Intergroup Violence: Testing and Lower Limits of Stereotyping of Blacks," *Journal of Personality and Social Psychology* 34 (1976): 590-98.

30.   D. M. Taylor and V. Jaggi, "Ethnocentrism and Causal Attribution in a South India Context," *Journal of Cross-Cultural Psychology* 5 (1974): 162-71.

31.   D. E. Kanouse and L. R. Hanson, "Negativity in Evaluations," in Attribution: Perceiving the Causes of Behavior, ed. Jones, Kanouse, Kelley, Nisbett, Valins, and Weiner.

32.   Hall, *Beyond Culture,* p. 79.

16

The Phenomenological Approach

JOSEPH J. PILOTTA • *Ohio State University*

AN OVERVIEW OF PHENOMENOLOGY

Phenomenology regards as restrictive the notion that the world consists of either things or a system of objects, and that persons are interpreted either as objects or subjects. Phenomenology exhibits the experiential assumptions implicit in the avowal of any particular world; what the world "looks like" under certain conditions may not correspond in total or in part to what the world looks like under another set of conditions. This is because the world is experienced qualitatively and meaningfully. Thus, "object" for phenomenology is treated as a quality and valuative meaning that governs in conjunction with an entire matrix of compossible meanings as "attitude" involving not only nature, but man and even the "super-natural."[1] Yet these various matrices, the religious versus the material, for example, are not *ex hypothesi* either discrete or irreconcilable. Whether in fact they are or are not is a matter to be ascertained only through the phenomenological determination of their fundamental assumptions about the world. We should add, there is good reason to maintain that they are neither. Phenomenology is empirical in the strongest sense of the word. This means that whatever is "given" or "appears" to consciousness in experience has an intrinsic quality and lawful manner of constitution. The notion of empirical is in the narrow sense, namely, whatever can be measured or, at least, seen.

For phenomenology, human behavior, including science, is a meaningful process of living a situation.[2] The human world is defined by phenomenological thought as a nexus of experience respecting both the human and the world, not as the object which *has* experiences. Human behavior is primarily the experience of meaning. Hence, it is the meaning and the experience that provide the integrative element for the study of humans. It must be noted that experience is inevitably meaningful, for indeed, the experience of meaninglessness is as well meaningful. All methods, even scientific methods, are human responses to the world assuming particular ways of experiencing the world.

Phenomenology has set out to be a science of phenomena in so far as they are given as meaningful experiences. Hermeneutics has demonstrated that there is an assumed cultural interpretation of the world; phenomenology reveals what interpretation is.[3] Interpretation is an experience of meaning and phenomenology clarifies how that interpretation is constituted in experience.

This hypothesis, namely human beings are experiencing beings whose experience is primarily the experience of meaning, seems at first almost trivial but is, in fact, potentially quite powerful. "Experience," taken phenomenologically, refers generically to the "appearing" presented to human consciousness of the world and self across various specific experiential domains. Phenomenologists have analyzed various accessations of consciousness upon the world; such domains include perception, corporeality, valuation, vitality, the aesthetic, the psychological, the theoretical, and the spiritual. This is made possible by phenomenology's building upon the assumption that all of these contexts of experience share the characteristic of involving qualitative-signification or sense-making processes. Phenomenology aims at an "archaeology of meaning," displaying how a particular meaning or meaningful manifold arises in experience and attempts to circumscribe that meaning in terms of the precise limitations established for it *by* experience.

Phenomenology is not a system. Yet it is neither arbitrary analysis, a sort of introspectionism, nor a description plain and simple. It is based on the character of experience itself. Experience itself is lawful, rather than arbitrary or vacuously subjective, and is interpretative-integrative. It is important to distinguish between phenomenology and "phenomenography." Rather than mere description, phenomenology points to the "logic" of the phenomena experienced, which are illuminated by the descriptive orientation. It identifies the significative texture of phenomena: values, aesthetic objects, religious beliefs, and so on and their genesis in experience. *The phenomenological description may indeed be the first and an important step of phenomenological study, yet such a description is obtained under a strictly controlled thought that weeds out inessentialities, delimits necessities, and exhibits the distinctive contours of various types of phenomena.* Phenomenology does not disavow the subjective factor that is operative in experience; rather it points out that subjectivity—"my own experience of the world"—is determined only in a much more encompassing context. No element is derivable from the subject. For example, the experience of subjectivity is a precondition for subjective experience as well as for experiences by the subject. Hence, while introspectionist psychology attempts to generalize about human experience on the basis of the subject's experience, phenomenology claims that one of its preconditions, namely, the assumed experience of subjectivity, involves a complex set of conditions such as "myself and other," "subject and other," "subject and object," "here and there," and so forth, the analysis of which probably leads to the analysis of an entire cultural, or at least theoretical, milieu. The elements of experience and meaning provide and integrative accessation to the comprehension of human in all contexts of their humanity. These elements are experientially prior to the category of person, since before there was a man who distinguished himself or herself from a meaningful milieu an experience is presumed. Since phenomenology does not assume a set of theoretical conditions and selected empirical features but rather seeks to discern them, the guiding question of phenomenological analysis is "how" a particular meaning is experienced and the preconditions for that experience. Only on the basis of such analysis can theoretical principles be generated. Since phenomena are meaningful and those meanings are integrated in terms of an entire matrix, experience is always situated in a particular matrix in which these experienced meanings function. The implications of this hypothesis for a theory of culture are patent. Finally, the recognition on the part of phenomenology that significations are not given in isolation formulated by Edmund Husserl as "life-world" *(Lebenswelt),* encourages the combination of phenomenological procedures with the hermeneutical. Phenomenology, in this extended sense, and hermeneutics proper share the intention of a rigorous and verifiable articulation and elucidation of this matrix of significations. Hermeneutics provides certain salient insights, and phenomenology supplies the method and the requisite theoretical framework.

The principle discovery that the world is mediated in terms of experienced meanings and that these meanings are constituted lawfully and function within an entire matrix of meanings through which various domains of human interation with nature, self, and one another are established points indicating the focus of a phenomenological-hermeneutical analysis of culture. Our method claims that all phenomena, from natural to supernatural, play a role and are comprehensible within a cultural matrix which establishes for these phenomena their characteristic locus, signficance, import, and stress. Thus, any cultural phenomenon must be investigated in its own right in light of the particular culture in which it is meaningful. Moreover, the manner in which the cultural element is expressed, in a symbol for example, must also be accorded its inherent value; for the manner in which an element of cultural life is expressed is "transparent with" the phenomenon expressed. In turn, the phenomenon expressed serves to express the particular cultural world and is interrelated with other expressions existing in that world. Thus if one speaks of "material conditions" one is referring to an expressed significance having its place within a particular matrix of a particular cultural world in which its functions meaningfully and to which it contributes a vehicle for self-interpretation. In other words, they both are defined by and help to define the cultural world to which they belong. This suggests that all phenomena are significative of the context in which they function; they are "transparent with" it. These phenomena in turn have a range of delimitations constituting an entire "field" of implications for experience: vectors signifying other phenomena that manifest that same context. This is important for the ascertaining of (1) the basic structure of the "cultural-consciousness" and (2) the interconnected "field" of phenomena revealing such consciousness. This refers of course to the hermeneutical principle of the part-whole relationship. If diverse phenomena manifest a specific consciousness-structuration, then this structure can be employed to select additional phenomena as potentially rewarding for analysis that are implied in that culture.

The concepts of "cultural-consciousness" and "cultural world" are in principle closely related to the concept of "transparency."

Jean Gebser[5] has suggested that modes of experience are institutionalized in languages, arts, sciences, social organizations, and the like. Institutionalized modes of experience in their turn interpret and shape the lives of individuals, and these various modes serve to organize and correlate the complexity of meanings into a whole. This is possible, he maintains, because the various phenomena of experience are "seen through" or "in light of" a particular experience. *Experience, in short, is correlated to a texture of meanings which do not number among the visible and tangible things or persons of the world. Rather they are "in light of" and the phenomena of experience are "in light of" the basic significative whole.*

Therefore, cultural-consciousness itself consists of basic significative dimensions. Significative dimensions or the matrix of meanings establish a cultural world. Cultural-conciousness and its expressions cannot be derived from any particular scientific analysis of perception. Erwin Strauss[6] attempted to correlate a particular spatiotemporal structure to a particular field of perception, and has demonstrated that the rhythmic temporal structure correlates to the audial field of perception and the linear temporal structure correlates to the visual field of perception. But this does not establish the derivability of such structures from the respective fields. The characteristic predominance of one perceptual field only means that the particular character of that field, including the metaphors that depend on it, it is best suited to express the particular mode of experiencing the world. A careful reading across cultures shows stresses on a particular perceptual field and its expression by a particularly apt organic component. For example, visuality-mind-linearity and audiality-soul or heart-rhythmic circularity are correlative fields, and the expressions rooted in this perceptual field are carried across all other perceptual fields to such an extent that diverse fields are overlayed by the expressions rooted in the predominant field. Thus, the specific fields of perception are laden with signficance, which provides expressive facility for the particular cultural-consciousness subtending them. At the same time, a particular stress in the perceptual field provides are important indication of the character of the cultural matrix (e.g., Western "visualism" and Eastern "audialism"). Culture thus comprises a world-matrix that is manifest through all "artificial and natural phenomena." This underscores the dubitability of the assumption of such ontological principles as materialism, idealism, and mentalism, for the investigation of cultural phenomena, if, such principles are not already part of the significative matrix. For example, if we were to say that "ultimately material components" determine the character of a particular people, we would misunderstand those people *if* in their experience such components are not expressed.

Significations (or meanings) are "detachable" from any particular event, geographical location, and natural environment and therefore can be "transposed" across time and space. This is relevant for the analysis of (1) atavism and survivals, (2) emigration and immigration, (3) expressive coincidences between otherwise unrelated cultures, unrelated either spatially or/and temporally, (4) cultural assimilation and dissimilation, (5) a cultural heritage and its ramifications, (6) cross-cultural investigation using the technique of comparison, and (7) chronologization. At the same time, it is the assumption of a signficative matrix that enables the investigation of "dead" or "past" cultures. For what distinguished the artifact from the mere refuse of the past is the signficance with which the "thing" is transparent, and which the investigator painstakingly undertakes to establish. Only the assumption of a cultural matrix not lost to time allows the "reconstruction" or the past culture. The "meaning" is not identical with the things, yet it is discerned through them.

Gebser has asserted that any particular element of a culture refers inevitably to a whole that establishes the significance of those elements, and hermeneutics requires that there is a reciprocal relationship of understanding obtaining between a particular feature and the whole of which it is a feature. The expression, while transparent with the significance, must at the same time coimply other expressions thus composing a matrix of interconnected significations revealing at their fundamental level the manner in which the significances comprise a unitary world. Thus, each expression, while manifesting the basic cultural outline, implicates as well other expressions revealing the same cultural matrix. One significance, thus, reveals all signficances and cannot be completely understood without them, while all significances are implicitly present in one signficance. This is the basis for the understanding of cultural linguistics. A word spoken in a sentence does not gain its sense from the relationships of the words within a sentence; rather the sense arises from a system of a total linguistic field carried by "tradition" and present to the speaker and hearer. The total linguistic field is a latent background out of which a sentence emerges and within which the individual words acquire their meaning. Each sentence implicates the entire language and the entire language is manifest in each sentence. The entire linguistic field and all that is signifies must be present if the specific words and sentences are to be understood, and they will be understood to the extent that the linguistic field is present. (This is the cultural basis for "communicative competence.") Of methodologically significance is the recognition of the intrinsicality of the relationships obtaining between elements of culture enabling the correlation of points of view of culture with an eye to comprehending the integrative character of experience. Moreover, it suggests the dubitability of a totalizing perspective that attempts to provide an ultimate explanation and encourages research upon various levels while maintaining that these levels are not ultimately discrete. At the same time, it indicates that we are justified in using the locution "culture" in a way other than as an empirical or simply pragmatic abstract concept comprising essentually heterogenous elements, viz. nature, economics, religious, literary, psychological, and so forth. Without neglecting the natural environmental factors and functions, the biopsychological and mental functions, the socioenvironmental functions, we are concerned with the significative-experiential functions. It has been shown quite extensively that similar environmental-natural conditions yield vastly diverse cultural configurations; at the same time it has been shown that similar biopsychological and mental conceptions assume differing significance in differing cultures. It can be shown step by step that there is no one-to-one correspondence between the environmental-natural conditions, between biopsychological and mental states and what such states signify in a particular culture. Moreover, the concepts of "environment," "psyche," "society," and "mind" depend on a meaning that may be absent in some and present in other cultures. Signification constitutes an experiential stress on particular functions and particular environmental components and excludes others. It means that in a final analysis, signification is not derivable from the environmental, biopsychological, social, or mental conditions, although such conditions are selected and defined in terms of their meaning. The "non-coincidence" between the "real" factors and their meaning indicates that the exchange-ability of factors in terms of similar functions is based on the meaning of such functions. Similar functions and factors may have diverse meaning in diverse cultures, and diverse factors and functions may have a similar meaning in differing cultures, suggesting the requirement for the understanding of the significative dimension as prior to factorial and functional analysis.

There is neither one-to-one correlation between the "real" functions and significative aspects, nor one-to-one correlation between the structurally discoverable "similarities" or "identities" and their significance in cultural life.[7] The structures may be constant but their significance in different cultures may vary; conversely, the structures may vary, yet their significance through various cultures may be the same. This variation is valid for all areas of cultural life, from socioeconomic to aesthetic. This is not to deny the importance of structural analysis of cultural processes and functions; it does correlate facts and make them manageable, yet such facts themselves must be investigated with respect to their signficance in cultural life, and the structures must be surveyed with respect to their meaning and meaning implications. This is to say that the fundamental dimension of cultural life is that of signification and not structure or function.

It may be contended that structure provides a context for meaning, that meaning is comprehensible and functional when the context is understood; without a context no meaning could be specified and hence confusion would reign. *This is precisely the first requirement for cross-cultural studies:* to appreciate the contextual differences, delimited by structural analysis, whereby meaning retains its universality. Differences are understood as differences of the same meaning within different hermeneutics and provide a point of transition between different contexts without the loss of comprehension. This is the point of conjunction between phenomenological analysis of signification aiming to discover the identity and its hermeneutical deployment across various times and cultures. This is called the principle of identity and difference in cross-cultural investigations.

This significative dimension is involved in every experiential aspect and hence is applicable to the socioeconomic as well as religious and aesthetic processes in culture. Doubtlessly, the socioeconomic process is necessary for human survival and welfare, yet as even structuralism has pointed out that social factors and economic processes depend upon the structural arrangement and interrelationships constituting the context for socioeconomy.

Another major role played by signification consists of the process of selectivity. While the environment, inclusive of nature, society, and the subjective states of individuals, may be present in toto, *what is present as an "environment" for a particular people is highly selective.* The selective process has been attributed to the structure of a society, yet such an attribution fails to account for various phenomena of cultural life; (1) while the structural components may remain constant, the functions of such components may assume differing significances at differing times; (2) the very significance of the total structure may be placed in question by a process of resignification such as is the case of revolution and major upheaval; (3) structure as such does not permit the transgression of its boundaries for the incorporation of factors outside the scope of its limits; (4) the process of resignification, while dealing with the social and cultural structure, is not based on such structures; it is a process distinct from such structures and belongs to the experiential dimension. This is not to say that the experiential dimension is not "influenced" by the structural components; it is simply to say that such components are evaluated and such structures are judged by a more fundamental process that makes sense and demands of the entire structure transformations that the structure cannot offer. This means that a particular structure is not completely "self-maintaining" as if it were an organism designed for "survival." *The process of sense-making is the basic selective-process of the environmental components and structures in terms of their signficance.* Institutional domination of the experiential process is thus circumvented, leaving an area of choice of selectivity and resignification. Although subjectivism is avoided, the experiential dimension retains its function in evaluating the entire sociocultural process and itself as either part of transcending the process.

The investigation of cultural phenomena requires a multileveled analysis of signification and the shifts of signification due to the various possible combinations of intersections of signification. There are meanings of the material phenomena, the psychological, the sociological, the valuative, the aesthetic, the religious and even the theoretical. The locus of each must be investigated with respect to the rest, their mutual influences noted and implications drawn concerning the results of the various significative interconnections. What is to be noted at the same time is the manner of interpretation of such significations by the various peoples or cultural groups. This would lead to the notion of cross-cultural influence, acceptance, or rejection of various factors from other cultures. It is necessary therefore to correlate the significative interconnections in order to determine what meaning newly introduced factors, be they technological, valuative, aesthetic, or religious, may assume within a differing cultural significative interconnection. In terms of cross-ethnic relationships such investigations are crucial. What value, for example, things may possess for one group and what meaning such values hold for that group may or may not be compatible with the meaning of the same things and values for another group. Hence the questions is not what things, values, and so on are, but what do they mean for the particular group and the individuals within the group. The question of adjustments need not be resolved at one level of meaning but must be investigated "vertically": A particular thing may have different value meanings for different groups; or while divergent in terms of religious meaning of events, the meaning of religion for one group may be similar to the meaning of human person for another, whereby convergence of meaning for differing contexts is made possible.

This theoretical framework allows for the tracing of the "significative implications" due to the introduction of factors or structures belonging to their cultures or ethnic groups. This assumes that the cultural significative interconnection functions in terms of the hermeneutical circle: A part, such as a new cultural factor or introduced structure, will affect the whole and in turn the whole will affect the part. Researchers must be initiated concerning the extent to which an introduction of a "foreign" element into a culture will affect the entire culture and to what extent the cultural context will be able to absorb and reinterpret such an element in terms of the cultural context. For example, would an introduction of the ethos of women's liberation disrupt the political, religious, and other functions in a Moslem world and to what extent? Would such a world be able to incorporate the ethos without major disruptions? Structuralism would seem to say there cannot be a disruption, since the cultural structure, like an organism, perpetuates itself and maintains the identity of the system; yet hermeneutics points out that in cross-cultural communication and understanding, there is a mutual communicative influence between the parts, by they old or new, and the whole leading to the conclusion that an introduction of new factors into a culture must be investigated in terms of the "hermeneutical circle": mutual influence between the whole and the part.

By using the phenomenological-hermeneutical process it is possible to investigate the mutual communicative influence among cultures through their various factors with full understanding of the range of their significative implications. At the same time it allows a student of cross-cultural communication to understand cultural interconnections stemming from the past, since such interconnections can no longer be witnessed expirically.

APPLICATION TO
INTERCULTURAL COMMUNICATION

We must remember that phenomenologically we are interested in delineating the criterion necessary for intercultural communication. The fundamental tenet of phenomenology that is consciousness is always consciousness of *something*. Hence, all communication is communication *of something*. This means the fundamental human experience is *prepositional*. Phenomenologically, culture is a network of symbolic human relationships to the world. Based on the paradigm of sameness and difference we may understand how the same meaning can be expressed in many ways by the use of different empirical media. Such media are languages, pictorial representations, writing, institution, and so on. Each can carry a distinct meaning as a symbolized perspective of things. We must remember that symbols are symbols of *something*; therefore, the symbol always must symbolize something that is other than itself. Basically, our knowledge of meaning is derived from our interaction about something. The meanings can be symbolized by media that are man-made. For example, language is not an entity analyzable in itself but rather a symbolic or presentational[8] structure used to communicate the meaning of the situation. By looking at terms alone, we could never know its meaning. Culture provides the symbolic media by means of which the individual can be shown a multitude of perspective of things. Symbols created by past generations *point to* the particular relationship that the past generations had to their world. While it is impossible for us to be transported to ancient Greece, we can understand their view because the meaning of their world was preserved symbolically.

Cultural symbols indicate the possibility of the subjects' self-interpretation. Our understanding of the meaning of symbols depends upon our understanding of our own possibility of assuming the same perspective to the world and interpreting ourselves in terms of that perspective. The symbolized meaning can become our own mode of relationship to the world as our own possibility of being human. Therefore, a temple is not an expression of some subject's relationship to and knowledge of each other, but is symbolic of the particular group's relationship to a Deity. We understand this relationship as expressed through the given cultural symbol because it points to our possibility of taking the *same* relationship to the Deity and interpret ourselves as Catholic, Protestants, or Buddhists. Cultural products are symbolic presentations of a particular meaning of the world. Cultures are expressions of and dependent upon human relationship to their world. Culture is a preserver of meanings. We must not confuse symbolically transmitted meanings with individual psychological investment. Cultural products are symbolic expressions of the acquired meaning. Symbols preserve and transmit meaning to future generations. The sphere of symbolized meaning is present to the individual as a particular way of being in contact with the world of things without being perceptually present to it. In other words man is a product of his or her culture, but a particular culture is equipped to communicate symbolically the perceptual meanings of a particular system of cultural relationships. Intercultural communication presupposed the differentiation between cultures, and the possibility of communication presupposes an interactional process. Yet, for diverse cultures to interact, one must know what the interaction expresses: One must know that one is interacting about something. This means that intercultural communication is possible in terms of the subject's capacity to take up the *same* position and perspective to the state of affairs in order to understand the other's self-interpretation in terms of this perspective. Intercultural communication is based on establishing a commonness. We must guard against the subjective interpretation of culture. Culture cannot be a literal imprint of the thoughts or wishes of the subject. If it were, then it would be difficult to comprehend how the same projection can present itself with implications contrary to the wishes of the subject. The culturally symbolized meaning contains more than the interaction of the subject as a group of subjects. Meaning implies more than the particular intention of the subject. The subject correlates him or herself to it and expresses it in the communicative process. The possibility of viewing the other's world from his or her perspective widens our own horizons and is the evaluative criterion for successful intercultural communication. Intercultural communication is possible given the multitude of cultures or "world views" because the multitude of world views are nevertheless views of the *same* world. Intercultural communication phenomenologically demands that humans living in different cultures can have a common world. Having a common world means being able to be in communication with one another. Therefore, in all conceivable cultures, there is something that is shared before all differences. The common or the invariant meaning is that which is the beginning of all communication and that to which intercultural communication specifically attends.

Phenomenologically, intercultural communication attends to the belief in "a given world common to all" that is the principle which underlies intercultural communication and is the principle which grounds the possibility of investigating and translating the significances of cultural groups in their own right.

NOTES

1. David Stewart and Algis Mickunas, *Exploring Phenomenology: A Guide to the Field and Its Literature* (Chicago: American Library Association, 1974).

2. Maurice Merleau-Ponty, *The Phenomenology of Perception,* trans. Colin Smith (London: Routledge & Kegan Paul, 1962).

3. Hans Georg Gadamer, *Truth and Method* (New York: Seabury Press, 1975).

4. Jean Gebser, *Unsprung and Gegenwert* (Stuttgart: Deutsche Verlag, 1966).

5. Ibid.

6. Erwin Straus and Richard Griffith, eds., *Aisthesis and Aesthetics: Fourth Lexington Conference on Pure and Applied Phenomenology* (Pittsburgh: Duquesne University, 1970).

7. Martin Heidegger, *Identity and Difference,* trans. Joan Stambaugh (New York: Harper & Row, 1969).

8. Joseph Pilotta, "Presidential Thinking: A Contemporary Hermeneutic of Communicative Action," *Western Journal of Speech Communication* 43 (1979): 288-300.

17

Toward a Grounded Theory

BERNARD I. BLACKMAN ● *University of Miami*

Literature in the field of intercultural communication reflects a concern with self-analysis, developing theory, collecting information, and discovering a satisfactory definition of the field. In reading the literature, I have moved from a bleak critical assessment of the underdeveloped state of research and theory to an optimistic view based on the emerging consensus about fruitful directions for further study. My purpose in this chapter is to better understand intercultural communication by moving from a focus on what is wrong or where are we going to how to bring about the needed changes.

There is a consensus among researchers in the field regarding the present lack of theory and methodology. Therefore, I want to discuss how to develop a theory that simultaneously provides explanation, direction, and practical information. I agree with Gudykunst and Nishida that we "need to begin constructing theories of intercultural communication,"[1] but I also believe that it is imperative to begin at the beginning.

Glaser and Strauss's[2] model of developing a grounded theory can put us somewhere near the beginning. Their model presents a methodological framework for

(1) developing theory and directing research in a systematic fashion in any field of inquiry;
(2) developing theory and a body of knowledge that is practical, relevant, and accessible to practitioners; and
(3) developing theory that encourages greater specification and clarification of intercultural communication.

In this chapter I will discuss criticisms of intercultural communication and identify the most important recognized issues, particularly the need for complex, holistic models that can describe and explain intercultural communication. Then, I will describe grounded theory and finally discuss some implications of this model for the field of intercultural communication.

CRITICAL ASSESSMENT

As a field of study, intercultural communication is a preteen, scarcely ten years old and comparatively undeveloped as well. Heretofore, practitioners have been meeting novel situations with limited experience. Rich[3] and Smith[4] have recognized the lack of information that could enable practitioners to increase effectiveness. Moreover, little research has been directed toward solving practical problems.

Part of the difficulty in intercultural communication is conceptual: A common definition of the field is elusive, its boundaries of study unsettled. Saral[5] and Gudykunst and Nishida[6] report a growing interest in definitions, but a lack of a commonly accepted definition. Without such a common conceptual direction, it is difficult for one to develop systematically theory and to isolate intercultural communication as a unique field of study from communication study in communication as a unique field of study. How, for example, can we distinguish intercultural communication study from communication study in general if we cannot establish how intercultural variables differ from communication variables? Saral[7] says that perhaps part of the problem rests with the relationship between the concept and the data. The starting point for a definition and a delineation of intercultural communication, as well as a pragmatic data base, should be rooted in the intercultural experience itself. However, intercultural communication has rarely been studied directly and there is a lack of theory and method for theory development employed in intercultural communication. Four issues in developing theory should be of particular interest to theorists: (1) the type of model used, (2) the model's connection or fit to phenomena under study, (3) how hypotheses are generated, and (4) the presumption of objectivity.

Since intercultural communication is a young field, most of its theorists and researchers received their training in other areas. They imported social science theories and other models as part of their intellectual tradition from the areas of their training. Some of these theories and research paradigms have been criticized for their failure to perform as intended in the social sciences.[8] Similar criticism has been evident in the area of intercultural communication.[9]

For example, the empiricist-positivist models employed in the social sciences are predominantly linear/causal models that center on fragments or parts of the world. This reductionistic tendency is inadequate to deal with the complex, processual nature of communication.[10] Saral suggests that we may have to discard unidimensional and unidirectional causality models for models that focus on multiple causation.[11] Holistic models that are more complete, richer in information, and tolerate multiple explanations of phenomena are more appropriate to the study of communication.[12]

Importing linear, reductionistic models from the physical sciences via the more established social sciences often reduces the fit between data and theory. Theories are neither developed from intercultural experiene nor geared toward the study of intercultural variables. These theories have bypassed the essential inductive or descriptive state of theory development.[13] Imposed theories typically provide little direction in problem-solving and offer little direction in guiding research. Burk pointed out there is "no coherent tradition to guide the collection and analysis of data in intercultural communication research."[14]

Directly related to the fit of theory and methodology is the source of hypotheses themselves. In the empiricist-positivist paradigm hypotheses are deductively generated from the theory. These hypotheses are directed and limited by the theory and are tautological; that is, they are derived logically and are selected for testing on the presumption or appearance of being true.[15] McGuire suggests that scientific investigation is reduced to theory verification with an emphasis on demonstrating truth rather than testing truth.[16]

The tendency to base theory development solely upon deductive hypotheses is limited in explanatory power. When deducing hypotheses, we often make intuitive judgments aside from what the evidence indicates on its surface. We tend to build theory upon those studies that support our particular reasoning, even when the evidentiary base may be flawed conceptually or methodologically. Jones's discussion of his proxemic behavior investigations is a rarely reported case in which persistence and curiosity led him to conclude that sole reliance on deductively derived hypotheses is insufficient.[17]

Finally, the empiricist-positivistic paradigm aims at objectivity while failing to acknowledge the subjective intrusion of the theorist/researcher into the process of developing theory. Redding, in a penetrating discussion of organizational communication, points up the effects of ideology on theory development (regardless of whether or not it is acknowledged).[18] Asante, Newmark, and Blake have suggested that communicologists impose concepts derived from rhetoric in the study of intercultural communication.[19] Moreover, Saral identified several biases underlying Western conceptualizations of theory development, biases that are usually unstated and unacknowledged, and that, as Redding suggests, pervade every stage of the research process.[20]

The growing acknowledgment of our premature theorizing about intercultural communication has led to a call for more descriptive research.[21] However, while description may be required for the initial stages of research, it is not sufficient for theory development. Description does not necessarily lead to substantive theory, nor does it necessarily enhance pedagogy. Descriptive studies may be unsystematic and impressionistic or restricted to single cases. Such studies may provide insights or interesting commentary, but still do not contribute directly to theory development. In addition, descriptive data may be directed at validating existent theories rather than generating new hypotheses. If descriptive research is to be valuable in developing useful research information, methods aimed at description must be specifically oriented toward theory development.

Not all scholars agree that description is the answer to the lack of theory development in intercultural communication. Gudykunst and Nishida appear to take a position contrary to those recommending elementary, descriptive research. They suggest that "to purposefully ignore theorizing will hinder the development of the field."[22] I agree with Gudykunst and Nishida, but see no particular need to emphasize theorizing over description or vice versa. My position is that theorizing and description can occur simultaneously. Moreover, a model that can intimately connect theory to description of intercultural communication can develop theories capable of explaining how ordinary people function.

GROUNDED THEORY

Qualitative methods, participant observation, and Grounded Theory have often been used synonymously. However, there are some useful distinctions among them. Bogdan and Taylor use the term "qualitative" to indicate subjective participation with data collection.[23] They say "qualitative methodologies refer to research procedures which produce descriptive data: people's own written or spoken words and observable behavior."[24] Van Maanen suggests that the qualitative method is an umbrella term without precise meaning. It describes many types of techniques "which seek to describe, decode, translate, and otherwise come to terms with the meaning, not the frequency, of certain more or less naturally occurring phenomena in the social world."[25]

Participant observation describes a particular method of obtaining qualitative data. Bogdan and Taylor say that participant observation is "characterized by a period of intense social interaction between the researcher and the subjects, in the milieu of the latter. During this period, data are unobtrusively and systematically collected."[26] McCall and Simmons use participant observation as a more general method. They say that participant observation is "a characteristic blend or combination of methods and techniques."[27] These techniques include direct observation, direct participation, interviewing, and document analysis.

Participant observation, whether considered a specific technique or a general method that includes different techniques, is empirical data collection.[28] The researcher typically enters into the investigation with few a priori hypotheses and specified variables. Through the researcher's subjective immersion in the phenomenon of study, variables are identified and hypotheses generated.

Theory, however, does not evolve automatically from the data, but rather is generated through the process of analytic induction. Grounded Theory is a method of analytic induction. The Grounded Theory approach typically (but not necessarily) relies upon participant observation methodology and design. Grounded Theory has a unique information processing style aimed specifically at systematically generating theory through constant comparative analysis.[29]

Glaser discusses three types of analytic induction.[30] The first approach relies on generating ideas or theories through unsystematic, impressionistic contact with the data. The researcher inspects and codes the data intuitively. Categories or theories are not systematically verified and therefore remain descriptive and impressionistic.

In the second approach, termed overall grounding, hypotheses are generated from the initial impressionistic inspection of data and then subjected to verification. Explicit coding is conducted to verify the hypotheses generated from the data. McCall and Simmons say that the grounded hypotheses can be modified or verified through case studies. McCall and Simmons and Glaser recognize that this approach limits what is examined. Once hypotheses are formed, the only cases examined are those in which phenomena relating to the hypotheses are formed. Cases where the phenomena do not occur are excluded.[31] The initial intuitive and creative process moves rapidly from hypothesis generation to hypothesis verification, which then controls subsequent sampling and data collection. Consequently, hypotheses are verified and remain grounded in the data, but remain few in number as well. In addition, while the method is more systematic than the impressionistic analysis, it is limited in scope and generality.

The third type of analytic induction, Grounded Theory, combines the first two into a single method directed at theory generation. The processes of generating hypotheses, testing hypotheses, collecting data, integrating categories, and constructing theory occur *simultaneously* and are "guided and integrated by the *emerging* theory."[32] Typically, the researcher compares data and identifies similarities and differences from which abstract categories and their properties are generated. Familiarity through comparison of similarities and differences among categories and properties suggests to the researcher hypotheses about relationships, which he or she records and later verifies by further data collection and comparison. Concepts, categories, and hypotheses are *constantly* verified, added to, or modified as more data are collected in such a scheme. As the researcher is working with the data to verify theory, he or she is forced to reduce the amount and diversity of the data. "To make theoretical sense of so much diversity in his data, the analyst is forced to develop ideas on a level of generality higher in conceptual abstraction than the qualitative material being analyzed. He is forced to bring out underlying uniformities in data."[33]

The emphasis on generating theory through constant comparisons rather than verifying hypotheses results in multiple hypotheses about general phenomena. Description and interpretation are not rstricted to single cases, but are more general explanations of phenomena. Grounded Theory, therefore, can account for complex behavior in complex situations. Consequently, the emergent theory is "integrated, consistent, plausible, close to the data."[34]

Glaser and Strauss identify four interrelated properties of Grounded Theory that make it accessible for application by practitioners. First, since the theory was developed from direct contact with the data, it fits the data better than deductively derived theories, which are imposed from a priori premises. Second, Grounded Theory is attractive because its postulates parallel natural human processing, albeit under strict procedural conditions. Third, it works. That is, in Grounded Theory, variables can be identified and predictions about the relationships and outcomes can be made. Since the theory has been constantly verified as it develops, the theorist has been forced to be pragmatic. Finally, Grounded Theory is flexible and modifiable. It is a process of constantly verifying hypotheses and of evolving descriptions and interpretations as new data are collected. Application serves to further test and validate the theory and force the roles of practitioner and theorist to merge.

Recent studies demonstrate the utility of Grounded Theory.[35] Browning used Grounded Theory to study hierarchy in a government agency.[36] He began the study by intentionally avoiding reviewing and interpreting literature and formulating hypotheses. Instead, he initiated his investigation with the goal of describing "how individuals communicate interpersonally in an organizational setting," and "what variables influence the ways individuals communicate."[37] By using the constant comparative methods of analysis on data gathered through interviews and direct observation, Browning obtained 24 categories and 36 propositions clustered under three grand theoretical power concepts.

Blackman used Grounded Theory in the investigation of Iranian and American intercultural communication in public forums. The study began with four broad questions.

(1) What is the nature and type of behavior exhibited by Iranian students in public forums where they are attempting to influence Americans?
(2) What is the nature and character of the interactions between Iranian and American students?
(3) What is the nature and character of American reactions to Iranian behavior and attempts at persuasion and information dissemination?
(4) What are the sources of misunderstanding between Iranian and American students?

Data were collected through participant observation, interviewing, and document analysis. Once categories and hypotheses were established through the comparative analysis, a literature review of Iranian culture was conducted and compared with the emerging theory. After one year, a field experiment was conducted to further substantiate the emergent hypotheses. The results describe and interpret several interdependent characteristics of Iranian behavior, as well as several ways in which Americans interpret Iranian behavior. In addition, three critical features were proposed that consistently contributed to communication problems between the two cultures.

IMPLICATIONS OF GROUNDED THEORY FOR FOR INTERCULTURAL COMMUNICATION

In each of these studies, the researchers recognized the subjective nature of the research, and attempted to control for it by limiting initial presuppositions and hypotheses, consistently reporting their thoughts and impressions in their notes, and by employing convergent or multiple methods to decrease the limitations of any single method. In addition to the benefit derived from the control of researcher bias, intercultural communication theory can benefit when researcher bias is studied directly. In the Grounded Theory method, the researcher reacts holistically to the research context and creates and organizes categories and a framework through the constant/comparative process. When the researcher begins to identify concepts and to make connections between them, he or she is "no longer a passive receiver of impressions, but is drawn naturally into activity generating and verifying his hypotheses through comparison."[39] The process of perceiving and organizing and interpreting sensory data has been described as a likely focal point for intercultural communication research. Newmark and Asante emphasize the need to probe "how humans think, feel, and experience in the arena of intercultural communication."[40]

Redding suggests that there are two types of researchers. One sets out to discover the ideology of the object of study and usually fails to account for his or her own subjectivity. The second recognizes some of his or her assumptions and biases and incorporates them into the research product. The biases of the first contaminate a study, while the biases of the second are identified and compensated for with the aim of limiting their effects on the investigation.[41]

I suggest a third type of researcher who engages in the systematic study of his or her own reactions in addition to those of the target population. In this case, the researcher demonstrates the same care and gives the same procedural attention to the study as does Redding's second type of researcher. But in addition, he or she would go beyond mere reportage of perspective to the study of how his or her perspective changed in the course of the study. McCall and Simmons say that the comparison of data derived from different methodological probes sensitizes the observer to his or her biases and framework.[42] Schwartz and Schwartz suggest that research is a process of discovering and grappling with one's limitations and blocks,[43] and Bogdon and Taylor suggest that at its best research changes one's perspective, one's logic, and one's assumptions.[44] Moreover, Jacobs describes research as a kind of transcendence.[45] Therefore, Grounded Theory is a process of generating self-knowledge as well as generating theory.

Since in the constant comparative method of Grounded Theory observers make notes on their thoughts and feelings, content analysis could begin to discover the observers' changing perspective via the intercultural contact. The recorded insights, thoughts, feelings, and resulting concepts, hypotheses, and theoretical frameworks can provide a valuable source of information on intercultural processing. Moreover, O'Keefe suggests that critical analysis and public disscussion of theoretical frameworks are a means of clarifying theory as well as of identifying cultural dimensions of human affairs.[46] Therefore, Grounded Theory provides an opportunity to develop substantive theory about a particular social phenomenon as well as develop theory about the researcher's experience in the intercultural encounter.

NOTES

1. W. B. Gudykunst and T. Nishida, "Constructing a Theory of Intercultural Communication," *Speech Education* 7 (1979): 13-25.

2. B. G. Glaser and A. L. Strauss, *The Discovery of Grounded Theory* (Chicago: Aldine, 1967).

3. A. L. Rich, "Definition and Process Observation of Intercultural Communication," in *Proceedings of the Speech Communication Association Summer Conference*, ed. N. Jain et al. (New York: Speech Communication Association, 1974).

4. A. G. Smith, "Research and Theory in Intercultural Communication," in *Overview of Intercultural Education, Training and Research*, Vol. I, ed. D. Hoopes et al. (Pittsburgh: Society for Intercultural Education, Training and Research, 1977).

5. T. B. Saral, "Intercultural Communication Theory and Research: An Overview," in *Communication Yearbook 1*, ed. B. Ruben (New Brunswick, NJ: Transaction, 1977).

6. Gudykunst and Nishida, "Constructing a Theory of Communication."

7. T. B. Saral, "Intercultural Communication Theory and Research: An Overview of Challenges and Opportunities," in *Communication Yearbook 3*, ed. D. Nommo (New Brunswick, NJ: Transaction, 1979).

8. W. J. McGuire, "The Yin and Yang of Progress in Social Psychology," *Journal of Personality and Social Psychology* 26 (1973): 446-56; D. J. O'Keefe, "Logical Empiricism and the Study of Human Communication," *Communication Monographs* 42 (1975): 169-83; W. C. Redding, "Organizational Communication Theory and Ideology," in *Communication Yearbook 3*, ed. D. Nimmo (New Brunswick, NJ: Transaction, 1979); D. H. Smith, "Communication Research and the Idea of Process," *Speech Monographs* 39 (1972): 174-82.

9. W. S. Howell, "Theoretical Directions for Intercultural Communication," in *Handbook of Intercultural Communication*, ed. M. Asante et al. (Beverly Hills, CA: Sage, 1979); Saral, "Intercultural Communication Theory and Research."

10. Smith, "Communication Research and the Idea of Process."

11. Saral, "Intercultural Communication and Research."

12. Smith, "Communication Research and the Idea of Process."

13. L. Hawes, "Alternative Theoretical Bases: Toward a Presuppositional Critique," *Communiction Quarterly* 25 (1977): 63-68.

14. J. L. Burk, "Intercultural Communication Vistas: Description, Concept, and Theory," in *International and Intercultural Communication Annual, Vol. 1*, ed. Fred Casmir (New York: Speech Communications Association, 1975), p. 31.

15. McGuire, "The Yin and Yang of Progress."

16. Ibid.

17. S. E. Jones, "Integrating Etic and Emic Approaches to the Study of Intercultural Communication," in *Handbook of Intercultural Communiction*, ed. M. Asante et al. (Beverly Hills, CA: Sage, 1979).

18. Redding, "Organizational Communication Theory and Ideology."

19. M. K. Asante, E. Newmark, and C. A. Blake, eds., *Handbook of Intercultural Communication* (Beverly Hills, CA: Sage, 1979).

20. Redding, "Organizational Communication Theory and Ideology"; Saral, "Intercultural Communication and Research."

21. Asante et al., *Handbook of Intercultural Communication.*; Burk, "Intercultural Communication Vistas"; Howell, "Theoretical Directions for Intercultural Communication"; R. Shuter, "The Promise of Participant Observation Research," *Journal of Applied Communication Research* 4 (1976): 1-7; A. G. Smith, "Research and Theory in Intercultural Communication."

22. Gudykunst and Nishida, "Constructing a Theory of Intercultural Communication," p. 14.

23. R. Bogdan and S. J. Taylor, *Introduction to Qualitative Research Methods* (New York: John Wiley, 1975).

24. Ibid., p. 4.

25. J. Van Maanen, "Reclaiming Qualitative Methods for Organizational Research," *Administrative Science Quarterly* 24 (1979): 520.

26.   Bogdan and Taylor, "Introduction to Qualitative Research Methods," p. 5.

27.   G .J. McCall and J. L. Simmons, eds., *Issues in Participant Observation* (Reading, MA: Addison-Wesley, 1969), p. 1.

28. S. T. Bruyn, *The Human Perspective in Sociology* (Englewood Cliffs, NJ: Prentice-Hall 1966).

29. Glaser and Strauss, *Discovery of Grounded Theory.*

30. B. G. Glaser, *Theoretical Sensitivity* (Mill Valley, CA: Sociology Press, 1978); B. G. Glaser, "The Constant Comparative Method of Qualitative Analysis," in McCall and Simmons, *Issues in Participant Observation.*

31. McCall and Simmons, *Issues in Participant Observation.*

32. Glaser, *Theoretical Sensitivity,* p. 2.

33. Glaser and Strauss, *Discovery of Grounded Theory,* p. 114.

34. Glaser, "Constant Comparative Method of Qualitative Analysis," p. 218

35. B. Blackman, "Intercultural Communication Patterns of Iranian Students in Public Forum Situations" (Paper delivered at the Speech Communication Association convention, San Antonio, TX, November 1979); B. Blackman, "Intercultural Communication Patterns of Iranian Students in Public Forum Situations: A Participant Observation Investigation" (M.A. Thesis, University of Texas at Austin, December, 1978); L. Browning, "A Grounded Organizational Communication Theory Derived from Qualitative Data," *Communication Monographs* 45 (1978): 93-109; L. Harper and L. R. Askling, "Group Communication and Quality of Task Solution in a Media Production Organization," *Communication Monographs* 47 (1980): 77-100.

36. Browning, "Grounded Organizational Communication Theory."

37. Ibid., p. 93.

38. Blackman, "Intercultural Communication Patterns of Iranian Students," p. 5.

39. Glaser and Strauss, *Discovery of Grounded Theory.*

40. E. Newmark and M. Asante, "Perception of Self and Others: An Approach to Intercultural Communication," in *International and Intercultural Communication Annual, Vol. 1* (New York: Speech Communication Association, 1975), p. 54.

41. Redding, "Organizational Communication Theory and Ideology."

42. McCall and Simmons, *Issues in Participant Observation.*

43. M. Schwartz and C. Schwartz, "Problems in Participant Observation," in McCall and Simmons, *Issues in Participant Observation.*

44. Bogdan and Taylor, *Introduction to Qualitative Research Methods.*

45. G. Jacobs, ed. *The Participant Observer* (New York: George Braziller, 1970).

46. O'Keefe, "Logical Empiricism and the Study of Human Communication."

18

Toward Multiple Philosophical Approaches

MOLEFI KETE ASANTE • *State University of New York, Buffalo*
ERIKA VORA • *St. Cloud University*

The Speech Communication Assocation held a colloquium in 1980 on intercultural communication theory focusing on different philosophical approaches in its studies. The participants expressed a deep concern about the intercultural theories lying locked into Western ways of discovery and validation. In order to facilitate multiple philosophical approaches, the work group suggested that an openness of vision was necessary to allow sufficient understanding and theorizing about cultural interactions.

Intercultural communication involves symbolic transformation at the fundamental level of human interaction. Our study of intercultural communication cannot rest upon ethnocentric assumptions about the nature of that symbolic transformation. Rather, it is essential for a reasonably useful explanation of the intercultural phenomenon to include as wide a research perspective as possible.

WESTERN PERSPECTIVE ON
INTERCULTURAL COMMUNICATION

Our analysis of an interaction between a person from a Western culture and a person from another culture may be jeopardized by the insistence on theories explaining only what the Westerner does. If our theory answers questions raised in Western society, there is nothing inappropriate about that per se. Scholars usually seek to generate answers to questions raised in a particular culture, perhaps even in a particular age as well. But intercultural communication carries with it a concern with at least two cultures. The interaction is not merely Western in context if one of the interactants is other than Western. That is why our analysis of the interaction must not impose Western categories, otherwise we make the mystification of the intercultural encounter insoluble because we operate in a cultural closet. By misunderstanding the complexity of the intercultural questions, we short-circuit all reasonable answers.

By now we have an understanding of cultural diversity, but we are still applying methods acceptable in cultural unity of a Western kind. Few scholars have been willing to relinquish their hold on methods designed for nonintercultural forms of dialogue and interaction. Thus, our emphasis is on the intercultural event, but we believe we can study it as if it were an interpersonal event within the same culture. There are too many voices harmonizing on this theme. These scholars would simply pack their tools from Western organizational or interpersonal theory, make camp at the intercultural interaction, and unpack the same instruments for work. A few Western theories and philosophies affecting intercultural communication studies are discussed below.

The development of communication theories is historically based on the concept of expansion. Questions of influence and persuasion are at base questions of power and domination; that is, the essential motive of Western inquiry into communciation is an inquiry into how to sell ideas to other people. The corroboration of non-Western scholars trained in the West further entrenches the domination motive in communication theory. Although it is possible to detect in the works of some intercultural communication scholars an attempt to deimperialize communication theory, the preponderance of the studies still favor the expansive notions promulgated by most communicationists.[1]

Another Western perspective in communication is the emphasis and reliance on overt behavior to measure effectiveness of a communication effort. The philosophy is that the end results are the primary measure of success. If the receiver of a message behaves as expected by the sender of the message, the communication is considered effective. Isn't it possible that the behavior may have occurred despite poor communication or may not have materialized in spite of effective communication? Effective communication is being measured by the message reaching the receiver as it was intended by the sender. The emergent behavior (action or lack of it) may be affected by many variables, such as immediate issues, technological infeasibility, and resistance to change. Behaviorism is not applicable to human language because it is vague and tautological, and language is not behavior.[2]

Behavioral emphasis in Western philosophies has also led to the development of theories by simplifying situations into categories of stimulus and response activities, and by relating them as cause-effects in a single time period or instance. Although feedback is conceptualized in many models to indicate circular relationships, it is the most neglected element in the studies. Western perspective focuses on effects of a stimulus (message) from a person in Western culture on a person from another culture. It seldom studies the dynamics in terms of affecting each other in an intercultural setting. Intercultural communication studies ought to rely heavily on the whole situation and dynamic interrelationships developing among many happenings over many periods of time.

Dissonance theories, balance theories, and other consistency theories have been accepted in Western studies to describe what happens when our dynamic state of equilibrium is challenged or disturbed. It has not always been confirmed in other cultures. Hiniker's Chinese experiments indicated a need for making modifications in either the theory or the testing procedure.[3] He noted some cultural biases in Dissonance Theory, particularly in the "follows form" phrase; that is, if the obverse of one element follows from the other, two cognitive elements are in dissonant relation.

The recognition and examination of other than Western cultures must be a major part of any intercultural communication enterprise. That does not mean, however, that we should abandon our study of European culture. What it does suggest is that we have a responsibility to understand cultures in order to understand what we say we are studying.

MULTIPLE PHILOSOPHICAL APPROACHES

We seem to be in a neoclassical stage of development in intercultural communication. As Fred Casmir[4] suggested, "The way in which we formulate our questions could have a decisive influence on the answers we may eventually develop." Questions have been raised about the validity, generalizability, and applicability of the existing theories in relation to intercultural communication. This field is young, growing and demanding. We are in a preempirical stage of knowledge in most areas of intercultural interactions. Even descriptive research is difficult because of complex cultural factors pervading throughout our communication phenomenon. Advanced predictive and manipulative theories are far from our reach, although many rules of thumb are suggested for effective intercultural communication.

What we need is a powerful metatheory capable of generating theories and research programs to accommodate intercultural interactions. Such a metatheory would make a place for and encourage competing theories, allowing for the consolidation of categories and concepts without any rigidly devised rules. In the rejection of internal rules the metatheory would reject the reliance on narrowly defined cultural categories. A metatheory useful for serving as the organizing place for a universe of theories about intercultural communication must not rely on sociocultural rules from Western society. Most behaviors are rooted not so much in rules as in the material conditions of a society. Therefore, it is necessary for our metatheory to possess flexibility; only in this way can it accommodate Afrocentric, Eurocentric, Asiocentric, and other perspectives.

While our present state of art does not allow us to establish a final and firm basis of a metatheory, we may initiate this worthwhile undertaking with the following general premises and approaches:

I. There are at least three perceptual versions of a culture. These are:
   (1) My perception of my own culture.
   (2) Perception of my culture by persons from a different culture.
   (3) My perception of their view of my culture.

In a dyadic intercultural communication setting, there are at least six such perceptions at work: three perceptual versions for each of the two cultures represented by the participants.

II. Theories of communication explaining an intercultural phenomenon should not be bound by Western philosophies and premises about human interactions and behaviors. Persons from each culture may develop their own theoretical frameworks based on their own perception of an intercultural experience.

Although a holistic view of the intercultural interactions is desirable, it may not be possible to achieve at the present state of research technology and skills. Many variables, such as differences in language, nonverbals, attitudes, value, and thought patterning orientations make the field very complex.[5] Investigations with nonjudgmental attitudes, high tolerance for ambiguity, low defenses, and multicultural capacity are rare.[6] Therefore, an intercultural framework should consider studying interactions from multiple culture perspectives rather than from a global or a noncultural perspective.

There are many more questions than answers in developing this new perspective. Should interaction be studied from the receiver's culture perspective or the sender's or both? Should such a situation be studied through some other cultural perspective to provide us with a third "objective" view of the situation? How many of these perspectives are needed to explain intercultural interactions sufficiently?

III. Methods of research should emphasize the use of instruments, researchers, and explanations from multiple cultural perspectives. Although episodic research is not recommended, observing intercultural dyads to secure systematic data for generating hypotheses should not be discarded as primitive research methodologies. How may one attempt such research? Here are some suggestions:

(1) Design a dyadic experiment that forms many similar dyads for comparisons and replications.

(2) Train each dyad partner in scientific and systematic observations and in reporting these as they happened. There are at least five major stumbling blocks in dyadic intercultural communication—language, nonverbals, stereotypes, tendency to evaluate, and anxiety.[7] Although the participants are trained to be objective observers and reporters of actual experiences and happenings, they are not trained to disregard their cultural perspectives. Videotapes may be used, if possible, for continued replay of events.

(3) Analysis of the data is to be done by at least two trained analysts from each culture involved in the dyads. This will allow coding data from those cultural perceptions and allow testing for intercoder reliability for each culture.

(4) Generate theoretical notions and frameworks, as suggested by analysts from each culture, for the explanation of the communication phenomenon.

(5) Develop a composite theoretical framework with the various hypotheses developed from multiple cultural perspectives of the dyadic interactions.

(6) Replicate and attempt field experiments and small group experiments.

(7) Develop instruments using persons from the cultures involved in the studies before attempting to test their reliability, validity, and use in future studies.

FUTURE RESEARCH AREAS

Three categories of studies were suggested at the 1980 Speech Communication Association's conference in an effort to conceptualize a powerful metatheory: (1) study interpersonal attraction within culture, (2) study interactions, and (3) study rituals and myths.

Our study of interpersonal attraction within cultures would consider analytical induction, linguistic theory, and demystification theory. Demystification theory would involve survey, inquiry, and action elements in any intercultural interaction. These categories of study constitute sources for creating a metatheory that would accommodate numerous philosophical approaches to theory in intercultural communication.

The study of a people's myths and rituals can give us more information about their communicative interactions with others. Myths constitute at the primary level the structural bases of a culture. Intercultural communication must understand the mythological bases of cultures if it is to mature as a discipline. In a people's myths and rituals we are introduced to their thinking about themselves and others.

By observing intercultural dyads we can secure more systematic data than by beginning with hypotheses. Phenomenological observations of intercultural dyads will supply us with the kind of data with which to theorize at a higher level about intercultural interaction.

The opportunities for creative research into non-Western perspectives are numerous. Collaborating with scholars from different cultural backgrounds, tapping international students, living in a different culture for a relatively long period of time, researching with persons from different but related disciplines in other cultures, and other approaches provide tremendously exciting avenues for broad intercultural studies. We have the intellectual capability to advance on this new frontier through the acceptance of openness toward non-Western ideas, perspectives, and philosophies.

NOTES

1. M. Asante, "Intercultural Communication: An Inquiry into Research Directions, in *Communication Yearbook 4*, ed. D. Nimmo (New Brunswick, NJ: Transaction, 1980); F. Casmir, ed., *International and Intercultural Communication* (Washington, DC: University Press, 1978); W. Howell, "Theoretical Directions for Intercultural Communication, ed. M. Asante et al. (Beverly Hills, CA: Sage, 1979).

2. F. A. Gruber, "Why Empirical Methods Can't Apply in Communication Research—A Case Against Behaviorism," in Casmir, *International and Intercultural Communication*.

3. P. J. Hiniker, "Chinese Reaction to Forced Compliance: Dissonance Reduction or National Character," *Journal of Social Psychology* 77 (1969): 7-41.

4. Casmir, International and Intercultural Communication.

5. M. H. Prosser, *The Cultural Dialogue* (Boston: Houghton Mifflin, 1978).

6. P. Adler, "Beyond Cultural Identity: Reflections on Cultural and Multicultural Man," *Topics in Culture Learning* (August 1974): 23-40.

7. L. Barna, "Intercultural Communication Stumbling Blocks," in *Intercultural Communication: A Reader*, ed. L. Samovar and R. Porter (Belmont, CA: Wadsworth, 1976).

INDEX TO VOLUME VII

NAME INDEX

SUBJECT INDEX

About the Authors

JAMES L. APPLEGATE is Associate Professor in the Department of Communication at the University of Kentucky. He received his Ph.D. from the University of Illinois at Urbana-Champaign. His major research interests include interpersonal and intercultural communication. He is coeditor of a forthcoming volume in the Sage Series on Interpersonal Communication, *Understanding Interpersonal Communication: Social Cognitive and Strategic Processes in Children and Adults*.

MOLEFI KETE ASANTE is Professor of Communication, State University of New York at Buffalo. He is editor of the *Journal of Black Studies*, and has authored or edited twenty books and written more than a hundred papers on a wide range of communication topics. Among his books are *Handbook of Intercultural Communication* and *Transracial Communication*. Dr. Asante was a Fulbright Professor to Zimbabwe in 1981-1982.

NOBLEZA ASUNCION-LANDE is Professor of Speech Communication at the University of Kansas. She has written over 30 articles on intercultural, development, and instructional communication and on sociolinguistics. She has also edited two books on intercultural communication and is coauthor of *The United States and Japan in the Western Pacific: Micronesia and Papua New Guinea* (1981). She is Chairperson of the Division of Intercultural and Development Communication of the International Communication Association, a member of the Legislative Council of SCA, and has served as consultant for AID, UNESCO, and NAFSA. She is currently a visiting professor at the Sheffield City Polytechnic in England.

GEORGE A. BARNETT received his Ph.D. from Michigan State University in 1976. He is currently Assistant Professor at the State University of New York at Buffalo. In 1979, he received a research fellowship from the East-West Communication Institute. This chapter is an outgrowth of the work he carried out with D. Lawrence Kincaid during that period. Dr. Barnett has written a number of articles about intercultural communication, as well as political, organizational, and technical communication theory and methods.

BERNARD I. BLACKMAN has researched Egyptian-American communication in multinational organizations and Iranian-American communication in public forums. He holds a Master's degree in Intercultural Communication and is presently a lecturer in the Department of Communication at the University of Miami.

IN MEMORIAM
RALPH E. COOLEY
1932-1982

The field of intercultural communication lost one of its scholars this year. Ralph Cooley, Associate Professor of Communication at the University of Oklahoma, died suddenly on September 28, 1982, a the age of 49. In eight short years, Ralph contributed four books, six chapters, and numerous articles and convention papers. His strong sense of identification with the communication discipline led him to shape his finely honed linguistic skills into a concern for what he could meaningfully contribute to our discipline. He was a leader, sensitive to the needs of students and his colleagues: He worked to improve the communication skills of foreign students whose English was a second language. He chaired the University of Oklahoma's interdisciplinary program in linguistics. He taught courses in intercultural and nonverbal communication. Perhaps most important of all, he helped the University of Oklahoma meet its social responsibility to the Native American people in the teaching of both Indians and Anglo-Americans the importance of intercultural relationships. Ralph's colleagues remember him as a warm, caring person. At the same time he held high standards of scholarship. His colleagues throughout the discipline will miss him. [Written by L. Brooks Hill]

VERNON E. CRONEN is Professor of Communication Studies, University of Massachusetts, Amherst. He received his B.A. degree from Ripon College and his M.A. and Ph.D. from the University of Illinois, Urbana-Champaign. Cronen and his colleague, W. Barnett Pearce, developed the theory of Coordinated Management of Meaning; Cronen developed with Kenneth Johnson and John Lannamann a theory of reflexivity and paradox in social action. Cronen is coauthor of the book *Communication, Communication Monographs, Journal of Social Psychology, Human Communication Research,* and elsewhere. He has also contributed to various volumes, including *Human Communication Theory, Rigor and Imagination, Communication Yearbook 3,* and *Intercultural Communication Annual.* Cronen is currently chairman of the Interpersonal and Small Group Communication Division of the Speech Communication Association.

PETER C. EHRENHAUS is Assistant Professor in the Department of Communication at Rutgers University. He received his Ph.D. in speech communication from the University of Minnesota. His research interests include attribution processes in ongoing conversation, frame analysis, and the relationship between culture, cognitive structure, and communication.

HUBER W. ELLINGSWORTH (Ph.D., Florida State University) is Professor and Chairman of the Faculty of Communication at the University of Tulsa. He has written on intercultural themes for the ICA *Yearbook* and is coauthor of *Communication and Social Change in Latin America* and *Administration of Family Planning Programs in the Phillippines and Malaysia.* Former appointments include Connecticut; Michigan State, where he served as Director of the AID Communication Seminars; and Hawaii, where he was also Senior Colleague of the Communication Institute of the East-West Center.

WILLIAM B. GUDYKUNST (Ph.D., University of Minnesota) is currently Associate Professor of Rhetoric and Communication at the State University of New York at Albany. He is editor of Volumes 7-9 of the *International and Intercultural Communication Annual.* Bill's major research interests are the development of interpersonal relationships across cultures and adjustment to new cultural environments. He is coeditor of *Readings in Intercultural Communication* with Tsukasa Nishida (Tokyo: Geirinshobo) and coauthor of *Communicating with Strangers: An Approach to Intercultural Communication* with Young Kim (Addison-Wesley).

CARL B. HOLMBERG is Assistant Professor and member of the graduate faculty of the Department of Interpersonal and Public Communication at Bowling Green State University, Ohio. His interests in figurative rhetoric as qualitative mathematics has also led to applications in gaming, horticulture, music phenomenology, and problemsolving. Currently he is studying nineteenth-century American popular culture documents as intercultural evidence of black African rhetoric.

D. LAWRENCE KINCAID has been Research Associate at the East-West Center's Communication Institute in Honolulu since 1973. He earned his Ph.D. degree in Communication from Michigan State University in 1972, his B.A. in Psychology from the University of Kansas in 1967. His major interests are in communication theory and research methodology. His work on the convergence theory of communication was published recently in *Communication Networks: Toward a New Paradigm for Research* (Free Press, 1981), coauthored with Everett Rogers.

JOLENE KOESTER is Assistant Professor of Speech and Dramatic Art at the University of Missouri—Columbia. She received her Ph.D. from the University of Minnesota in 1980. Her primary research interests are in intercultural communication and organizational communication.

HAMID MOWLANA is Professor of International Relations and Director of International Communication Studies at the School of International Service, American University, Washington, D.C. He has written extensively on communication, international relations, and political sociology. Among his books are *International Communication, Social Communication in Iran, and Watergate: A Crisis for the World.* He is an editor of *Journal of Communication* and *USA Today.* He has his Ph.D. from Northwestern University and has been a visiting professor in England, Argentina, and Iran.

ROICHI OKABE (Ph.D., Ohio State University, 1974) is Associate Professor of Communication, Faculty of Foreign Languages. Nanzan University in Nagoya, Japan. He has coauthored *Supiichi Kuritishizumu no Kenkyu* (A Study in Speech Criticism), has translated into Japanese Michael Prosser's *The Cultural Dialogue: An Introduction to Intercultural Communication,* and published many articles on intercultural rhetoric.

W. BARNETT PEARCE is Professor of Communication Studies at the University of Massachusetts, Amherst. He earned his Ph.D. at Ohio University in 1969. He is best known for his work in developing the theory of the Coordinated Management of Meaning, described in Pearce and Cronen, *Communication, Action and Meaning: The Creation of Social Realities.* His current work consists of applying this theory to intercultural communication. In addition, he has published another book, more than a dozen chapters in edited volumes, and about 50 articles in scholarly journals. He has served as President of the Eastern Communication Association and as a member of the Board of Directors of the International Communication Association.

JOSEPH J. PILOTTA, is Assistant Professor in the Department of Communication at Ohio State University. He has a Ph.D. in Interpersonal Communication (Ohio University) and a Ph.D. in Sociology (University of Toronto). Current research interests are intercultural evaluation theory, refugee resettlement and the legal delivery system, and intercultural communication in technological transfer. He has edited the collection *Interpersonal Communication: Essays in Phenomenology and Hermeneutics* and is a member of the International Board of the Center for Advanced Research in Phenomenology.

BRENT D. RUBEN is professor and Chairperson of the Department of Communication, Rutgers University. His work in the areas of communication systems theory and cross-cultural communication includes *General Systems Theory and Human Communication* (Hayden, with J. Kim), the forthcoming *Communication and Human Behavior* (Macmillan), and articles in *International Journal of Intercultural Relations,* the *International and Intercultural Communication Annual, Quarterly Journal of Speech,* and *Group and Organization Studies.*

L. E. (LARRY) SARBAUGH is Assistant Dean of the College of Communication Arts and Sciences, and professor in the Department of Communication at Michigan State University. His B. A. is in Agricultural Education from Ohio State University, M.A. in Journalism and Communication from the University of Illinois, and Ph.D. from the Department of Communication at Michigan State University. His major interests are in intercultural communication and communication and change.

ROBERT SHUTER is Director of the Center for Intercultural Communication at Marquette University, and has published widely on intercultural communication. His articles have appeared in *Journal of Social Psychology, Journal of Communication, Communication Monographs, Journal of Applied Behavioral Science, and numerous others.* He has published two books with Harper & Row and Holt, Rinehart & Winston, and is on the editorial board of *Communication Education* and the *International and Intercultural Communication Annual.* Active in national and international associations, Dr. Shuter has also been a consultant for CBS and other multinational organizations.

HOWARD E. SYPHER, who received his Ph.D. from the University of Michigan, is Assistant Professor of Communication at the University of Kentucky. His research interests include communication theory, interpersonal communication, and social cognition and communication. He is coeditor of a forthcoming volume in the Sage Series on Interpersonal Communication, *Understanding Interpersonal Communication: Social Cognitive and Strategic Processes in Children and Adults.*

DENNIS W. TAFOYA (Ph.D., University of Michigan, 1976) is Assistant Professor of Communication Studies at the University of Massachusetts. His main area of research interest is interpersonal conflict. The purpose of his research is to describe physiological, psycho-emotional, cognitive, and behavioral responses to conflict-producing situations. Currently this research program is designed to isolate, describe, and account for strategies children select to manage conflict situations between them and their parents, peers, authority figures, and coexisting cultural groups.

ERIKA VORA is Assistant Professor at St. Cloud State University. Minnesota. She has directed an international studies program in West Germany and consulted with multinational organizations in India, Europe, and the United States. Her numerous publications include such topics as concept diffusion across cultures, diplomatic communication, female-male communication, and effective listening. She is one of the founders of the International Listening Association, and is coauthoring a book on effective listening. She was a visiting professor at Gujarat University in India and at the State University of New York at Buffalo.

RICHARD L. WISEMAN is Associate Professor at California State University, Fullerton. His interests include intercultural communication, interpersonal persuasion, and communication theory. He has published articles in the *International Journal of Intercultural Relations, Communication Monographs,* and *Communication Quarterly.* He earned his Ph.D. at the University of Minnesota, Minneapolis.